T0100284

Our Lives in Their Portfolios

Our Lives in Their Portfolios

Why Asset Managers Own the World

Brett Christophers

VERSO

London • New York

This paperback edition first published 2024
First published by Verso 2023
© Brett Christophers 2023

1 3 5 7 9 10 8 6 4 2

Verso
UK: 6 Meard Street, London W1F 0EG
US: 388 Atlantic Avenue, Brooklyn, NY 11217
versobooks.com

Verso is the imprint of New Left Books

ISBN-13: 978-1-83976-899-6
ISBN-13: 978-1-83976-900-9 (UK EBK)
ISBN-13: 978-1-83976-901-6 (US EBK)

British Library Cataloguing in Publication Data
A catalogue record for this book is available from the British Library

The Library of Congress Has Cataloged the Hardback Edition as Follows:

Names: Christophers, Brett, 1971– author.
Title: Our lives in their portfolios : why asset managers own the world /
  Brett Christophers.
Description: London ; New York : Verso, 2023. | Includes bibliographical
  references and index.
Identifiers: LCCN 2022051845 (print) | LCCN 2022051846 (ebook) | ISBN
  9781839768996 (paperback) | ISBN 9781839769016 (ebk)
Subjects: LCSH: Asset allocation. | Portfolio management.
Classification: LCC HG4529.5 .C488 2023 (print) | LCC HG4529.5 (ebook) |
  DDC 332.6—dc23/eng/20230104
LC record available at https://lccn.loc.gov/2022051845
LC ebook record available at https://lccn.loc.gov/2022051846

Typeset in Sabon by MJ & N Gavan, Truro, Cornwall
Printed and bound by CPI Group (UK) Ltd, Croydon, CR0 4YY

Contents

Abbreviations

APPR   Société des Autoroutes Paris-Rhin-Rhône (France)
ASCE   American Society of Civil Engineers
AUM   assets under management
BAM   Brookfield Asset Management
BREIT   Blackstone Real Estate Income Trust
BREP   Blackstone Real Estate Partners
BRI   Belt and Road Initiative (China)
BRT   bus rapid transit
BTR   build to rent
CEO   chief executive officer
COP26   2021 United Nations Climate Change Conference
CPP   Canada Pension Plan
CPPIB   Canada Pension Plan Investment Board
DfE   Department for Education (UK)
ESG   environmental, social and governance
G20   Group of Twenty
G7   Group of Seven
GIIA   Global Infrastructure Investor Association
GIP   Global Infrastructure Partners
GND   Green New Deal
GP   general partner
GSE   government-sponsored enterprise
HUD   Department of Housing and Urban Development (US)
IFC   International Finance Corporation
IIJA   Infrastructure Investment and Jobs Act (US)
IMF   International Monetary Fund
INREV   European Association for Investors in Non-Listed
          Real Estate Vehicles

IPO	initial public offering
IRR	internal rate of return
LP	limited partner
MAp	Macquarie Airports
MEIF$_3$	Macquarie European Infrastructure Fund III
MIM	Manulife Investment Management
MIRA	Macquarie Infrastructure and Real Assets
MKIF	Macquarie Korea Infrastructure Fund
MOIC	multiple of invested capital
MSIP	Morgan Stanley Infrastructure Partners
NHP	Nursing Home Properties
OECD	Organisation for Economic Co-operation and Development
OMERS	Ontario Municipal Employees Retirement System
PFI	Private Finance Initiative (UK)
PGII	Partnership for Global Infrastructure and Investment
PIF	Public Investment Fund of Saudi Arabia
PPA	power-purchase agreement
PPP	public–private partnership
PSERS	Pennsylvania Public School Employees' Retirement System
REIT	real-estate investment trust
RTC	Resolution Trust Corporation (US)
S&L	savings and loan
SEK	Swedish kronor
SHP	Swedish Hospital Partners
SIB	Washington State Investment Board
SMG	Seoul Metropolitan Government
SPV	special purpose vehicle
SVT	Sveriges Television
SWF	sovereign wealth fund
UKIB	UK Infrastructure Bank
UNDP	United Nations Development Programme

Introduction

Summer House

Plenty of stories about the modern world are told through the lens of Silicon Valley, the famous region nestled at the southern end of the San Francisco Bay. Home to the world's leading tech companies, the Valley has come, for many, to assume the status of nothing less than a metonym for contemporary capitalism, a symbol of its relentless dynamism, ingenuity and potential for wealth creation, the source of much of the innovation that drives national and global economic growth.

A very different story about the modern world can be told through the lens of a little-known place some fifty kilometres north-west of the Valley, situated directly across the Bay from it. Adjacent to Oakland and in the lee of the Bay Bridge is the island of Alameda, today home to around 75,000 people. In the neighbourhood of Woodstock, which was one of the first areas of the island to be settled, is a seemingly inconspicuous apartment complex comprising 17 buildings and 615 dwelling-units. Abutting Poggi Street to the west and Buena Vista Avenue to the south, the complex is today called Summer House. In its own way, it, too, is a metonym for the modern world.

Originally built in the mid 1960s as the Buena Vista Park Apartments, in the early 1990s the Summer House units were known as the Bridgeport Apartments. They, and the tenants that lived in them – these were (and still are) rental homes – were about to embark on a decades-long, ongoing journey of upheaval.

The second half of the 1990s and the first few years of the new millennium represented one long, drawn-out period of disinvestment and decline. The property, local writer Rasheed Shabazz would later recall, was allowed to deteriorate to the point that the city appointed a dedicated taskforce to address repeated code violations.[1] Shabazz was in a position to know: his family lived there during the period in question. 'Tenants at this 615-unit complex', editorialised a local newspaper in 2004, 'all seem to have horror stories about their landlord: plumbing failures, electrical problems, leaky roofs, broken appliances'.[2]

That year, 2004, turned out to be a seminal one in the history of the complex. At the height of summer, all tenants suddenly received eviction notices, and despite putting up an almighty fight – with notable support from sections of local government – within twelve months every single one of them was gone, Shabazz's family included.

In the meantime, rents were going up – and they have continued to do so. In the early 2000s, prior to the mass eviction, tenants were paying in the region of $1,100 per month for a two-bedroom let. By late 2006, rates for a two-bedroom unit started at $1,425.[3] During the financial crisis of 2007–09, and the foreclosure crisis that followed on its heels, rents actually dipped temporarily – a small two-bed could be had for as little as $1,299 in 2010, for instance; but, since the early 2010s, they have headed vertiginously upwards. By 2015, $1,900 was the approximate minimum for a two-bed let.[4] Today, two-beds start at around $2,350 and go up to in excess of $3,500.[5]

And rising prices have not been the only matter exercising tenants. 'In addition to rising rents,' Shabazz reported in 2018, 'many residents expressed concerns about living conditions. At a recent meeting, residents shared tales of sewage, vermin, leaky roofs, and delayed responses to repairs over the years.'[6] Nor, by any means, had the spectre of evictions gone away. A 2016 study

---

1   R. Shabazz, 'Wall Street Comes to Alameda', 23 May 2018 – at eastbay express.com.

2   'Exploited, Then Evicted', 19 August 2004 – at sfgate.com.

3   L. Teague, 'Buena Vista Reinvents Itself', 18 December 2006 – at eastbay times.com.

4   Shabazz, 'Wall Street'.

5   'Floorplans' – at summerhousealameda.com (as at mid 2022).

6   Shabazz, 'Wall Street'.

by the Anti-Eviction Mapping Project identified the number of unlawful detainers – essentially, eviction lawsuits – enacted in different parts of Alameda between 2006 and 2016. Which location had the highest number? Summer House.[7] Moreover, as Shabazz remarked, the study actually underestimated the actual extent of involuntary tenant turnover, inasmuch as it did not include people who moved because they could not afford rent increases, but before eviction proceedings could force them out.

So how might we understand this local story of consistent upward pressure on rents, allied to – and to one extent or another, enabled by – consistent displacement pressure on tenants, not to mention recurring concerns ('horror stories') about living conditions?

Inevitably, there have been many relevant factors. But the argument to be developed in this book is that it is not possible to understand stories such as Summer House without paying close attention to asset ownership; and more than that, to a particular *type* of quintessentially late-modern, financial-capitalist ownership.

In the early 1990s, the then-owner of Bridgeport Apartments was their original builder, the Gersten Company of Los Angeles. But in 1996, the apartments' fate changed forever when Gersten filed for bankruptcy and the complex was sold to a new owner, the Fifteen Group of Miami. It was under Fifteen Group's ownership that the apartments – which it renamed Harbor Island Apartments – entered into long-term physical decline. And it was Fifteen Group that initiated the mass eviction of tenants in 2004. It did so, it said, to allow it to undertake wholesale renovation of the properties. The evictions feature in a 2008 documentary film, *Civic Unity: Five Years in the West End of Alameda*. An extraordinary seven-minute clip entitled 'The Battle of Harbor Island' can be viewed online.[8] In it, tenants facing eviction front up to the Fifteen Group's executives, Mark and Ian Sanders, at an open meeting. The clip is full of jaw-dropping moments,

7 'Counterpoints – Alameda County Report, 2016' – at antievictionmap. com.

8 'Civic Unity, excerpt 1 "The Battle of Harbor Island"' – at lunaproductions. com.

not least when the tenants are offered a $750 'per-unit moving stipend' and howls of derision ripple through the hall.

Fifteen Group would not own the apartments for much longer, however. In 2005, it sold them to the Beverly Hills–based Kennedy Wilson for $122 million.[9] The latter – which renamed Harbor Island as Summer House – would forge ahead with the renovations (which Fifteen Group had barely started), announcing its plan to spend $20 million on improvements. Asked about the mass eviction, the new owner insisted that it was part of the past. 'We're going to try to forget about that and move forward', said Bob Hart, senior managing director at Kennedy Wilson.

As we have seen, the 2006–2016 period was one of rising rents – but also of continuing evictions and complaints about living conditions. Ownership-wise, the period corresponding to the financial crisis is somewhat murky. We know that Kennedy Wilson sold Summer House in 2007; but, despite digging, it is unclear (to this author, at least) to whom, or how much for.[10] What is clear, though, is that Kennedy Wilson reacquired Summer House in 2010. One might ask, why? The answer is that the opportunity was too good to pass up. Whoever the new owner was, they were clearly in difficulty, rents having dipped, and Summer House was available at the knock-down price – it was, in the vernacular of the trade, 'distressed' – of just $86 million: 30 per cent less than Kennedy Wilson had paid in 2005. Kennedy Wilson's chief executive, William McMorrow, called the 2010 repurchase 'probably the greatest opportunity we have seen in our careers on the buy side for distressed real estate'.[11]

Quite how bounteous the opportunity was (for Kennedy Wilson, if not its tenants) became plain in the fullness of time. Perhaps even McMorrow was surprised by the riches it ultimately delivered. The abovementioned rent increases translated into a near-doubling of net profit from Summer House between

---

9   D. Levy, 'Biotech Gamble Gets Under Way', 18 September 2005 – at sfgate.com.

10   Kennedy Wilson has merely said the sale was to 'one of its equity partners'. See kennedywilson.com/case-studies/summer-house.

11   G. Winfrey, 'Kennedy Wilson Secures $100m Investment', *Private Equity Real Estate*, 19 May 2010 – at perenews.com.

2010 and 2015, from around $6 million to $10 million per annum.[12] And it was around that point that Kennedy Wilson began taking steps to sell for good. In 2017, it did. That November, it disposed of Summer House for $231 million, nearly three times the amount the complex had cost just seven years earlier. Kennedy Wilson's own return was not three times its investment, though. Because it had funded the purchase with large amounts of debt ('leverage'), its return was 700 per cent.[13] We will explore how this works later.

The report of the 2017 deal in the *San Francisco Business Times* contained a striking line: 'Kennedy Wilson declined to disclose the buyer.'[14] Just as had been the case a decade previously, the company did not reveal who it had sold Summer House to. The identity of the new owner was, initially at least, a mystery. Tenants first learned of the sale from the local press; they paid their rents to managing agents, not the ultimate owner. Already exhausted by Kennedy Wilson's period of tenure – 'annual rent increases, evictions, rotating property managers, and repeatedly ignored requests for repairs and renovations' – residents told Shabazz that, under the new owners, they feared things might now get even worse: 'Are they going to kick us out? Will they raise our rents? *Who are they?*'[15]

In time, it emerged who the new owners were: the New York–based Blackstone Group.[16] But this was not through Blackstone itself disclosing the fact: again, to the best knowledge of this author, Blackstone has never publicly revealed itself as the owner; Summer House is managed by another firm. In any event, in the five years since Blackstone took over, rumblings of tenant discontent have persisted, and the rents continue to rise.

---

12   Q2 2015 Kennedy Wilson Holdings Inc Earnings Call Transcript – at seekingalpha.com.

13   Q4 2017 Kennedy Wilson Holdings Inc Earnings Call Transcript – at seekingalpha.com.

14   R. Li, 'Apartments Sell for $231 Million in Bay Area's Biggest Multifamily Deal of the Year', 15 November 2017 – at bizjournals.com.

15   Cited in Shabazz, 'Wall Street'; emphasis added.

16   L. Shaver, 'For the First Time Since 2009 Apartment Sales Decline', *Units Magazine*, 1 March 2018.

Owning the World

In what sense, then, is the story of Summer House a story about the modern world more generally? Very different entities on the surface, among other things in terms of scale – the Fifteen Group has about thirty employees, Blackstone about 3,000 – the three corporate owners of Summer House since 1996 are, in fact, substantively identical in terms of their core business model: all three are *asset managers*.

The most well-known being the likes of BlackRock, and indeed Blackstone itself, asset managers are private financial firms that manage money on behalf of investors, typically institutional – as opposed to household or 'retail' – investors, and in particular pension schemes and insurance companies. Pension schemes and insurance companies collectively hold enormous amounts of money to invest. In the past, they carried out most of that investment directly themselves. In recent decades, however, a growing share of the money held by institutional investors has been invested indirectly, namely by specialist asset managers who charge fees for their investment services. The metric typically used to measure the size of the global asset management sector is *assets under management*, or AUM. In 2020, estimated AUM globally – that is, the value of the indirect investments managed by asset managers – surpassed $100 trillion for the first time.[17]

Much of the money managed by asset managers is invested in financial assets, such as shares (in the United States, 'stocks') and bonds – but not all of it; and, in relative terms, less and less of it. In recent times, asset managers have been investing ever more of the money with which pension schemes, insurance companies and the like entrust them not in financial assets but in assets of

---

17   BCG, 'The $100 Trillion Machine', July 2021 – at bcg.com. AUM is an analytical and hence representational minefield. There are differences (often significant and material) between financial institutions both in terms of definition (i.e., what is and is not included) and measurement (whether based on cost or market valuation, for example). For this reason, AUM data will be used relatively sparingly in this book. The important point to remember is what AUM aspires to measure: in the most basic terms, how much money an asset manager manages for its clients.

two other kinds. It is their investment in these 'alternative' assets, rather than financial assets, that this book explores.[18]

The first of the two consists of various types of housing – 'multi-family' apartment blocks such as Summer House, standalone homes, student housing, care homes, and even manufactured-housing ('mobile home') communities. The second kind of asset includes all those physical things typically grouped together under the capacious term 'infrastructure'. This term denotes the basic physical 'stuff' that enables modern society to function, from water-supply networks to roads, and from hospitals to electricity-transmission grids. Infrastructures, the geographer Deborah Cowen says simply, 'build and sustain human life'. 'Without infrastructure', she goes on, 'life as we know it stops.'[19]

As increasingly significant owners of housing and infrastructure, asset managers today are directly and intimately implicated – albeit often without most of us even being aware of it – in everyday social existence. They own, and extract income from, things – schools, bridges, wind farms and homes – that are nothing less than foundational to our daily being. Forty years ago, it would have been more or less unthinkable that we would buy our gas from, make our parking payment to, or rent our home from a company like Blackstone. But today, for growing numbers of people around the world, such is the social reality.

It is this reality that the book terms *asset-manager society*: a society in which asset managers increasingly own and control our most essential physical systems and frameworks, providing the most basic means of social functioning and reproduction.

---

18   The reader may already have noted a point of potential terminological difficulty. This concerns uses of the crucial word 'asset'. Confusingly, this word is widely used to refer to both the money that asset managers invest (they invest their clients' capital 'assets') *and* the things they invest that money in (they invest it in 'assets' of various kinds). In this book, I will also (unavoidably) be using the word in both ways. But I will endeavour to be as clear as possible about which meaning applies in any particular context. And to help with clarity, I will often simply use the term 'money' to refer to the client assets that asset managers pool together, invest, and earn fees on.

19   D. Cowen, 'Infrastructures of Empire and Resistance', 25 January 2017 – at versobooks.com.

Summer House is a metonym for this burgeoning reality. Most of us – poor and rich, in Global North and South alike – now live in asset-manager society to one extent or another, with this embeddedness spreading, expanding and intensifying at a tremendous pace: just one single asset manager (among thousands), Macquarie of Australia, now owns infrastructures on which over 100 million people rely each day; meanwhile, asset managers collectively own global housing and infrastructure assets worth, at a minimum, $4 trillion.[20] And, as the Summer House story suggests, the reality of asset-manager society is not a pretty one – except, of course, for the asset managers themselves.

In a very physical, if also strangely intangible respect, all of our lives are now part of their investment portfolios. Asset managers increasingly own the physical as well as financial world around us.

Summer House is prototypical of this modern, asset-manager-ruled world in at least three crucial respects, each to be explored in detail in the chapters that follow. First, asset managers are relentless in squeezing maximum profits out of the homes and infrastructures they own. They cut to the bone the costs incurred in operating those assets – which is obviously less than ideal if you happen to live in one of those assets. And they do whatever they need to do to maximise the incomes (such as rents) that the assets generate. If mass eviction is what it takes, then, à la Fifteen Group, mass eviction is what it will be.

---

20 The reported number of daily users of Macquarie-owned infrastructure is from *Macquarie Group Annual Report, Year ended 31 March 2021*, p. 16 – at macquarie.com. As for the value of all asset-manager-owned housing and infrastructure assets, there are no reliable estimates publicly available for either asset class. There are certainly estimates for infrastructure (albeit not housing) AUM, but such estimates refer to the value of equity holdings, which is not the same as the value of the physical assets themselves, principally because most investments are leveraged. My best estimate of the value of housing owned by asset managers – conservatively, some $1 trillion – is contained and explained in Chapter 3. My best estimate of $3 trillion for the minimum value of infrastructure owned by asset managers is based on the reported fact that the 100 largest managers controlled infrastructure AUM of around $1.65 trillion in mid 2022: $3 trillion in physical asset value would imply average leverage of 45 per cent, which is conservative. See R. Lowe, 'Top 100 infrastructure investment managers 2022', July/August 2022 – at realassets.ipe.com.

Second, asset managers both buy and sell housing and infrastructure assets. It is difficult to overemphasise the significance of the latter activity. Selling is as much a part of the business model as owning. In fact, one might say that asset managers buy such assets generally *in order to* sell them; and the fact that ownership is a mere means to that end has all manner of deleterious consequences – all too visible in the case of Summer House – during the period of proprietorship. At nine and seven years, respectively, Fifteen Group and Kennedy Wilson's periods of ownership of Summer House were actually on the long side by asset managers' standards. On average, ownership is shorter than that. Blackstone, as far as one can discover, still owns Summer House five years on from purchasing it. But for how much longer?

Third, asset-manager society is in significant measure invisible. Partly, this is because much of the buying and selling occurs in private, with limited, if any, requirement for disclosure: as we have seen, Kennedy Wilson did not say who it sold Summer House to on either occasion that it did so. But the invisibility also pertains partly to actual asset operation. Whether it is a toll road, a school, a gas pipeline or an apartment block (such as Summer House), the asset manager that owns it almost never manages it, and hence evades scrutiny for this reason, too. 'We're in the business of owning the backbone of the global economy. [But] what we do is behind the scenes. *Nobody knows we're there*', the CEO of Brookfield Asset Management, one of the world's leading asset managers in the housing and infrastructure space, has observed, 'and we provide critical infrastructure to people that somebody pays a small amount for ... the road you drive on, most people think it's owned by the government. Even if it is a toll road, they wouldn't actually know who owned it'.[21] This book's aim is to ensure that people do know – and know why it matters.

---

21 J. Evans and P. Smith, 'Bruce Flatt of Brookfield on Owning the Backbone of the Global Economy', *Financial Times*, 22 September 2018; emphasis added.

The Age of Asset Management

The business of capitalist asset management has existed in one form or another for as long as private-property rights, surpluses of financial wealth and meaningful opportunities for wealth investment have coexisted. Among the holders of wealth surpluses, there have always been corporations and individuals keen not to handle investment of those surpluses themselves, but rather to outsource such activity to expert, professional managers. Investment managers referred to as *trusts* were already an institutional fixture in the City of London by the mid nineteenth century, for instance.

Nevertheless, it would be another century before anything resembling the modern asset-management industry began to take shape. And it was not until the beginning of the 1980s that that industry began to enjoy significant growth: precise consolidated figures for that period are not readily available, but global AUM – which, as we have seen, breached $100 trillion in 2020 – probably amounted to not much more than $100 billion (one-thousandth of the 2020 sum) four decades previously. The subsequent growth has had two basic drivers.[22] Total global financial wealth has increased dramatically; so also has the proportion of that wealth invested via asset managers.

The first area of the mushrooming asset-management business to receive meaningful critical attention in terms of its implications for wider society was, interestingly, a relatively small business niche: private equity. The label 'private equity' is often used to signify a type of business – *Carlyle Group is a private-equity firm*, people will say – but it is more accurately applied to a type of asset, or what is commonly referred to as a particular 'asset class'. Private equity, in short, is one of the various things that asset managers can and do invest in – specifically, equity (company shares) that is not traded on public exchanges, as distinct from tradeable 'public equity', such as shares in Apple or Amazon.[23] What people call private-equity firms, then, are in

---

22   R. Greenwood and D. Scharfstein, 'The Growth of Finance', *Journal of Economic Perspectives* 27: 2 (2013), pp. 3–28.

23   Although an asset manager's purchase of publicly traded equity would

fact better understood as asset managers that happen to invest mainly or exclusively in the private-equity asset class.

Though the value of AUM invested in private equity was (and remains) much smaller than AUM channelled into publicly traded equity and debt securities via vehicles such as mutual funds, it was nonetheless private equity that predominantly caught critics' eyes in the 1980s and 1990s. This was unsurprising: in its most high-profile, publicly visible form, asset managers' private-equity investment activity involved hostile takeover bids and the use of copious amounts of debt (the term 'leveraged buyout' was widely preferred), and often resulted in asset-stripping and large numbers of redundancies at acquired firms. This was a world away from the dry fare of most asset-management business practice. The standard-setter among critiques of private equity was Bryan Burrough and John Helyar's best-selling 1990 book *Barbarians at the Gate*, subsequently made into a television movie.[24] The 'barbarians' in question were the asset-management firm Kohlberg Kravis Roberts, today known simply as KKR & Co. Founded in 1976, in 1988 KKR completed the deal chronicled in *Barbarians at the Gate*. This was the bitterly contested $25 billion acquisition of the US tobacco and food-product conglomerate RJR Nabisco – by far the largest leveraged buyout in history to that point.

For private equity, the global financial crisis of 2007–09 was a key moment. Until then, banks, and especially investment banks, had been widely regarded as the dominant, most powerful players in the world of global finance. But banks were now widely held responsible for the crisis, and – in Western nations, at least – they had their wings clipped by regulators as a result. As big banks became 'more heavily regulated and scrutinized', a *Bloomberg* report later observed, private-equity firms moved forcefully out of their shadow: 'Almost everything that's happened since 2008 has tilted in [private equity's] favor.

nonetheless be classed as a private-equity investment if the result of the purchase was the de-listing of the shares from the exchange on which they previously were traded – a so-called 'take private' transaction.

24   B. Burrough and J. Helyar, *Barbarians at the Gate: The Fall of RJR Nabisco* (New York: Harper & Row, 1990).

Low interest rates to finance deals? Check. A friendly political climate? Check. A long line of clients? Check ... Private equity managers', the report concluded, 'won the financial crisis.'[25]

But it was not just private-equity-focused managers who 'won' the financial crisis: this was also true of asset managers more generally. From some $46 trillion in 2008, global AUM leapt to $74 trillion six years later, on which the industry earned annual net revenues of approximately $260 billion.[26] Not only that, but the burgeoning business of asset management was proving immensely profitable – 'among the world's most profitable businesses', as the authors of a Boston Consulting Group analysis put it.[27]

By the mid 2010s, then, commentators were unanimous that global finance had seen nothing less than a deep-seated structural shift. Being increasingly 'risk-averse', banks, intimated Landon Thomas in the *New York Times*, were yesterday's news. Amid 'super-low interest rates', the balance of power on Wall Street had instead shifted decisively towards institutions with bigger risk appetites – in particular, towards 'asset managers, which have been inundated with cash from investors desperate for higher returns'.[28] Little wonder that, so as not to lose sight of their ascendant rivals, global investment banks increasingly ploughed resources precisely into expanding their own asset-management arms.[29] Andrew Haldane, the cerebral Bank of England economist, in a 2014 speech at the London Business School, perhaps captured the mood best. After – and as a result of – the financial crisis, he surmised, we had finally arrived in 'the age of asset management'.[30]

---

25   Bloomberg, 'Everything Is Private Equity Now', 3 October 2019 – at bloomberg.com.

26   BCG, 'Sparking Growth with Go-to-Market Excellence', July 2015 – at bcg.com.

27   Ibid., p. 3.

28   Landon Thomas Jr, 'Blackstone's Deal with GE Highlights Its Real Estate Holdings', *New York Times*, 12 April 2015.

29   B. Braun, 'From Exit to Control: The Structural Power of Finance Under Asset Manager Capitalism', October 2021, p. 13 – at osf.io.

30   A. G. Haldane, 'The Age of Asset Management?', 4 April 2014 – at bankofengland.co.uk.

From 'Asset-Manager Capitalism' ...

'Academics, practitioners and regulators', Haldane observed in the same speech, 'have been studying banks, their behaviour and failure, for several centuries. Analysing and managing the behaviour of asset managers is, by contrast, a greenfield site.'[31] Haldane, of course, was not quite right on this score: as I have noted, the private-equity business had already been in the critical spotlight for several decades by the time he declared that the age of asset management was upon us.[32] Private equity aside, though, Haldane spoke the truth. For all that asset management was now a $260 billion global annual business, it remained, circa 2014, a remarkably under-studied and poorly understood one. That, Haldane insisted, needed to change.

And, to a significant degree, it has. Not only has private equity itself stayed very much in the critical spotlight; scholars and other close observers have also begun to spend much more time studying and analysing what we might call the 'mainstream' of global asset management. This specifically entails asset-manager investment in publicly listed financial securities (especially shares and bonds), and it accounts for the lion's share of the asset-management business in terms of money under management. Some $88 trillion of the $103 trillion that asset managers collectively held under management globally in 2020 was invested in these mainstream asset classes. Private equity, by way of contrast, accounted for 'only' $5 trillion of AUM.[33]

That critical attention should have been directed to the mainstream as well as private equity is entirely understandable. For one thing, as we have seen, this is where most client capital – all the money that asset managers receive from pension schemes, and so forth – is put to work. Moreover, such has been the surge in the scale of the mainstream asset-management business in recent times, that such growth has to some extent structurally transformed financial markets. At the beginning of the 1980s,

31   Ibid., p. 14.

32   And the year of Haldane's speech saw the publication of E. Appelbaum and R. Batt's indispensable *Private Equity at Work: When Wall Street Manages Main Street* (New York: Russell Sage Foundation, 2014).

33   BCG, 'The $100 Trillion Machine', pp. 8, 18.

asset managers' collective ownership share of, for example, the public equity circulating in US stock markets was close to zero. Today, their ownership share of the average S&P 500 company is in the region of 30–40 per cent.[34]

The wider implications of this barely need spelling out. Stock markets in general, and the US stock market in particular, are the beating heart of contemporary global capitalism, where shareholders convene and the fortunes of the world's biggest capitalist firms are evaluated, traded and even, in some measure, decided. Thus, to transform the dynamics of stock markets and the structural composition of shareholder registers – as the rise of mainstream asset management in recent decades unequivocally has done – is at once to transform the dynamics of capitalism itself. It is for exactly this reason that one observer of the growth of mainstream asset management, the political economist Benjamin Braun, has taken to referring to contemporary capitalism as 'asset manager capitalism'.[35]

At the same time, however, it is also the case that the particular ownership structures and dynamics examined by Braun and others are very distant from most people's everyday lives. If the question of who (other than households themselves) owns Apple and Amazon's shares affects ordinary households at all, it does so only indirectly, and often only marginally.

But the question of who owns the homes we live in and the infrastructures we depend upon to go about our daily lives is another matter entirely. As this book will show, it matters to households very much who owns such assets, in a way that is typically experienced very directly, even viscerally. Simply recall

---

34   I have not been able to find exact estimates. In mid 2021, it was reported that the largest three asset managers together owned about 22 per cent of the average S&P company (S. Potter, 'BlackRock-Led "Big Three" May Forestall Chaos in Stock Markets', 20 July 2021 – at bloomberg.com). Various other data points suggest that those three managers' combined market share of total industry AUM invested specifically in S&P 500 equities is likely to be in the range of 55–75 per cent, which is how I derived the 30–40 per cent estimate.

35   B. Braun, 'Asset Manager Capitalism as a Corporate Governance Regime', in J. S. Hacker, A. Hertel-Fernandez, P. Pierson and K. Thelen, eds, *The American Political Economy: Politics, Markets, and Power* (Cambridge: Cambridge University Press, 2022).

Summer House. Housing and infrastructure belong within what the asset-management industry defines as a wider class of so-called 'real assets', which is to say, investible assets that possess physical substance, as opposed to existing (like financial assets) only in digital form, or at most as paper certificates. Asset-manager investment in real assets has been growing apace since the 1990s.

The concept of an 'asset-manager society' is intended to denote the substance and significance of this trend. Whereas, after Braun, growing asset-manager investment in mainstream financial assets such as publicly listed shares and bonds power-fully reshapes business and the economy (hence, 'asset manager capitalism'), growing asset-manager investment in the 'real' assets that are housing and infrastructure powerfully reshapes social life itself.

To gain a preliminary appreciation of how asset-manager society differs from asset-manager capitalism – and to see why the former, too, is worthy of overdue study – consider briefly how an asset such as housing is differentially positioned within these two contrasting investment constellations.

In asset-manager capitalism, you might find yourself living in an apartment owned by a corporation such as Avalonbay Com-munities. Avalonbay is a publicly listed US real-estate company, and a longstanding constituent of the S&P 500. Asset managers collectively might own 40, 50 per cent, or even more, of Avalon-bay's shares; and one of the biggest mainstream asset managers, such as BlackRock, might individually own as much as 10 per cent of the company. In asset-manager society, by contrast, *you live in an apartment owned by BlackRock*. Your relationship with the asset manager is altogether less ambiguous, much more direct, and considerably less mediated by other stakeholders.

Now, this is not to suggest that the phenomenon of renting an apartment under asset-manager capitalism does not have its own special features worthy of examination. Two features in particular make it noteworthy, and potentially problematic. First, the great likelihood is that BlackRock owns not just, say, 5–10 per cent of Avalonbay: it is also likely that it owns a com-parably sized stake in every other major publicly listed owner of residential property – not just in the United States, but in every other territory with advanced securities markets. It is, in the language of political economy, a *universal owner*. Second, it is not just BlackRock that owns 5–10 per cent of every major publicly listed corporate residential landlord: so too, almost certainly, do Vanguard and State Street, the other two of the so-called 'Big Three' universal owners, who between them now own more than 20 per cent of the average S&P company.[36] That these three own significant stakes in *all* major publicly listed corporations, not just in the housing sector but across the whole economy, such that *common ownership* dovetails with universal ownership, has its own special implications, not least relating to corporate governance – but such implications are not the concern of this book.[37]

... to Asset-Manager Society

When, in the 1980s, asset managers first started investing in 'real' (as opposed to just financial) assets on a significant scale, the initial locus of that investment was real estate – specifically, commercial real estate. Offices, hotels, warehouses, shopping centres and so on: all became, and would remain, valuable institutionalised asset classes (or 'sub-classes').

Yet, in reality, even in this new context of physical investment, asset managers were still just as economically distant from most people's everyday lives as when they invested in the shares of an Apple or Avalonbay. To be sure, many of us work in offices, visit hotels, and shop in shopping centres. But we do not live in them.

---

36 Potter, 'BlackRock-Led "Big Three"'.

37 See, for example, J. Fichtner, E. M. Heemskerk and J. Garcia-Bernardo, 'Hidden Power of the Big Three? Passive Index Funds, Re-Concentration of Corporate Ownership, and New Financial Risk', *Business and Politics* 19 (2017), pp. 298–326; J. Azar, M. C. Schmalz and I. Tecu, 'Anticompetitive Effects of Common Ownership', *Journal of Finance* 73 (2018), pp. 1513–65; B. Christophers, 'How Financial Giants Might Come to Rule Us All', 18 June 2019 – at jacobinmag.com; M. Backus, C. Conlon and M. Sinkinson, 'Common Ownership in America: 1980–2017', *American Economic Journal: Microeconomics* 13: 3 (2021), pp. 273–308; Braun, 'Asset Manager Capitalism'.

And the rents paid to real-estate owners by, for example, office-block tenants, hotel operators or shops in shopping centres tend to affect us only indirectly and intermittently.

But the impact became much more direct and continuous – at least for tenants – when, starting around a decade later, asset managers began buying substantial quantities of housing. As far as real estate is concerned, then, it is asset managers' ownership of housing, and only housing, that this book explores.

What of infrastructure? Asset managers' move into direct investment in infrastructures of various kinds began around the same time as their entry into home ownership, in the 1990s – it, too, in other words, is a relatively recent phenomenon. It encompasses six main infrastructure categories, all integral to quotidian social reproduction, and all examined in this book. The first category is *energy* infrastructures, which include power generation facilities and fuel storage and distribution networks. The second is *water and wastewater* infrastructure, such as water mains and pumping stations. The third is *transportation* infrastructure – roads, tunnels, bridges, parking facilities, train rolling-stock, and so on. The fourth is *telecommunications* infrastructure, including broadcast towers, data centres and fibre networks. The fifth category is *social* infrastructure – principally schools and hospitals. And the sixth and final category is the main infrastructure of *food production*: farmland.

In asset-manager society, then, to return to the above example, BlackRock not only owns your home; it also owns the land from which your food originates, the wind farm that generates your electricity, the road you drive on to work, and much else besides. Your life depends intimately on BlackRock – and especially on how it decides to commercialise those various proprietary real 'assets'.

One of the most interesting and important aspects of asset-manager society, however, is that its cast of dominant institutional characters is very, very different to that which presides over asset-manager capitalism. BlackRock, for its part, does indeed feature: it owns various infrastructures, especially in the energy sector, and some housing, though not large amounts at the time of writing. But real assets are, in relative terms, a tiny part of its business, largely peripheral in broader corporate terms, representing less than 1 per cent of its AUM at the end of 2020.[38] And Vanguard and State Street, the two other goliaths of mainstream asset management, play essentially no role at all in direct infrastructure and housing investment. Real assets are simply not their thing.

The market leaders are demonstrably others. One, we have already substantively encountered: the US firm, Blackstone, which owns a vast international housing portfolio, of which Alameda's Summer House is one small part. Australia's Macquarie is another market leader, in its case specialising in infrastructure investment. But if one had to pick one asset manager that epitomises the institutional dimension of asset-manager society, that firm would have to be Canada's Brookfield Asset Management. With huge investment operations in both housing and infrastructure, Brookfield is the real-asset asset manager par excellence.

And there are countless other significant players. To get a sense of the variety, and also of quite how fully asset-manager society has flowered in particular places, consider the county of Kent in the south-east of the UK. Like Alameda, it is seemingly innocuous, but no less a metonym for the world of contemporary real-asset investment. Quietly, without attracting much attention, asset managers have colonised the local physical landscape, stitching themselves into the very fabric of the region's social metabolism. The entire infrastructure of wastewater collection and treatment in the county, including tens of thousands of kilometres of sewers, is controlled by Macquarie. Macquarie also controls much of Kent's infrastructure of water supply, the rest of which is controlled by another Australian asset manager, namely Morrison & Co. Meanwhile, a joint venture between two asset managers – Global Infrastructure Partners of the US and the aforementioned Brookfield – and one Canadian pension scheme owns the entire network of pipes through which gas is distributed to heat Kent's homes.

If these represent the most comprehensive examples of colonisation, numerous more discrete examples exist in more or less all

---

38   To be precise: $48 billion, composed of equal amounts in real estate and infrastructure. See BlackRock, Inc., *Annual Report for the Fiscal Year Ended December 31, 2020*, p. 8 – at ir.blackrock.com.

the other sectors we are interested in. Housing? Blackstone owns rental properties in Paddock Wood. Student housing? Chicago-headquartered Harrison Street owns digs in Canterbury. Care homes? New York–based Safanad controls homes in Dartford and Gravesend. Electricity generation? The UK's Foresight Group owns solar farms at Abbey Fields and Paddock Wood. Transportation? Legal & General Investment Management owns parking spaces; Sweden's EQT Partners owns rapid-charging stations for electric vehicles; PSP Investments of Canada owns train rolling-stock. Telecommunications? Luxembourg's Cube Infrastructure Managers owns a large ultra-fast fibre broadband network. Last but not least, there is social infrastructure: asset managers whose investment portfolios contain Kent hospitals or schools include Amber Infrastructure, Innisfree and Semperian PPP Investment Partners, all UK companies.

Asset-manager society, as will already be abundantly clear, is thus nothing if not a thoroughly multinational constellation of investment institutions.

As these institutions have discovered over the past few decades, owning real assets is very different from owning financial assets. For one thing, it entails different responsibilities. Owners of financial assets do not really have any formal responsibilities as such: while shareholders are expected out of self-interest to ensure that the companies in which they own shares are well managed, through for example the exercise of their voting rights, they can and do treat this 'responsibility' with widely varying degrees of consideration. But if you own a house or a wind farm or a toll road, and especially if that asset is relied upon by others – for accommodation, electricity and travel, respectively – it is your legal responsibility to maintain it. Such responsibility is one more reason why asset managers tend to have a far more direct impact on people's lives in asset-manager society than under asset-manager capitalism.

Furthermore, real assets generate different kinds of income from financial assets. The latter generate interest payments (on fixed-income securities) and dividends (on shares), and it is these that asset managers have historically been accustomed to receiving. Real assets, by contrast, generate things like housing rents, payments per kilowatt-hour for electricity, and road-toll fees – and innumerable other types of income stream besides. This fact alone makes real-asset asset management a very different, and arguably much more complicated, type of business.

And if we need to study and understand asset-manager society because of the asset manager's direct influence on people's everyday lives when it owns housing and infrastructure, it is crucial also to appreciate the profound significance of real-asset asset management *as a capitalist business*. There is in fact a very considerable irony, and perhaps even paradox, here. Asset-manager capitalism – and the firms that dominate it – receives outsized critical attention partly because of the sheer scale of the relevant operations: during 2021, AUM at BlackRock alone, for example, passed $10 trillion, and Vanguard and State Street were not far behind. And yet, to use a boxing metaphor, asset-manager society tends on a pound-for-pound basis to be much the more lucrative, profitable territory for asset managers to operate in.

Take the following comparison. In 2020, BlackRock, which, as we have seen, operates overwhelmingly in the mainstream of the asset-management business, ended the year with $8.7 trillion under management, and it earned net income (profit) of $4.9 billion. Thus, it needed to have approximately $1,770 of client capital under management to earn each single dollar of profit. Across the three years 2018–20, the average figure for this particular metric was $1,604.[39] The equivalent ratios for Vanguard and State Street would be broadly similar.

Now look at Blackstone, and specifically its real-estate operation, which is focused predominantly on logistics, residential and office assets. In terms of AUM, it is dwarfed by Black-Rock, managing (at 2020 year-end) only $187 billion of client money: BlackRock (as a whole) is nearly fifty times larger than Blackstone Real Estate, in other words. But the latter's profits ('distributable earnings' is the firm's preferred measure) in the same year were $1.7 billion – less than BlackRock's $4.9 billion, to be sure, but not that much less, and clearly of a comparable order of magnitude. Thus, Blackstone Real Estate needed to have

---

39 Ibid., p. 2.

only $110 of client capital under management to earn a dollar of profit in 2020, and only an average of $105 across 2018–20.[40] Compare that with BlackRock's $1,604 over the same three-year period. Pound for pound, in terms of returns on AUM, Blackstone Real Estate is fifteen times more profitable than BlackRock as a whole – that is, it is a machine that is fifteen times as efficient in converting managed client capital into asset-manager profit. Not for nothing did one industry observer argue in 2007 that, even as it managed much less capital than giants like State Street, Australia's Macquarie was effectively the world's largest asset manager.[41]

Thus, as well as explaining how asset-manager society affects the ordinary households whose lives are embedded in it, this book will explain how and why it is such a financially rewarding commercial terrain.

Before we can get to the question of these respective costs and benefits, however, we need to learn much more about what asset-manager society consists of in practice, and when and where it emerged historically and geographically.

---

40   The Blackstone Group Inc., *Annual Report for the Fiscal Year Ended December 31, 2020*, pp. 94, 108 – at sec.report.

41   This was Peter Doherty of Capital Partners, as reported in G. Haigh, 'Who's Afraid of Macquarie Bank?', 4 July 2007 – at themonthly.com.au.

1

Asset-Manager Society: The Basics

The Investment Fund

At the heart of the asset-management industry, and thus of asset-manager society, is the investment fund. Insofar as asset managers invest money entrusted to them by assorted third-party clients, they require one or more vehicles to enable them to pool together that third-party capital, and then invest it on their clients' collective behalf. The investment fund is the pre-eminent such vehicle. All of the major asset managers discussed in this book operate several such funds. Some operate hundreds. The investment fund is as central to asset-manager society as the commodity is to the capitalist mode of production. It is its elementary form, the analysis of which therefore represents the logical place to begin our investigation. The wealth of societies in which the asset-management industry prevails appears as an immense collection of investment funds.

Often described as a 'collective investment scheme', the investment fund is effectively an aggregation of capital belonging to multiple investors, and used to make purchases of certain assets. In practical terms, the fund itself is a legal creation, formed usually (but not always) under company law, using arcane legal documents. Most investment funds established and operated by asset managers have a stated focus on one or more asset types, and often also a particular geographic focus.

Thus, where the assets that interest us in this book are concerned, a manager might for instance set up a fund to invest in 'real assets' of various kinds and located across numerous geographies – as the US asset management firm HarbourVest Partners did in 2020 with its Real Assets Fund IV (its fourth fund of that type, in other words). Alternatively, a manager might create a fund with a tighter focus. In 2019, for example, Greystar established a fund – Greystar China Multifamily Venture I – to invest specifically in Chinese multi-family rental housing.

Meanwhile, for institutional investors wanting to put money into infrastructure, the same year saw the launch of an abundance of new funds. Among the most niche were funds such as Parking Fund Europe, established by Germany's AIF Capital to invest solely in parking garages. At the other extreme were several considerably more diversified 'mega' funds. A notable one was Global Infrastructure Partners' (GIP) latest global infrastructure fund, GIP IV, which was created to invest in energy, transportation, water and waste-management assets primarily in OECD markets, but with up to 15 per cent of fund capital earmarked for selected non-OECD countries.[1] GIP, as we will see, is a major player in infrastructure asset management. Created in 2006 by former executives of the bank Credit Suisse and the multinational conglomerate General Electric, and operating out of New York, GIP's earliest investments were in assets ranging from Argentine ports to US gas pipelines and Indian oil-storage facilities.

Once asset managers have legally created a new fund, they set about the crucial task of raising capital from third-party investors to pool into that fund and to be invested by it. They ask investors to make binding *commitments*: pledges, essentially, to invest a given amount in the fund, which the asset manager can draw down (via the 'capital call') when the time comes to purchase assets. GIP IV can serve as an illustration, albeit one of unusually large size. For this fund, GIP set an initial fundraising target of $17.5 billion, and required potential investors to commit a minimum amount of $25 million. In the event, demand from clients exceeded expectations, and when the fund

---

1 Global Infrastructure Partners (GIP), 'Global Infrastructure Partners IV', February 2018.

was closed to new investors in December 2019 some $22 billion had been committed to it, making it the largest infrastructure fund ever raised.[2]

In total, 240 external investors from around the world put money into GIP IV, including public and private pension plans (the New York State Common Retirement Fund committed $500 million, for example, in one of the largest single investments), sovereign wealth funds, and insurance companies. Approximately 70 per cent of these external investors were existing GIP clients, having invested in previous GIP funds. Although high-net-worth individuals and family offices sometimes feature among investors in real-asset funds, the vast bulk of investors, as in the case of GIP IV, are always institutional, and are typically led by pension plans. There is nothing mysterious about this: investing in such funds requires not just large amounts of capital but a willingness to commit it for several years, and pension plans are the world's largest custodians of capital meeting these two criteria. By way of illustration, Figure 1.1 shows the breakdown by investor category of the 5,920 separate reported institutional-investor commitments to infrastructure funds globally between 1990 and 2020. Note that this represents *numbers* of commitments rather than commitment *value*; as we will see in Chapter 5, different types of investor tend to make investments of smaller or larger average size. As the chart shows, over 60 per cent of these thousands of individual commitments were made by pension schemes.

If its size made GIP IV unusual (by way of comparison, the aforementioned HarbourVest real-asset fund and Greystar housing fund both raised 'only' around $500 million, and the AIF parking-garage fund, in turn, only around half that amount), on another important dimension GIP IV was more typical: namely, the amount of capital that GIP itself put in. When asset managers create real-asset funds, they almost always invest some of their own money alongside that of their clients as a way of explicitly aligning interests, or having 'skin in the game'. GIP

Figure 1.1

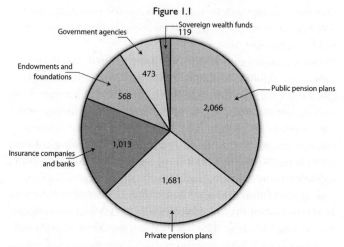

Number of institutional-investor commitments to infrastructure funds globally, by investor type, 1990–2020

Source: Andonov, Kräussl and Rauh, 'Institutional Investors and Infrastructure Investing', *Review of Financial Studies* 34 (2021), p. 3888.

pledged to commit the equivalent of 1.5 per cent of total commitments made by external investors, up to a maximum of $300 million; since $22 billion was raised, GIP's commitment was indeed the maximum $300 million, representing a 1.4 per cent share of fund value. Asset managers' commitments to their own real-asset funds generally range from 1 to 5 per cent of the total; GIP's, then, was at the low end, but not unusually so by any means. The important point – one to which we shall return – is that asset managers generally do not have very much skin in the game, relative either to their clients or to the outsized share that they successfully capture of any financial gains generated by the investment fund.

Investment funds such as GIP's are often referred to as 'limited partnerships', which is the legal form they usually take. A principal reason that the funds are established as limited partnerships is that, unlike corporations, such partnerships are generally not subject to tax; instead, tax is incurred by investors on distributions from the fund. The external investors that put money into the fund are its 'Limited Partners' (LPs), so called because they have limited liability (the most they can lose is the amount they have invested in the fund) and limited control (they are not actively involved in the management of the fund). As well as LPs, funds also have a General Partner (GP), which controls the fund. The GP is not the asset manager itself, but rather an entity (usually another partnership) constituted and owned by that manager. The GP generally contracts the management of the fund to the asset-management firm and its investment professionals. There are several reasons why the GP is constituted as a separate entity, perhaps the most important being to insulate the investment professionals employed by the asset manager from unlimited liability.

Real-asset funds vary not just in terms of size and the types of assets they invest in (and where they invest geographically), but also in terms of their commercial structure. Most are *unlisted*, meaning that it is not possible to buy and sell shares in them on the open market. Instead, investors deal directly with the asset manager, and are issued with fund units, which cannot be traded. There are also *listed* real-estate and infrastructure funds – which, like company shares, are quoted on public exchanges. We will encounter such listed funds periodically in the pages that follow. But they are in the minority, representing less than 10 per cent of infrastructure funds, for example.[3] Just as importantly, and for reasons explained later in this chapter, the typical characteristics of listed funds mean that most exist outside asset-manager society as this book conceives of it. Certainly, unlisted funds are asset-manager society's core investment vehicles. This partly explains why asset-manager society is so difficult to research, and remains largely in the shadows: unlisted funds tend to have extraordinarily limited disclosure requirements. Unlisted often means unknown, except to the asset manager itself and its investor clients.

There are two main types of unlisted real-asset vehicles – 'closed-end' and 'open-end' funds. Three of the examples of specific funds previously mentioned – GIP's, Greystar's and HarbourVest's – are closed-end funds. This means they have

---

3   A. Andonov, R. Kräussl and J. Rauh, 'Institutional Investors and Infrastructure Investing', *Review of Financial Studies* 34 (2021), pp. 3880–934, at p. 3887.

a predetermined term or lifespan, usually of seven to twelve years, and a predetermined subscription period, usually lasting from twelve to eighteen months – at the end of which the fund is 'closed' – during which capital can be committed. Also prescribed is the period during which managers of such funds are able to make new investments, which is typically the first four to six years of the fund's life. Once committed to closed-end funds, investors' money is locked up for the duration. All assets in which the fund invests must be sold prior to fund termination. Generally speaking, it is primarily from capital gains generated through these asset sales that such funds aim to make money for their investors.

Open-end funds, such as AIF's parking-garage fund, are different, inasmuch as they have no specific term: unless actively wound up for some reason, they are 'perpetual' vehicles. Subject to certain constraints (frequently including initial lock-up periods of two to five years), investors are free to commit and redeem capital as they choose from one quarter to another. Whereas closed-end funds typically prioritise capital gains, open-end funds generally aim to maximise recurring income over the long term. Many of them periodically distribute cash-flow to investors. Such funds are increasingly common in the real-estate and infrastructure spaces: indeed, the ability to generate income consistently and predictably is seen by asset managers and their investor clients as one of the most appealing and valuable features of the real-estate and infrastructure asset classes. In 2018, for example, Brookfield Asset Management, one of the world's leading real-asset asset managers, created its first open-end infrastructure fund, Brookfield Super-Core Infrastructure Partners.

At any rate, whatever the exact structure of the fund used in any particular case, the critical point is that it is *through investment funds* that asset managers do business. Funds are the kernel of their operating and financial model. Funds are where asset managers and their investor clients 'meet', so to speak, as it is in those funds that clients' all-important 'assets under management' (AUM) are held. Crucially, it is funds, not asset managers themselves, that make purchases. It is common to read that, say, BlackRock or Carlyle or KKR has bought such-and-such an asset; but, except in rare circumstances, it is not in fact the asset-management firm itself but rather one or more of the funds it manages that makes the investment and becomes the owner.[4]

An example may help make the point. Two Norwegian wind farms at Tellenes and Guleslettene respectively, which the huge US asset manager BlackRock was reported to have acquired in 2016 and 2018, were in fact bought by BlackRock Global Renewable Power II, a closed-end fund to which sixty-seven external investors committed a total of $1.65 billion.[5] The wind farms thereby became the property of the fund, meaning that their actual ultimate ('beneficial') owners were the dozens of investors that supplied the fund with capital, in proportion to their respective holdings of fund units. That the asset manager 'owns' the acquired assets in such instances is a useful and ubiquitous shorthand – readers familiar with the world of asset management know that 'BlackRock' typically means 'BlackRock-controlled investment funds' – but it is technically incorrect. We, too, will follow the custom: where, in this book, an asset manager is identified as acquiring or owning an asset, it is actually its fund(s) that is the acquirer and owner, unless explicitly stated otherwise.

Not for nothing, in short, is the asset-management business often instead labelled 'fund management'. Managers do indeed manage client assets – but they also manage the funds through which those assets are invested.

A Capsule Industry Ecology

All manner of different types of corporations are active in asset-manager society. Beyond the fact that they are all in the business, to one degree or another, of establishing investment funds to

---

4   Some asset-management firms do sometimes purchase assets themselves, using their own proprietary capital rather than collective-investment fund vehicles. In such instances, however, they are not acting *as* asset managers, but instead as institutional investors.

5   J. Shankleman, 'BlackRock Busts $1 Billion Green Power Goal with Second Fund', 5 July 2017 – at bloomberg.com.

pool investor capital and invest specifically in housing, infra-structure, or both, it is often the case that very little connects the firms in question. Take three examples. The US firm, Digital-Bridge, describes itself as a 'digital infrastructure' firm. The UK's Legal & General describes itself as a 'financial services' firm. Only the third, France's Amundi, calls itself an 'asset manager'. But asset management, including real-asset asset management, is an important part of what each one does.

To get a handle on asset-manager society, it is essential to gain a basic grasp of the primary kinds of institutional participant. At the risk of over-simplifying what is, in reality, a highly complex and heterogeneous landscape, we can identify three main types (see Table 1.1). The three aforementioned companies belong to one each of the three categories.

The first type is the *pure-play asset manager*. Asset manage-ment – investing third-party investor capital through pooled investment funds – is what such firms do, if not necessarily exclu-sively (they may engage peripherally in other business activities), then certainly at their core: asset management is their principal line of business, and is what they are known for.

Of the three categories, this one in particular warrants further segmentation – specifically according to where housing and infra-structure fit among the asset classes in which the manager invests. It helps to think about this question in terms of a spectrum. At

Table 1.1 Types of firm operating asset-management businesses that invest in housing and/or infrastructure

Pure-play asset managers			Financial services companies	Operating companies
Generalists	Diversified alternative asset managers	Specialists		
E.g. • Amundi (Fra) • BlackRock (US) • Franklin Templeton (US) • Invesco (US)	• Blackstone (US) • Brookfield Asset Management (Can) • Carlyle (US) • KKR (US) • Nuveen (US)	• Abacus Capital (US) • Global Infrastructure Partners (US) • Griffis Residential (US) • Stonepeak Infrastructure Partners (US)	• Allianz (Ger) • Goldman Sachs (US) • Macquarie Group (Aus) • Morgan Stanley (US) • Legal & General (UK)	• DigitalBridge (US) • Greystar (US) • Grosvenor Group (UK) • Tricon Residential (Can)

Source: Author

one end of the spectrum are generalists, who invest across the full gamut of asset classes – publicly listed equities and bonds (corporate and government-issued), commodities, currencies, private equity and commercial real estate, as well as housing and infrastructure. Amundi is one such generalist. Another, and the largest in the world in terms of AUM, is BlackRock.

At the other end of the spectrum are specialist asset managers, which invest only in housing, infrastructure or both. Global Infrastructure Partners, for example, which we encountered earlier, is a specialist infrastructure pure-play asset manager. Meanwhile, an example of a specialist housing asset manager is Abacus Capital Group, a US firm headquartered in New York that invests only in residential property (indeed, only in a particular type of residential property, namely multi-family housing). A recent report claimed that, of some 1,422 firms that in 2021 were managing active funds targeting investments that included (but in most cases were not limited to) European housing, only ninety-five specialised in residential investment.[6]

Lastly within the pure-play asset-manager category, in the middle of the spectrum we find more diversified 'alternative' asset managers. As well as investing in housing or infrastructure (or both), these firms are also active in one or more of private equity, hedge funds, commodities or private debt. But they differ from the aforementioned generalists inasmuch as they do not invest in the 'conventional' asset classes of publicly listed stocks and bonds – hence the very label, 'alternative'. The best-known such pure-play, diversified alternative asset manager is Blackstone. Interestingly, as their names suggest, Blackstone and BlackRock – commonly confused with one another – have a shared history. The former, founded in 1985, helped finance the creation of the latter in 1988, initially owning 50 per cent of the new business, and remaining a significant shareholder until 1994.

---

6 D. Gabor and S. Kohl, 'My Home Is an Asset Class: The Financialization of Housing in Europe', January 2022, p. 51 – at greens-efa.eu. Note here that not all of these 1,422 firms (nor indeed all of the ninety-five-strong subset of residential specialists) were pure-play asset managers: some belonged to one of our other two categories.

Moving on from pure-play operators, our second main type of institutional actor in asset-manager society is the diversified *financial services company*. Many of the major players in asset management in general (that is, across all asset classes) are financial institutions for which asset management is just one of the services it offers to clients: other services typically include commercial banking, investment banking, foreign exchange, securities custody, and sometimes also insurance and reinsurance. Some of these diversified financial services companies are active only in conventional asset management, while avoiding alternative asset classes such as real assets. But a large number do invest substantially in real assets, including housing and infrastructure, on behalf of their clients. Examples include the US firm Goldman Sachs, Australia's Macquarie Group, and the UK's Legal & General.

One of the things that makes asset-manager society particularly complex is that financial services companies are often *clients of* asset managers, rather than (or even as well as) operating as asset managers themselves. This is especially (though not only) true of insurance companies, which, after pension schemes, have traditionally been the largest source of the capital that is committed to asset managers' investment funds (see Figure 1.1). But, even if it complicates the picture, it is important nonetheless to recognise that some of the world's biggest and most influential asset managers – including in the real assets space – are indeed companies whose core business is the provision of insurance and reinsurance services.

The prime example is Germany's Allianz Group, founded as long ago as 1890, and frequently identified today as the world's largest insurance firm. Not only does Allianz mostly not rely on third-party asset managers to invest its own considerable capital, instead carrying out that investment in-house, but, through its twin asset-management businesses, PIMCO and Allianz Global Investors, it also manages and invests huge sums of external capital, these third-party AUM having grown to no less than €2 trillion by the end of 2021.[7]

---

7   Allianz Group, *Annual Report 2021*, p. 83 – at allianz.com.

Our third and final category of major participant in the business of real-asset asset management is *operating companies*. These are companies whose core business is owning and operating residential property or infrastructure using their own capital, but which additionally engage in the same activity – that is, investing in income-generating real assets – using third-party investor capital pooled into discrete investment funds. Although the nature of the intervention into the built environment is the same regardless of whose capital is used, the company's business model is notably different in the two cases: while the core business earns revenue in the form of charges levied on users of the housing or infrastructure, the asset-management side-business earns revenue principally in the form of fees paid by its investment funds' limited partners. I will explore the nature of such fees later in this chapter.

On the infrastructure side, consider the example of the Florida-based DigitalBridge Group. Its core business (labelled 'Digital Operating') involves using DigitalBridge's own balance sheet to buy, own and operate digital telecommunications assets, including cell towers, fibre networks and, in particular, data centres. But it also has a growing asset-management business ('Digital Investment Management'), which uses a range of investment funds to own and operate the same types of assets on behalf of third-party investors, whose cumulative commitments to such funds – representing DigitalBridge's third-party AUM – amounted to $44 billion at the end of 2021. At the time of writing, the core business is approximately four times the size of the asset-management business when compared in terms of revenues, which totalled, respectively, $763 million and $192 million in 2021.[8]

Such hybrids between operating company and asset manager are somewhat more common on the housing side. Three well-known examples are the UK's Grosvenor Group, Canada's Tricon Residential, and the US firm, Greystar, all of which invest in rental housing using both their own and third-party capital. The split between these two parts of the business is difficult to

---

8 DigitalBridge Group, Inc., *Annual Report for the Fiscal Year Ended December 31*, 2021, pp. 50–1 – at ir.digitalbridge.com.

discern in the case of Greystar (a privately held company with limited information disclosures), but clearer in the two other cases, which proportionally are very similar to one another.

Tricon, which invests solely in residential property (mainly in the United States, and mainly in the form of single-family units), and which at the end of 2020 had $2.6 billion in limited-partner capital under management within funds such as Tricon Housing Partners US I and II, earns fourteen times as much from letting its own property ($478 million in 2020) as from its asset-management business (£34 million).[9] Grosvenor, the property vehicle of the Duke of Westminster, which invests in commercial as well as residential real estate, earns ten times as much from letting its own property (£164 million in 2020) as from its asset-management business (£16 million).[10] The involvement of the Duke – the quintessential aristocrat – in the asset-management business provides a useful signal that, for all the relative novelty of asset management as a model of capital ownership and allocation, in the UK at least it remains bound up with some of the longest-standing and most ingrained structures of wealth distribution and inequality.

Equipped now with this basic picture of the main types of company that compete in the creation and commercial exploitation of asset-manager society, we may move on to begin to delineate the key contours of that society itself.

The Contours of Asset-Manager Society

The importance of asset control

Once an asset manager has secured sufficient commitments to a fund, it can begin investing this capital. On rare occasions, real-asset funds only ever make one investment. More commonly, a fund will make multiple 'portfolio' investments; and sometimes, especially where particularly large sums are involved,

9 Tricon Residential, 2020 Annual Report, pp. 43, 89 – at investors. triconresidential.com.

10 Grosvenor Group Limited, Financial Statements for the Year Ending 31 December 2020, p. 48 – at grosvenorlive.b-cdn.net.

Figure 1.2

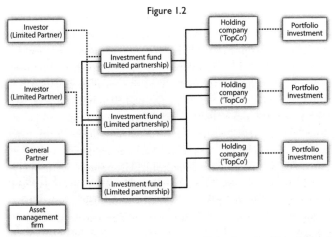

Pro forma structure of the asset-manager-controlled, private-fund-based pooled investment mechanism

Source: Author

investments in a single asset – for instance, a network of gas pipelines or a chain of care homes – are effected via multiple funds (Figure 1.2). By way of example, Global Infrastructure Partners' first flagship global fund, GIP I, which was launched in 2006, invested a total of around $5 billion in twelve separate assets during its twelve-year life, among them airports, ports, gas pipelines, oil-storage facilities and renewable-power plants.[11]

The assets acquired by real-asset funds can themselves exist at varying points of their own lifecycle. Real estate, and especially infrastructure investments, are often placed in one of three life-cycle categories. The first is 'greenfield', meaning that investors are actually financing the construction of an asset that does not yet exist. 'Brownfield' refers to assets that exist, but which need substantive renovation or upgrading. Finally, 'secondary' assets are fully operational. Data suggest that around three-quarters of investments by infrastructure funds are of this last type; of the remainder, greenfield outnumber brownfield investments by approximately two to one.[12] In other words, the asset manager is financing new infrastructure in less than one in five cases.

---

11 GIP, 'Global Infrastructure Partners IV', pp. 6–8.
12 Andonov, Kräussl and Rauh, 'Institutional Investors', p. 3889.

Meanwhile, in the housing space, investment by asset managers has historically been almost exclusively in existing assets. Only since the mid 2010s has that begun to change (and then only slowly, and thus far on a relatively small scale) with the emergence in countries such as Australia, Ireland, Spain and the UK of the 'build to rent' market, in which asset managers have latterly been establishing a growing presence.

The analysis of asset-manager society elaborated in this book would be considerably more straightforward than it is if all real-asset investments by asset managers were of the sort that BlackRock and its Global Renewable Power Fund II made in the abovementioned Norwegian wind farms in 2016 and 2018. In those two cases, the investments were in the assets themselves – the physical 'real things', as I referred to them in the Introduction. Now, I have not visited either Tellenes or Guleslettene, and I do not know whether either facility bears a plaque naming its owner. But, if they do, 'BlackRock' or 'Black-Rock Global Renewable Power Fund II' would presumably be the inscription.

Asset managers – or rather, their funds – very often do own in this direct, immediate fashion the real, physical assets that provide the scaffolding for asset-manager society. Tellenes and Guleslettene are not outliers, in other words. Countless other examples could be cited, involving physical assets of various types. In 2018, for instance, Canada's Brookfield Asset Management paid $1.1 billion to acquire thirty-one data centres in ten countries on four different continents from the telecommunications group AT&T.[13] In 2020, the US asset manager Manulife Investment Management bought an almond orchard in New South Wales, Australia, for $98 million.[14] And the following year, another US-based manager, PGIM, spent $120 million on six multi-family apartment blocks, containing 353 residential rental

13   Y. Sverdlik, 'AT&T Sells 31 Data Centers to Brookfield for $1.1B', 22 June 2018 – at datacenterknowledge.com.

14   M. Tracey, 'US Investor Snaps Up Almond Orchard for $98m', 5 September 2020 – at farmweekly.com.au. At that time, Manulife Investment Management operated under the brand Hancock Agricultural Investment Group, only adopting the Manulife brand in November 2021.

units, in the Japanese cities of Tokyo and Yokohama.[15] Such deals are the core transactional building-blocks of global asset-manager society, directly connecting managers – and, behind them, their institutional investors – to a vast, disparate array of vital physical systems of social reproduction.

Often, however, the connection between the asset manager and the physical asset is, or at least appears to be, somewhat less direct and immediate. Another company frequently sits between the two. This can come about in two main ways. First, and probably most commonly, instead of buying the physical asset per se, an asset manager buys the company that owns the asset. In 2010, for example, the Australian asset manager Macquarie Infrastructure and Real Assets (MIRA) spent approximately €574 million to take control of the Czech Republic's principal infrastructure for the transmission of terrestrial television and radio signals, comprising over 800 towers and masts, as well as a 2,600-kilometre fibre-optic backbone network.[16] The deal was notable not only for the fact that three different Macquarie funds co-invested, but because they bought the infrastructure's owner-operator – a company called České Radiokomunikace – rather than the assets themselves. Today, České Radiokomunikace remains in business as the infrastructure owner-operator; the Macquarie funds sold the company in 2021.

Second, asset managers sometimes create new companies specifically as vehicles to acquire, and then operate, real assets. One of the best-known examples of recent times concerns a company called Invitation Homes, which the US asset manager Blackstone created in 2012 to acquire and then let US single-family houses. Whereas, in the Czech case mentioned above, several Macquarie funds bought a company that already owned physical assets, in this latter case several Blackstone funds – the main one being Blackstone Real Estate Partners VII – capitalised a new company in order to enable it to purchase assets. That company, Invitation Homes, then carried out such purchases on a vast scale, spending

---

15 C. Caillavet, 'PGIM Buys Greater Tokyo Multi-Family Apartment Portfolio for $120m', 7 January 2021 – at mingtiandi.com.

16 'Macquarie-Managed Funds Acquire Ceské Radiokomunikace', 6 December 2010 – at macquarie.com.

in the region of $10 billion to become, by the end of 2016, the country's biggest owner of single-family homes, with a portfolio of some 48,000 properties.[17]

But the key point to be made here is that, in cases of both such types – of buying or creating a real-asset-owning company – the asset manager, even if more 'remote' from the physical assets legally than when directly owning the assets, is scarcely more remote practically, still less financially. If, through its funds, it is the owner of the intermediary company that in turn owns the assets, it enjoys both asset control (typically exercised via majority appointments to the board) and all the financial benefits associated with direct equity ownership. As Blackstone's long-time chief executive, Stephen Schwarzman, responded when recently asked about the advantages of the particular approach to investment – owning firms outright, either by buying or creating them – favoured by Blackstone and its plethora of investment funds: 'You have complete control.'[18] Our hypothetical ownership plaque nailed to the Czech broadcast towers may read 'České Radiokomunikace', but, for a decade, 'České Radiokomunikace' effectively meant 'Macquarie'. Those broadcast towers were no less substantively a part of asset-manager society than are the Tellenes wind farm or Brookfield's data centres.

Here, then, we have one of the most important differences between asset manager *society* – that is, growing asset-manager ownership specifically of physical systems integral to social reproduction – and so-called asset manager *capitalism* – growing asset-manager ownership of equity stakes in publicly listed corporations of all kinds, increasingly through tracker or index funds that hold positions in all shares included within certain market indices. In asset-manager society, the asset manager controls the physical asset. Indeed, such control is definitive of asset-manager society, being integral to its very constitution. It is the asset manager that decides how the asset is commercially

17   J. Berr, 'Blackstone's Plan to Cash In on a $10 Billion Housing Bet', 7 December 2016 – at cbsnews.com.

18   M. K. Flynn, '"Complete Control" Is the Beauty of Private Equity, Says Blackstone's Stephen A. Schwarzman', 17 September 2019 – at themiddlemarket.com.

exploited: who electricity is sold to, whether road tolls should be increased, how farmland should be tenanted, and so forth. And this is true even where a wholly owned intermediary portfolio company exists; as Blackstone's Schwarzman said: *You have complete control.*

Under asset-manager capitalism, by contrast, the asset manager does not control the companies in which it holds shares. Typically in the 5–15 per cent range, the stakes held by the giant universal owners BlackRock, Vanguard and State Street are too small to give even them formal control. Moreover, as Lucian Bebchuk and Scott Hirst have pointed out, these managers own stakes in so many companies – Vanguard, for instance, had holdings in over 13,000 worldwide in 2019 – that, even if they did possess the legal power to exert control, they clearly do not possess anything like the necessary operating capacity to do so in meaningful fashion: Vanguard's team of stewardship personnel, tasked with engaging with portfolio companies, numbered a grand total of twenty-one in the same year.[19] More importantly still, asset-manager capitalism's 'Big Three' do not even want control of the companies in which they hold their thousands of minority positions. Control is not part of the business model. As Benjamin Braun has persuasively argued, the hallmark of asset-manager capitalism is precisely asset-manager passivity. It is a capitalism of large, universal and 'disinterested' shareholders.[20]

Asset-manager society is fundamentally different. Control is one of its calling-cards. And therefore, those generalist asset managers that straddle both worlds – BlackRock is perhaps the prime example – in reality comprise (at least) two different

19 L. A. Bebchuk and S. Hirst, 'Index Funds and the Future of Corporate Governance: Theory, Evidence, and Policy', *Columbia Law Review* 119: 8 (2019), 2029–146, at p. 2077. On BlackRock, Vanguard and State Street's general lack of engagement with portfolio companies in which their index funds own minority stakes, see also D. Heath, D. Macciocchi, R. Michaely and M. C. Ringgenberg, 'Do Index Funds Monitor?', *Review of Financial Studies* 35: 1 (2022), 91–131.

20 B. Braun, 'Asset Manager Capitalism as a Corporate Governance Regime', in J. S. Hacker, A. Hertel-Fernandez, P. Pierson and K. Thelen, eds, *The American Political Economy: Politics, Markets, and Power* (Cambridge: Cambridge University Press, 2022), pp. 270–94.

businesses. On the one hand is the largely passive, mainstream business of buying up small financial stakes in essentially all significant publicly listed corporations. On the other is the business we are interested in in this book, represented in BlackRock's case by its Real Assets investment team, which operates almost entirely separately from the team of managers of BlackRock's vast index funds. This is the highly active, hands-on business of buying up much smaller numbers of real, physical assets or the companies that hold them – and, in the process, shaping in direct and tangible ways the conditions of everyday life for ordinary people.

Issues of demarcation

If the phenomenon of asset managers controlling housing or infrastructure via wholly owned intermediary companies is very much part of asset-manager society, the contours of asset-manager society arguably begin to seem more ambiguous in a couple of other important and relatively common investment scenarios. The first involves fractional ownership. To illustrate once again using the case of BlackRock, it turns out that, even in the case of its real-asset business, there are instances in which BlackRock's funds enjoy only part-ownership of the physical assets, or of the company that holds the assets. In such instances, the distinction between asset-manager society and asset-manager capitalism can itself appear somewhat blurred.

Generally speaking, as the proportion of ownership of an asset declines, so also does the degree of control – as well, of course, as the extent of potential financial gain – that a capitalist shareholder enjoys. However imperfect, this generalisation serves to provide us with a useful and relatively straightforward rule of thumb in delimiting asset-manager society – which is to say, in determining whether particular cases of fractional ownership are or are not of relevance to our study. Specifically: the less that the types of real assets examined in this book are under the control of asset managers, the less emphatically embedded in asset-manager society those assets can be assumed to be.

If this sounds unduly abstract or imprecise, consider two instructive examples. One is Invitation Homes, mentioned above.

In January 2017, Blackstone floated Invitation Homes on the stock market. But its funds initially retained more than 70 per cent of the shares, and Blackstone retained board control. Thus, at that particular juncture, Invitation Homes' approximately 50,000 rental properties were still essentially Blackstone's, and still very much part of asset-manager society: the asset manager continued to control them, and it therefore remained deeply implicated in the processes of social reproduction that those homes occasioned.

Over time, however, the homes in question became by degrees less part of asset-manager society, as Blackstone progressively sold down its shareholding and, eventually, ceded board control. In November 2019, Blackstone's funds finally cashed out.

This, of course, is not to say that asset managers do not hold Invitation Homes shares today. They do: all of the company's biggest shareholders are asset managers, predictably led, at the time of this writing, by Vanguard (whose index funds collectively hold a stake of around 13 per cent) and BlackRock (with around 8 per cent). But with respect to Invitation Homes, these two managers are mutually independent, minority, and passive shareholders. They do not control the company – management does. If the company's assets are operated in such a way as to privilege the interests of the company's asset-manager shareholders, it is because management has decided it should be thus. Perhaps the most precise we can be is to say that, in instances such as this, 'real things' like Invitation Homes' properties are not wholly external to asset-manager society, but neither are they at or near the core of it in the way that the properties in question categorically were when wholly owned and controlled by Blackstone.

Our second example shows, however, that there are nonetheless cases of fractional ownership, where asset manager control remains more or less absolute, and asset-manager society is precisely the correct conceptual framing. The example concerns the Thames Tideway Tunnel, a £4.2 billion 'super sewer' for London. When operational (currently projected for 2025), it will prevent millions of tonnes of untreated sewage from polluting the River Thames, with the cost of the tunnel's construction and operation ultimately being picked up by Thames Water's approximately 15 million wastewater customers.

The tunnel is being delivered by a company called Tideway, which has just four shareholders, all of which are asset management firms: Allianz Capital Partners (part of Allianz Global Investors), with 34.3 per cent; the UK's Dalmore Capital, with 33.8 per cent; Amber Infrastructure, also a UK firm, with 21.3 per cent; and the Netherlands' DIF, with 10.6 per cent.[21] In the ownership and operation of Tideway, these four are the very opposite of passive, mutually independent investors: they act as a single, integrated investor consortium. Each of the four has one seat on the Tideway board, thus ensuring that shareholder directors outnumber the board's three executive directors (in other words, management). Tideway, in effect, is run by the consolidated investor consortium that owns it.

Meanwhile, if fractional ownership is one of the main scenarios in which the contours of asset-manager society are perhaps less clearly defined than in the prototypical case of a single asset manager enjoying exclusive control of physical assets by virtue of ownership of them, the other such scenario is where those assets are held not via ownership but under long-term contracts.

Such contracts, which are more common with infrastructure assets than with housing, can take a variety of different forms. One common form is the concession, which is a time-limited franchise to manage and operate an asset and – crucially – receive any income that it generates. The body granting the concession is frequently, but not always, in the public sector. MIRA, a major Australian asset manager we have already encountered, is an example of a prolific acquirer and holder of infrastructure concessions. One significant such contract came into its hands in 2018, when, through its Macquarie Asia Infrastructure Fund II, it bid around $1.5 billion to secure a thirty-year concession to manage nine national highways in India, and to collect the tolls that the roads' users pay. It was not Macquarie's first such investment: it had been investing in Indian toll-road concessions since 2012.

---

21 It was announced in mid 2022 that DIF would be selling its stake to its co-shareholders, but at the time of this writing the necessary third-party approvals for the deal to proceed had not been provided.

Alongside concessions, the other principal type of long-term contract through which asset managers hold physical infrastructure assets is the much-discussed public–private partnership (PPP). Although it takes somewhat different forms in different countries, the core elements of a PPP can be simply stated. It involves the public sector commissioning a private-sector actor to build and then operate – over a defined period – a physical asset of some kind, which might for instance be a road, a hospital or a school. Often, as is the case under the UK's Private Finance Initiative (PFI), the contractor also arranges the borrowing to finance the build. The contractor is typically set up as a Special Purpose Vehicle (SPV), and this vehicle is frequently owned by an asset manager. Such is the case, for example, with the schools in Kent in the UK referred to in the Introduction. Ebbsfleet Academy in Swanscombe is one of those schools. Innisfree, a UK asset manager, has a 100 per cent equity interest in the SPV – called New Schools (Swanscombe) Limited – that built the school, and which holds the twenty-five-year PPP contract to maintain the buildings (2002–27).

Are such assets, held by asset managers under PPP and concessionary contracts, part of asset-manager society? Unquestionably, yes. To begin with, in a minority of cases, the manager does in fact own the asset, albeit only temporarily – specifically, until the end of the contract term. In 2019, for instance, the UK asset manager Aberdeen Standard Investments paid more than $1 billion to acquire the Carlsbad desalination plant in Southern California, which holds a thirty-year water-supply PPP contract signed in 2012 with the San Diego County Water Authority, the ownership of which will transfer (for $1) to said authority at the end of the PPP period.[22]

But, even where *de jure* asset ownership is absent, which it ordinarily is under long-term PPP or concessionary contracts, the control of the asset – not to mention the exclusivity of financial reward – during the contract term is certainly such as to parallel the conditions obtaining under legal ownership. If it were not, after all, asset managers would not invest. And then, finally, there

22   G. Tan, 'Aberdeen to Buy Desalination Plant for More than $1 Billion', 29 May 2019 – at bloomberg.com.

is the question of the condition of the asset that the contractee is left with once the contract is terminated. What is the asset's useful life? When, in the early 2000s, the city of Chicago and the state of Indiana granted concessions to the Chicago Skyway and Indiana Toll Road, they did so under ninety-nine- and seventy-five-year contracts, respectively. Each lease, as one commentator noted, was 'basically a sale, since its term exceeds the road's anticipated life'.[23]

Whether by long-term contract or outright ownership, therefore, asset managers increasingly control the basic physical building-blocks of global society and economy. As a result, they increasingly fashion the parameters of the daily lives that every one of us is able to lead. But how does all this really work in practice?

Asset-Manager Society in Operation

Whether it is housing or some type of infrastructure, none of the various real assets in which asset managers invest 'auto generates' income. Rental houses and data centres must be let. Farmland must be farmed – or alternatively, let to a tenant farmer. The demand and supply of electricity routed through transmission grids must be matched. Schools must be cleaned. Road tolls must be collected. And so on. Whatever form the income generated by real assets takes (and we will turn to those different forms of income shortly), there is always work of some kind involved in enabling the income generation to occur.

To recognise this is to raise an important question: Who does this work? Or, to put the question another way: Who operates asset manager society, and makes sure that real assets generate the cash-flows that asset managers invest in?

On the face of it, one would imagine that it would be unlikely to be asset managers themselves. After all, people do not join Global Infrastructure Partners or Blackstone in order to carry out gas-pipeline maintenance or take calls from disgruntled

23   S. Malanga, 'The New Privatization', Summer 2007 – at city-journal.org.

apartment tenants. Thus, it is indeed very often the case that the asset manager plays no active role, either directly or indirectly, in operating the real assets it owns.

Three examples from among the asset purchases we have already discussed can serve as illustrative cases. As we saw, Black-Rock acquired the Tellenes wind farm in Norway in 2016. But it plays no role in operating that farm. Instead, upon buying it, it entered a multi-year service agreement with a Swedish renewable power company, Arise AB, under which the latter handles all aspects of operations and maintenance. At the time of this writing, Arise manages a total of fourteen third-party-owned Scandinavian wind farms, the majority of which are owned by asset managers including not only BlackRock (four farms) but also Allianz Global Investors (three). A second example is the abovementioned Carlsbad desalination plant, which was acquired by the UK asset manager Aberdeen Standard Investments in 2019. Unsurprisingly, Aberdeen has no operational role, either. The plant is managed rather by Poseidon Water, a developer of water-treatment PPP projects, and the company that built the Carlsbad plant in the first place. The final example is MIRA's toll-road concessions in India, for which Ashoka Buildcon is its local operations and maintenance partner.

Several features of this fully outsourced model of asset operation are noteworthy. One relates to the implied nature of the asset manager's own business. Consider BlackRock and Tellenes. Given that all operational elements are contracted out, Black-Rock in this instance is neither an energy company itself *nor even an investor in an energy company*. Its investment is solely and specifically in a physical asset, and its business is maximising and extracting the income – *rent* – that that asset generates. It is, therefore, a pure rentier. The same is true of Aberdeen Standard Investments in the Carlsbad case and MIRA in the toll-road case.

Relatedly, there is the question of the nature of the business of the companies that handle operations for the likes of Black-Rock and Aberdeen. Again, consider Tellenes, and Arise AB. As it happens, Arise currently operates ten of its own wind farms (as well as the fourteen that are third-party-owned), and in those ten cases it is acting in the capacity of an energy company as we conventionally understand the concept – that is, a company generating and supplying power to one or more customer. But, at Tellenes, it is not. It is not an energy company, but a service provider: its customer is BlackRock, and BlackRock does not buy power from it. Similarly, Aberdeen buys services, not water, from Poseidon. In other words, these cases entail a fundamental reconfiguration of business models and relationships. There *is* no energy company or water company as such. There are rentier-owners on the one hand, and there are providers of services to those rentier-owners on the other.

A final noteworthy feature of the outsourcing-based rentier model is one that we return to in more depth in Chapter 4. Specifically: the asset manager's profits clearly increase to the extent that it can limit the amount it pays those who clean its apartments, sit in its tollbooths and patrol its parking lots. This is one of the costs of asset-manager society.

But if, in many instances, asset managers are entirely detached from the operation of their real assets, in other cases, the boundaries are more blurred, with managers becoming involved, if only indirectly, in asset operation. This typically occurs through a portfolio company that usually – but not always – is also the immediate owner of the asset.

The extent and nature of the asset manager's such involvement, and also the explanation for it, vary widely. Sometimes, it comes about simply as part of the deal: namely where, to take control of an asset, an asset manager buys the company that owns *and operates* said asset, as was the case for example when, in 2010 in the Czech Republic, MIRA purchased České Radio-komunikace's broadcast towers and masts and its business of operating that infrastructure. Other times, meanwhile, asset managers actively and strategically cultivate operational involvement. This was the case for instance with Blackstone's US single-family rental business, Invitation Homes, which handled property letting in-house. There was nothing inevitable about it doing so: letting was internally managed rather than outsourced because Blackstone decided that this was how things should be done.

Ultimately, the nature and extent of operational involvement reflects asset managers' investment decisions, based inter alia upon the consideration of relative risks and rewards. Invitation Homes represents an illuminating example, because while some activities, such as letting, were managed in-house, others *were* outsourced. As explained in the company's listing prospectus, only those activities where it was considered possible to 'capture additional economies of scale and operational efficiencies' – such as letting and procurement operations – were performed internally. Other activities were contracted out. 'For example', the prospectus indicated, 'we typically engage third party home improvement professionals with respect to certain maintenance and specialty services, such as heating, ventilation and air conditioning systems, roofing, painting and floor installations.'[24]

Another instructive example is the US-based asset manager Manulife Investment Management (MIM), which, it will be remembered, invested in an almond orchard in Australia in 2020. Farmland investment raises a whole range of different operational possibilities for asset managers like MIM. A pure rentier investor would simply own the asset, and outsource everything else, including the leasing of land to tenant farmers. A more 'involved' investor, meanwhile, would, like Invitation Homes, handle the leasing. And a still more involved investor might also buy or build an actual farming operation.

MIM, it transpires, is a very operationally involved investor. At the time of this writing, it owns, according to its website, some 434,000 acres of farmland in Australia (c. 111,000 acres), Canada (c. 12,000) and the US (c. 311,000).[25] Only in the region of 60,000 such acres, it appears, are pure rentier-type assets, where MIM *only* owns the land. Through various portfolio companies, such as Hancock Farmland Services in the US, it manages over 370,000 of its total acres. Most of these managed acres are leased: current figures are not publicly available, but in 2014, when MIM's US farmland portfolio was smaller than it is today, it leased over 200,000 acres in the US, on terms ranging from one to ten years.[26] The remainder of the acreage that MIM owns

---

24 Invitation Homes, 'Form S-11', 6 January 2017, pp. 6, 28 – at sec.gov.

25 At haig.jumpingjackrabbit.com (as at mid 2022).

26 Hancock Agricultural Investment Group, 'Farmland Investor', Fall–Winter 2014, p. 3 – at haig.jumpingjackrabbit.com.

and manages, however, it – or rather its portfolio companies, such as Farmland Management Services in the US – *also* farms.

As with Blackstone–Invitation Homes, the nature and extent of MIM's operational involvement vis-à-vis its farmland reflects strategic investment decisions. It typically leases properties growing row crops – those, such as corn and soy, planted each year and in rows wide enough to allow them to be tilled or otherwise cultivated by agricultural machinery. Meanwhile, it usually directly farms itself those of its properties given over to permanent crops such as vineyards of grapes. Why the different approaches? Because the different types of crops are associated with different levels of risk and thus call for different management styles. Leasing, MIM observed in 2014, 'is the lower risk management option and thus typically results in a lower income return. Direct operation is a higher risk farmland investment strategy and typically results in a higher income return.'[27]

Whatever the nature, extent and rationale, in all such cases of operational involvement, the asset manager is invested both in the physical asset *and* in the business of enabling that asset to generate income. It is, to be sure, a rentier; but it is not only that.

Who Pays, and How?

Asset-manager society is a society in which core physical systems of social functioning and reproduction – the shelters and infrastructures we rely upon to keep ourselves alive and well – are widely owned and controlled by asset managers. Asset managers, of course, would not invest in the ownership of those systems unless it paid to do so. And everything, even those systems allowing for something as elemental as social existence, comes at a price – especially today, when the idea that there is, in Milton Friedman's immortal words, 'no such thing as a free lunch' has assumed the status of a universal truth. In short, to access and use systems of social functioning and reproduction, society always

27   Ibid.

pays, in one way or another. Coming to grips with asset-manager society therefore requires coming to grips with the ways in which people make this payment.

Just as asset managers own real assets with varying degrees of directness – sometimes controlling them directly, at other times doing so at a greater distance and through one or more intermediary companies – so the ordinary people who depend upon such assets make payments to those asset managers in ways that are sometimes relatively direct and at other times much less so. Another way of expressing this is to say that asset managers' income streams from real-asset ownership sometimes take the form of payments by ordinary people themselves, while in other cases they represent payments by mediating bodies – although ultimately the ordinary citizen always ends up paying, however indirectly. The varying mechanisms of payment matter not just empirically, for understanding how asset-manager society works; they also matter socially, even politically. The further removed the ultimate payer is from the payee, the less visible, generally speaking, the latter is to the former. Much of the time, therefore, we live in asset-manager society – consistently making payments to asset managers – without even being conscious of doing so.

Consider, to begin with, two hypothetical individuals going about their everyday lives, one in Madrid and the other in Chicago. And consider some of the payments they make in the course of those lives: specifically, the Madrid resident's payment to rent her apartment, and the Chicago resident's payment to park her car outside the downtown office where she works. Living in an apartment block in Carabanchel in the southwestern part of Madrid, the Spanish resident pays her rent to the US asset manager Blackstone, which owns her dwelling. Meanwhile, the Chicago resident pays her parking fee to a consortium that is controlled by another US asset manager, Morgan Stanley Infrastructure Partners, which holds the seventy-five-year concession – granted in 2008 – of the Chicago Metered Parking System, encompassing approximately 36,000 parking spots throughout the city. The second-largest investor in the three-member Chicago consortium is another asset manager,

Allianz Capital Partners; the third is a sovereign wealth fund, the Abu Dhabi Investment Authority.

Such payments represent about as direct a flow of cash from ordinary people to asset managers as exists in today's asset-manager society. And yet, in reality, even here, most individuals making such direct payments probably have little idea of who the beneficiary of those payments actually is. While, in such cases, the asset manager does receive payments from ordinary people (rather than from independent mediating institutions, in ways I will examine shortly), it frequently routes such payments in a way that makes their destination opaque to the payer.

In the case of Blackstone's housing, the tenant in the apartment block at Carabanchel pays her rent to a Spanish entity called Fidere Patrimonio. Fidere is a vehicle controlled by a Luxembourg-registered entity called Spanish Residential (REIT) Holdco S.à r.l., which owns more than 99 per cent of Fidere shares. And this Luxembourg entity is in turn a vehicle controlled by various Blackstone funds, of which the one with the biggest holding is Blackstone Real Estate Partners Europe IV. In effect, Fidere is Blackstone. But it is far from obvious that this is the case.

In the case of Morgan Stanley's parking spots, as in the case of Macquarie and its Indian toll-road concessions, Morgan Stanley obviously does not get its hands dirty operating Chicago's parking meters. Operation is outsourced to a company called LAZ Parking, and it is thus with LAZ Parking that the Chicago driver interacts. But even if a driver were inclined to look beyond the identity of the company collecting her parking fee to the identity of the entity receiving it, things would not necessarily be much clearer. The consortium owning the concession is a company with the nondescript name of Chicago Parking Meters, LLC. Only if the driver were to enquire into the identity of the shareholders of this latter entity would she come across the names of Morgan Stanley, Allianz and the Abu Dhabi Investment Authority – the entities that she pays to park.

Such payments by ordinary people to access or use asset-manager-owned real assets like parking spots or apartments represent, in any event, the most direct real-asset-based incomes that such asset managers receive – even if the relationship generally does not appear particularly 'direct' to the payer. Road tolls would represent another payment of the same direct type.

The ordinary people who depend upon society's real assets exist at a greater financial remove from the asset manager–owner, however, when payment is made to that manager–owner not by those people themselves but by an independent, mediating entity. Typically, this is the case when that mediating entity relies in some way upon the asset in question in order to provide people with certain products or services. That entity can be either in the private or public sector, and it is helpful to consider these two scenarios in turn, not least because the way in which said entity passes on to ordinary people the cost of its payment to the asset manager – which it always ultimately does – can vary significantly between the two cases.

A good example of private-sector companies that rely upon real assets they frequently do not own in order to provide people with important products or services are private utility companies – in the energy or telecommunications sectors, for example. One such utility is SSE Airtricity, which sells electricity and gas to homes across Ireland. Although it has a significant electricity-generation portfolio of its own, this company also purchases large amounts of electric power from third-party generators under long-term power-purchase agreements (PPAs). In early 2017, it signed one such PPA, a fifteen-year contract, with what was then Ireland's largest operational solar farm, the 45 MW project at Bann Road in County Antrim. At the time, the Bann Road asset was owned by the German energy company BayWa. Later the same year, however, Bann Road was sold – to Greencoat Solar II, an investment fund of the UK asset manager Greencoat Capital. (BayWa stayed on as Greencoat's operations and maintenance partner.) The electricity generated by Bann Road and sold to SSE Airtricity powers an estimated 300,000-plus homes. SSE Airtricity's payments to Greencoat Capital are recouped via those homes' electricity bills. But the likelihood that the homes in question are aware of this fact is probably even smaller than the likelihood of Chicago drivers knowing that they pay Morgan Stanley for their parking.

Of course, utilities can be public entities instead of private ones, and where that is the case, their payments to asset managers such as Greencoat Capital are usually passed on to households in much the same way as with Bann Road and SSE Airtricity. Once again, we can take California's Carlsbad desalination plant, owned by the UK asset manager Aberdeen Standard Investments, as an example. Where Greencoat–Bann sells electricity to SSE Airtricity under a fifteen-year agreement, Aberdeen–Carlsbad sells water to the public San Diego County Water Authority under a thirty-year agreement: specifically, between 48,000 and 56,000 acre-feet of water per annum, approximating 10 per cent of the San Diego region's water needs.[28] Households paying for that water through their water bills have the same type of mediated relationship with Aberdeen Standard Investments as the aforementioned electricity-consuming Irish households have with Greencoat Capital.

Where scenarios involving a public-sector mediating entity typically present a substantively different mechanism of payment to asset managers being passed on to ordinary people, meanwhile, is in instances where the services provided by that public entity are free at the point of use. Here, perhaps the best example is public hospitals or schools built through public–private partnerships (PPPs). Let us return to Ebbsfleet Academy in Kent in south-east England. The vehicle that in 2001 was contracted to build and then maintain the school is owned by the UK asset manager Innisfree. As an 'academy' school, Ebbsfleet is independent of local-authority control – its educational services are provided by a charitable body, the Leigh Academies Trust – but is nonetheless non-fee-paying for students, and is directly funded by the Department for Education (DfE).

Like all other UK PFI contracts, the DfE contract with Innisfree for Ebbsfleet bundles payment to the contractor into a series of single ('unitary') annual charges to cover both the initial capital costs and ongoing maintenance and operation costs. Innisfree received its first such annual unitary payment in 2002; it will receive its final payment in 2027, when the contract

---

28 'Positive Operating Performance Boosts Carlsbad Desalination Plant's Bond Rating', 25 October 2019 – at businesswire.com.

ends.[29] But the school does not charge fees. If the DfE does not levy charges on students and their families to cover its payments to Innisfree in the way that San Diego's municipal water authority levies charges on water users to cover its payments to Aberdeen, how does it recoup its PPP costs? Who ultimately pays, and how? The answer, of course, is UK taxpayers. General taxation funds the UK's system of public secondary-school education. A tiny sliver of that vast pool of money eventually finds its way to the Kent village of Swanscombe, where Ebbsfleet Academy is located, and is divided up between Leigh Academies, which is responsible for teaching the schoolchildren, and Innisfree, which is responsible for the physical building in which they are taught.

Some might wonder whether any of this detail about how and whom we pay to occupy and use various vital properties and infrastructures really matters. If prices do not increase unreasonably and quality does not suffer unduly, who cares whether, say, a waterworks is owned by the government, a water company or an asset manager? As I will show, however, ownership does have implications for price and quality. And the details I have examined here are key pieces of the puzzle that explains why this is the case.

Manager Remuneration

As we have seen, the investment fund sits at the centre of asset-manager society; it is the hub around which that society financially spins. The fund owns the real, physical assets. The fund receives the income generated by those assets: tolls, parking fees, housing rents, water and electricity charges, unitary PPP payments, and so forth. And the fund receives the capital proceeds generated by the sale of assets. As we have also seen, the lion's share of the money deposited in the investment fund and

---

29   The contract with Innisfree is in fact for two Swanscombe schools, the other being Craylands, a local authority–controlled primary school. Total unitary payments to Innisfree over the life of the contract (2002–27) amount to £70.9 million. See 'Current Projects', 31 March 2018 – at gov.uk.

invested by it is not the asset manager's own. It belongs to the manager's clients – pension schemes, insurance companies and the like.

To recognise these various fundamental features in conjunction is to raise an equally fundamental question: How does the asset/fund manager itself make money? To render the question tangible, consider a simple hypothetical case of a fund investing in real assets, to which $100 million is initially committed, of which $3 million – a typical proportion – by the asset manager. By the time the fund is wound up ten years later, its value has swelled to $200 million, partly thanks to income generated by the acquired assets while under fund ownership, and partly thanks to capital gains upon asset disposal. If this $200 million were to be distributed strictly in proportion to initial equity commitments, the asset manager would receive $6 million – 3 per cent of the total. But in reality, of course, this is not at all what happens. The asset manager makes considerably more. Why, and how?

The asset/fund manager is remunerated principally through fees, and those fees are as important and central a feature of asset-manager society as the fund phenomenon itself. It is literally impossible to understand why asset-manager society is so profitable for asset managers and so problematic for more or less everybody else unless one understands the fee model. Fees are of several types, of which the first two are the most significant.

The first are management fees. All external investors that commit money to the fund pay the manager a fee for the work that goes with managing it: investing the money, managing the assets that are acquired, and (potentially) selling them. But real-asset investment comes in many varieties, with the result that fee terms are anything but standardised. Variance in those terms operates on two main dimensions.

One is the basis on which fees are levied. Specifically, management fees are always stated and charged as a percentage – but a percentage of what exactly? Usually the answer is: committed capital. In other words, if, say, an insurance company commits $50 million to a real-asset fund, it will be charged an annual management fee equivalent to a percentage of that $50 million – irrespective, notably, of whether the money has yet been invested.

But committed capital is not always the basis on which management fees are charged. Sometimes, the basis is invested equity. Sometimes, it is gross asset value – the estimated market value of the assets the fund owns.

The other key dimension of variance is the percentage itself. Here, the key consideration is how 'active' the manager is – or claims to be – in managing the fund. The greater the amount of work required, the higher the percentage. In the world of infrastructure and real-estate investment, funds are usually distinguished not only on the basis of their structure – that is, the open-end versus closed-end distinction outlined earlier in this chapter – but also according to their estimated risk–return profile. At one end of the spectrum are so-called 'core' funds, which are low-risk and generally invest in assets generating secure and predictable incomes, but with little potential for capital appreciation. At the other end of the spectrum are 'opportunistic' funds, where the risk is higher, but so also is the potential for capital gain and thus outsized investment returns. 'Value-add' funds sit in the middle. Industry convention has it that opportunistic funds, which are usually closed-end, require a considerably more active manager than core funds, which generate steady income with little need for oversight. Management fees for the former are therefore higher.

An analysis conducted in 2015 by Preqin, a leading provider of data on the real-assets investment business, indicated that average annual management fees for real-estate and infrastructure funds were around 1.5 per cent.[30] Opportunistic funds generally charged 2 per cent, and core funds closer to 1 per cent. Fees can also be charged on a sliding scale, to incentivise larger commitments. Investors in Global Infrastructure Partners' GIP IV, for example, pay 1.75 per cent up to $75 million of committed capital, 1.5 per cent on the next $75 million, 1.25 per cent on the next $75 million, and 1 per cent on any subsequent amounts, but with overall fees subject to a floor of 1.3 per cent.[31]

The model for these management fees is private-equity asset

---

30   Preqin, 'Interests Aligned? Infrastructure Fund Terms and Conditions', November 2015 – at docs.preqin.com.

31   GIP, 'Global Infrastructure Partners IV', p. 18.

management, which of course involves funds buying companies and holding their shares privately, and where a 2 per cent fee has long been the standard. In fact, asset managers adopting an opportunistic approach to real-estate investment are often referred to as 'private equity real estate', with a corollary in 'private equity infrastructure' (or sometimes, 'infrastructure private equity'). Many major players in real-asset asset management, it will be recalled, are also active in private equity per se, being referred to generically as 'alternative' asset managers. Indeed, the boundaries are fluid. If, say, KKR acquires a private company whose major assets are wind farms, is this a private-equity or infrastructure investment? The answer is: either, or both. Thus, it is not unusual in such cases for an asset manager's infrastructure and private-equity funds to co-invest. Each has its own rationale. Only if the acquisition is of the wind farms themselves, and not of a company owning and operating them, will this be a pure infrastructure play, with no role for a private-equity fund.

In any event, if management fees in infrastructure and real-estate asset management are modelled on private equity, so also is the second fee type: performance fees. The better the fund performs for its limited partners, the more those partners pay the general partner – which is to say, the asset manager. Again, performance fees are anything but standardised, but there is more uniformity across the market on these than there is on management fees. The most common performance fee is so-called 'carried interest' (or simply 'carry'), which is a form of profit share paid on the basis of any gains realised through asset disposal. Often, carry is only paid if the fund achieves a certain level of financial return for its limited partners, referred to as the 'hurdle rate', and typically set at around 8 per cent, annualised. If the hurdle rate is met, the general partner takes a cut – usually 20 per cent – of all realised fund returns.

Management and performance fees paid by a fund's limited partners thus represent the principal income streams for real-asset asset managers. As in the overlapping world of private equity (and indeed hedge-fund investment), it is common to hear the two sets of fees combined referred to with the moniker 'two and twenty' – that is, a 2 per cent management fee and 20 per cent performance fee. But, as we have seen, there is considerable variance around this norm. What bears emphasising is that the effect of these combined fees is obviously to generate for the asset manager a share of fund proceeds significantly exceeding the share of capital it commits to the fund in the first place.

I will closely examine this particular dynamic in Chapter 5. For now, let us make do with a brief illustration of just how lucrative a business it is we are talking about. Take Macquarie Infrastructure and Real Assets (MIRA), which invests largely in infrastructure. In the year to March 2021, its management and performance fees combined were A$1.6 billion.[32] But it had only around 750 employees, meaning that each had generated in excess of A$2 million. Little wonder that, with its renowned '"do anything for a bonus" entrepreneurial culture' (as one 2005 newspaper report put it), Macquarie – whose history is explored in Chapter 2 – has long been dubbed the Millionaires' Factory.[33]

It is also interesting to note the relative contributions of the two types of fees to MIRA's 2021 A$1.6 billion haul. Management fees accounted for 60 per cent, and performance fees for 40 per cent. Such a split is broadly typical in real-asset asset management, although of course it varies from year to year and from firm to firm. This is significant. Carried interest often captures the headlines (20 per cent!); but recurring, guaranteed management fees are asset managers' bread-and-butter.

Two final points are worth noting. One is that all of the above discussion of the fees charged by asset managers in the real-estate and infrastructure spaces refers to funds operating at the heart of asset-manager society – namely, where fund holdings confer on the asset manager significant, active control over the underlying physical assets. As we have seen, asset managers and their funds can also invest in real estate and infrastructure in much more passive ways – not least by taking minority shareholdings in publicly listed infrastructure or real-estate companies: say, a 5

---

32 Macquarie Group, 'Management Discussion and Analysis, Year Ended 31 March 2021', p. 21 – at macquarie.com.

33 C. Marriner, 'The Making of the Millionaires' Factory', *Guardian*, 16 August 2005.

per cent stake in Germany's Vonovia (one of the world's leading owners of rental housing) or the US's NextEra Energy (one of the world's leading owners of renewable-energy-generating capacity). As I have argued, such holdings are more peripheral to asset-manager society because, in such instances, the asset manager has much less influence on society; and they are not the main concern of this book. Nevertheless, funds investing specifically in real assets and in this more indirect, passive fashion do exist. They are generally labelled 'listed real estate' or 'listed infrastructure' funds: the fund itself, and usually also the multiple company stocks in which the fund invests, are publicly traded. One example among a myriad of such funds is the Lazard Global Listed Infrastructure Equity Fund, whose biggest holdings at the time of writing are an 8.5 per cent stake in the UK's National Grid (electricity and gas transmission and distribution) and 8.4 per cent of Spain's Ferrovial (transportation assets). Such funds' fee structures are very different. They rarely charge performance fees. Management fees, meanwhile, never exceed 1 per cent; at 0.85 per cent, Lazard's are typical.[34]

The second point to note is that, while management and performance fees represent a real-asset asset manager's main source of fee income, they are usually not its only such source. When acquiring controlling positions in infrastructure or real-estate companies, asset managers also generally charge those companies themselves two types of fee. The first is a one-off transaction fee, to cover the costs incurred by the manager in acquiring the company in the first place, such as banking and legal expenses. The second is an ongoing quarterly or annual monitoring fee, for the continuing advice provided to the company by the asset manager's investment professionals, including through board participation. As David Carey and John Morris have wryly observed, the acquired company thereby effectively pays the asset manager 'for the privilege of being [bought and] owned by it'.[35]

---

34 At least, for actively managed listed infrastructure or real-estate funds. Management fees on tracker funds – for example, Legal & General's Global Infrastructure Index Fund – are much lower still.

35 D. Carey and J. Morris, *King of Capital: The Remarkable Rise, Fall, and*

These additional fees are far from immaterial: analysing approximately 600 fund-based US buyouts (albeit not just of infrastructure or real-estate companies), Ludovic Phalippou and colleagues calculated that transaction and monitoring fees combined were equivalent to over 6 per cent of the value of the total equity invested.[36] Insofar as a fund's limited partners (LPs) are the main shareholders in a fund's portfolio companies (remember that the general partner usually commits only 1–5 per cent of fund capital), it is accordingly they who bear the burden of such costs. In the face of significant criticism, some asset managers have shown increasing willingness to share that burden – for instance by offsetting a proportion of transaction and monitoring fees against the management fees paid by LPs – but not always, and usually only to a limited degree.

The Role of Financial Engineering

In 2005, the UK firm Terra Firma Capital Partners, led by the renowned financier Guy Hands, achieved what at the time was the largest ever buyout of a residential real-estate company by an asset manager. One of its funds acquired Viterra, the property subsidiary of the German utility E.ON, which owned and let 150,000 apartments across Germany. The deal valued Viterra and its physical assets at over €7 billion.[37] But the Terra Firma fund did not itself invest €7 billion. For one thing, Viterra came with €1.25 billion of existing debt. More importantly, of the €6 billion that E.ON received for the sale, only €1 billion in fact came from Terra Firma and its limited partners in the investment fund. So where did the other €5 billion come from?

The answer will be obvious to anybody familiar with the business of real-estate or infrastructure (or indeed private equity)

Rise Again of Steve Schwarzman and Blackstone (New York: Crown Business, 2010), p. 50.

36   L. Phalippou, C. Rauch and M. Umber, 'Private Equity Portfolio Company Fees', *Journal of Financial Economics* 129 (2018), pp. 559–85.

37   A. Chambers, 'Record Deal Highlights German Opportunities', 26 May 2005 – at euromoney.com.

asset management. The other €5 billion was borrowed – specifically, from a group of banks including Citigroup, Barclays, Hypovereinsbank, Eurohypo, Royal Bank of Scotland and Société Générale. In the vernacular of finance, the deal was highly *leveraged* or *geared*. Terra Firma's own capital commitment to the fund that acquired Viterra was not disclosed, but if we assume for the sake of argument that 3 per cent – €30 million – of the €1 billion of equity invested was the general partner's (this being the industry average), then Terra Firma's equity contribution as a proportion of Viterra's enterprise value of €7 billion or more would have been less than 0.5 per cent.

Significant leverage/gearing of asset-manager deals in the real-assets space is not the exception, but the norm – even if the degree of financial gearing in the Viterra case was somewhat higher than average. When asset managers invest in housing or infrastructure, they invariably lever the deal. The same is true in private equity, which explains the name originally given to private-equity transactions in the 1980s – 'leveraged buyouts'. Debt represents the larger component of deal financing whether the asset manager is buying a company that owns physical assets (as in the case of Viterra) or physical assets themselves. As an example of the latter, consider BlackRock's purchase of the Guleslettene wind-farm project in Norway in 2018. Of the total of approximately €200 million in project financing, €141 million was long-term debt provided by DekaBank Deutsche Girozentrale.[38] At around 70 per cent, leverage on the Guleslettene deal was fairly typical of the infrastructure space more widely. Leverage ratios tend to fluctuate over time: in 2010 the average was 61 per cent; in 2013 it was 77 per cent.[39]

Asset managers predominantly use debt to finance their real-asset acquisitions for a simple reason: to boost returns. So integral is the power of leverage that Blackstone highlighted this power when explaining its business model to potential buyers of its shares when they were listed on the New York Stock Exchange

38 K. Gourntis, 'BlackRock Scores Guarantee for Second Norwegian Wind Deal', 3 July 2018 – at infrastructureinvestor.com.

39 Preqin, 'Infrastructure Industry Witnesses Leverage Boom', 22 May 2014 – at preqin.com.

in 2007. The relevant passage from its listing prospectus merits citation in full. It refers to private-equity funds, but could equally well refer to unlisted infrastructure or real-estate funds:

> A significant reason why many private equity funds may deliver superior returns on equity relative to traditional equity investments is the benefit of leverage. In the typical transaction effected by a private equity fund – a leveraged buyout acquisition of a company – the private equity fund borrows most of the purchase price and thereby magnifies the gain on its investment if the company's value appreciates (or its loss if the company's value declines). If a private equity fund were to acquire a company today with a total enterprise value of $1 billion, a typical capital structure for the transaction would be an equity investment of $300 million and $700 million of debt … If the private equity fund is successful in its objective of improving the operating performance of the acquired company over the period of its ownership of the company so that five years later it can effect a sale of the company at a total enterprise value of $1.3 billion, a 6% annual appreciation over the price it paid, it will have achieved a doubling of its equity investment or a gross annual internal rate of return of 15%.[40]

In this example, the profit on sale is $300 million ($1.3 billion minus $1 billion). The fund doubles its money, meaning a return of 100 per cent, because it put in $300 million but takes out $600 million ($1.3 billion minus repayment of the $700 million of debt). Had no debt been used, its return would have been only 30 per cent – putting in $1 billion and taking out $1.3 billion – even though the profit on sale would be the same. That is the power of leverage.

Crucially, when investing with leverage in infrastructure or housing, it is not the investment fund itself that borrows money and subsequently shoulders the debt. Rather, the debt goes onto the balance sheet either of the company that the fund has acquired or – as for example in the case of the acquisition not of a company but of a physical asset such as an apartment block

---

40 Blackstone Group, *Prospectus, 21 June 2007*, p. 149 – at sec.gov.

or wind farm – of a holding company established by the asset manager to hold the acquired asset. Furthermore, it is usually so-called non-recourse debt, meaning that creditors only ever have a potential claim specifically on those assets against which the debt is collateralised.

Hence, if trouble arises in repaying the debt, it is not the investment fund, still less its general partner, that is on the hook. Which, of course, is precisely the point. 'A key part of making the whole strategy work', Christopher Leonard wrote in *Kochland* in relation to Koch Industries' asset-management business,

> was the creation of a very deep and strong corporate veil. It shielded the private equity firm from catastrophic losses. The debt was loaded onto the target company, and if the company failed, the equity firm stood only to lose the money it had invested – often just a tiny fraction of the purchase price. The losses were contained, shifted, and kept off the balance sheet of investors.[41]

Gideon Haigh has written about how Macquarie quarantines risk in this manner, namely 'relying on big licks of non-recourse debt: debt that, in the event of default, won't destabilise other assets in the fund, or come back to bite Macquarie itself'.[42]

One of the advantages of using debt to finance real-asset investments is that the cash-flows generated by those assets while under fund ownership – whether housing rents, road tolls or PPP unitary payments – can be used to pay down the debt, thus further amplifying fund profits upon asset disposal. To see how this works, let us return to the example that Blackstone provided in its listing prospectus: that of a hypothetical company being bought for $1 billion, using $300 million of investor equity and $700 million of debt, and then sold for $1.3 billion. As we have seen, the fund behind the deal would double its money (from $300 to $600 million) if the full $700 million of debt remained to be repaid upon disposal. But now factor in the use of income

41   C. Leonard, *Kochland: The Secret History of Koch Industries and Corporate Power in America* (New York: Simon & Schuster, 2019), p. 319.

42   G. Haigh, 'Who's Afraid of Macquarie Bank?', 4 July 2007 – at themonthly.com.au.

generated by the company while under fund ownership to pay down debt: 'If over that period of time the company has used its operating cash flow to repay $300 million of the acquisition borrowings', Blackstone explained, then only $400 million of debt would remain to be repaid out of the $1.3 billion disposal proceeds, leaving not $600 million but $900 million to the investment fund. The fund has not now doubled its money, but trebled it.

Needless to say, given asset managers' use of large amounts of debt to finance their purchases of real assets, anything that can be done to reduce the cost of that debt also helps to boost returns – which is where more complex methods of financial engineering enter the picture. Philip Ashton and colleagues have noted, for example, that the consortium that purchased both the Chicago Skyway and Indiana Toll Road concessions in 2005 and 2006, respectively – namely, a partnership between Macquarie's American infrastructure fund and the Spanish transportation-infrastructure developer Cintra – used interest rate swaps to this end.[43] Similarly, while it was under the ownership and control of Blackstone funds, Invitation Homes used securitisation techniques to lower the cost of the debt that it raised to finance its single-family-housing acquisition spree. Specifically, it issued bonds backed by future flows of rental income from those homes. Approximately 75 per cent of the $10 billion or so that Invitation Homes invested in housing prior to its 2017 stock-market listing was raised with debt, and more than two-thirds of that debt was securitised debt rather than simple loans. The securitised debt was cheaper: the coupons (interest rates) on the rental-backed bonds ranged from 2.21 to 2.89 per cent; interest rates on the loans advanced to Invitation Homes ranged from 3.03 to 3.54 per cent.[44] When borrowing billions of dollars, that is a huge cost differential.

Moreover, there is an additional important rationale for such financial engineering: debt can be, and often is, used to hasten

---

43   P. Ashton, M. Doussard and R. Weber, 'The Financial Engineering of Infrastructure Privatization: What Are Public Assets Worth to Private Investors?', *Journal of the American Planning Association* 78 (2012), pp. 300–12.

44   Invitation Homes, 'Form S-11', pp. 77, 79.

fund returns from infrastructure and housing investments – to bring those returns forward in time. I will turn to the mechanisms of such hastening shortly, but first there is the question of motivation. Partly, this is straightforward: all other things being equal, partners in a fund prefer to earn returns sooner rather than later; time is indeed money. But there is more to it than that. One of the main criteria on which fund managers compete with one another for investor capital is the advertised returns achieved by their funds; and what is perhaps the industry's benchmark return measure, the internal rate of return (IRR), is profoundly influenced by the timing of returns: the earlier a positive cash-flow is received by a fund, the higher the fund's IRR. This provides a powerful incentive for asset managers to front-load returns – thus massaging the IRR upwards – to the extent that it is possible to do so.

Two main methods are used, although they amount to more or less the same thing. The first is so-called dividend recapitalisation. Imagine, in the hypothetical case outlined above featured in Blackstone's listing prospectus, that operating cash-flow has been used to pay down $300 million of the original $700 million of debt. In such a scenario, the portfolio company could then borrow a further amount – say, $200 million – of which some or all could be used to pay its shareholders a special dividend. This is dividend recapitalisation: essentially a way for equity investors to realise value from an investment without selling it. With infrastructure and real-estate assets often generating strong, predictable cash-flows, dividend 'recaps' are common in the real-assets investment world. In 2020, for example, Empark, a leading car-park concessionaire with over 500,000 parking spaces in the Iberian Peninsula, Britain and Turkey, issued €575 million of new bonds. About €92 million of the capital thus raised reportedly went towards paying a dividend to Empark's owner, the Macquarie European Infrastructure Fund 5.[45]

---

45 A. Ramnarayan, 'Divisive "Dividend Recap" Deals Return in Red Hot Debt Market', 22 January 2020 – at reuters.com. Macquarie's funds have long had a reputation for undertaking aggressive dividend recapitalisations. See in particular E. Chancellor and L. Silva, 'Macquarie's Secret Recipe', *Wall Street Journal*, 4 June 2007.

The second debt-based method of extracting value from ongoing investments is the use of shareholder loans, where some or all of the debt used to finance an investment is provided by the same institutions that invest equity. I shall have more to say about shareholder loans in Chapter 6. The critical point here is that the interest payments that such loans generate during the life of an investment are equivalent to dividends. A notable recent case of the large-scale use of shareholder loans in the real-assets space is the UK's Thames Tideway Tunnel, which is owned, as we have seen, by a consortium of four asset managers. Collectively, the four shareholders invested approximately £1.3 billion in the project in 2015. But only £510 million was equity; shareholder loans amounted to £765 million.[46] Although the tunnel will not be operational until 2025, the asset managers that own it have been receiving interest payments on those loans for several years already: the pay-out in 2017–18, for instance, was £51.6 million. Of course, interest payments must somehow be funded, and in the Tideway case they have been paid for by pre-emptive increases in household water bills.[47] For Londoners, this was – to quote one infrastructure finance expert – like 'being forced to pay for a meal at a restaurant before the restaurant has been built or opened, much less served any food'.[48]

It was a good analogy. Debt is like that: it is a promissory instrument, rooted in the promise to repay, which in turn is often also rooted in a promise to do something productive with the money borrowed. Debt becomes intrinsically political, however, when promises are essentially made on behalf of unwitting or impotent others. Asset-manager society is saturated in such debt.

It should by now be clear, at least in outline, what asset-manager society entails – the basic nature of the key economic forms, relationships and transactions that comprise it. We are thus on the way to being able to evaluate its significance. In Chapter 3, I will add flesh to the bones identified in this chapter: if we know who the main managers are, from whom they source

---

46 Tideway, *Annual Report 2019/20*, p. 57 – at tideway.london.

47 G. Plimmer, 'Investors Reap Rewards of London Super Sewer Long Before It Is Built', *Financial Times*, 8 November 2018.

48 Ibid.

their working capital, and where and in what they principally invest, we will know where exactly to direct our critique. First, in Chapter 2, I ask how, why and when asset-manager society came into being in the first place. Both its present and its future are inhabited and shaped by its past.

2

How It Came to Be

Blackstone in Berlin

In 2011, approximately 500,000 active and retired teachers within the public-school system of the US state of Pennsylvania came, indirectly, to own a share of a portfolio of thousands of rental apartments in the old East Germany, formerly owned and operated by that country's communist state. They did so because a significant chunk of the money held within their pension plan, the Pennsylvania Public School Employees' Retirement System (PSERS), had been committed to an investment fund managed by the US asset manager Blackstone, which in September of that year acquired approximately 6,800 German apartments, mostly in the eastern part of Berlin.

Two key questions are raised by this historical curiosity. Firstly, how and why was it that assets previously held within the German public sector came to be available for purchase by international financial investors? And secondly, why did PSERS not only invest in these particular assets, but do so indirectly – which is to say, specifically by way of its commitment of capital to a Blackstone investment fund?

This chapter begins with this case because its aim is to answer these two questions, but to do so in relation to asset-manager society more broadly. That is to say, how and why, firstly, have the various assets at the heart of contemporary asset-manager society – from farmland to wind farms, and from housing to toll roads – come to be available for ownership by asset-management firms? As we will see, many only became available for such ownership in the relatively recent past; it was not always thus.

Moreover, when they did become available, it was often far from inevitable that they would do so in a form and under conditions that firms such as Blackstone would consider financially attractive. How and why, in other words, did these myriad physical things forming the functional backbone of contemporary society become *commercially investible*? This brings us to the second broad question this chapter addresses. Why, in recent decades, has an increasing proportion of the capital held by the world's major capital-rich institutions – its pension schemes, insurance companies and sovereign-wealth funds – been invested specifically in housing and infrastructure assets, as opposed to other asset classes? And why, more pointedly, has such a substantial proportion of this real-asset institutional investment occurred via asset managers, rather than directly?

The case of PSERS, Blackstone and those 6,800 German apartments can begin to provide some clues. As will become clear, asset-manager society is a child of broader political–economic shifts, relating in particular to the changing role of the state: indeed, Blackstone and other leading real-asset managers can be usefully understood as, in one observer's words, 'an unelected elite ... increasingly standing in for the state', making 'big money' from owning assets that 'the public used to own [and] on which citizens vitally depend'.[1]

After German reunification in 1990, state-owned rental housing in the former East Germany was sold to the private sector, and rent controls were gradually removed. Beginning in 2005, a local real-estate company called Level One began buying up large stocks of such privatised rental housing, principally in Berlin. But it did so almost entirely with debt, and when the global financial crisis hit in 2008, Level One's unserviceable debt pile forced it into bankruptcy. Three years later, its creditors were still looking for buyers for the company's approximately 28,000 dwellings. Investor interest was growing in line with advertised market rents, which in Berlin were increasing faster than anywhere else in the country.

---

1 G. Haigh, 'Who's Afraid of Macquarie Bank?', 4 July 2007, at themonthly. com.au.

Meanwhile, in the same year that Level One entered bank-ruptcy, PSERS, with a pension plan valued at $67 billion, enlisted a consultancy called Wilshire Associates to advise on asset allo-cation. Alongside Wilshire's other recommendations – including a larger allocation to private equity – was one to lift the plan's allocation to real estate from 8 to 10 per cent. Following this recommendation, the PSERS board approved a series of new investments in March 2008, of which the biggest was a $200 million commitment to a new Blackstone fund – Blackstone Real Estate Partners ('BREP') Europe III.[2] Investing in real estate indirectly and specifically via Blackstone was already a favoured PSERS strategy: it had previously committed a combined $600 million to two Blackstone real-estate funds of older vintage (BREP V and BREP VI).[3]

Thus, the necessary ingredients were now in place. A large number of apartments formerly owned by the state were on the block in Germany; rising local rents made these attractive; and the possibility of securing the apartments at a 'distressed' price, from a company in administration, sweetened the investment proposition still further. Meanwhile, institutional investors such as PSERS were pouring money into asset managers' real-estate funds despite the shock of the subprime crisis: when Blackstone closed BREP Europe III in June 2009, it was with capital com-mitments of €3.1 billion, significantly above the €2.5 billion originally targeted. In any event, Blackstone eventually brought PSERS (and other limited partners in the new fund) and German rental housing together in September 2011, using BREP Europe III to acquire around 6,800 of the Level One apartments for around €220 million, representing a reported discount of more than a third to the price that Level One had paid for them.[4] Tenants of the apartments in question had entered asset-manager society.

2   M. Sorondo, 'PSERS Gets New Asset Allocation', *Investment Manage-ment Weekly*, 17 March 2008.

3   PSERS, 'Public Investment Memorandum: Blackstone Real Estate Debt Strategies III, L.P. – Real Estate Commitment', 14 November 2015, p. 5 – at psers.pa.gov.

4   B. Bomke, 'Blackstone zahlt 220 Mio. Euro für 7.000 Level-One-Wohnungen', 5 September 2011 – at immobilien-zeitung.de.

Pre-1990s Stirrings

Asset-manager society is a relatively novel historic phenomenon. It represents, as we have seen, a society in which the key physical systems supporting social life and its reproduction – so-called 'real assets' – are increasingly owned by institutional investors specifically through the mediation of dedicated asset managers and their investment funds. Traditionally, however, major institutional investors such as pension schemes and insurance companies generally did not use asset managers: overwhelmingly, they invested directly. Nor, moreover, did they invest significantly in real assets: they invested in corporate and (to a lesser extent) government-issued financial securities. In other words, neither of the two essential elements of asset-manager society – the centrality of asset managers and of real assets – obtained.

Consider the prototypical case of the United States. Figure 2.1 shows, for 1952 through to 2021, total assets held by US-based entities of two types. The first category is insurance companies and pension schemes, which are the dominant types of institutional investor. The second category is investment funds – that is, the investment vehicles established and managed by asset managers. Needless to say, there is considerable overlap (or double-counting) here, inasmuch as large amounts of the money held in investment funds is precisely capital that derives from insurance companies and pension schemes: it is predominantly their capital that investment funds invest. But the figure clearly demonstrates something very important: asset managers only began to play a significant role on the US investment scene relatively recently.

If asset managers are a phenomenon of recent historical vintage in the United States (and by extension also elsewhere: the United States is where asset management was effectively born), so also is institutional-investor investment in real assets. As recently as the mid 1970s, holdings by US pension schemes and insurance companies of anything other than equities, bonds and cash were so limited as to be immaterial. An important catalyst for change came in 1974, with the passage of the Employee Retirement Income Security Act, Section 404(c) of which imposed a series of

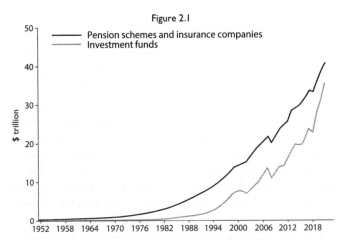

Figure 2.1

Assets held by selected US-based financial entities, 1952–2021
Source: OECD

investment diversification requirements on pension fund sponsors, thus setting the stage for meaningful allocations not just to real assets but to other 'alternative' classes such as hedge funds and private equity. But, to begin with, the diversification that occurred consisted only of baby steps. As late as 1985, comfortably in excess of 90 per cent of US institutional-investor capital remained invested in cash and publicly listed financial securities.[5] Furthermore, the bulk of that alternative investment which now existed was in private equity and commercial real estate; in 1985 the total US allocation to housing and infrastructure – the assets undergirding contemporary asset-manager society – was certainly less than 1 per cent, and almost certainly less than 0.5 per cent.

An important reason why institutional investors around the world historically did not substantially invest in housing and infrastructure was that such assets typically were not even available to invest in – or at least not in a form that would have made investment financially attractive. Take rental housing first. To be sure, in the initial post-war decades of growth in institutional investment in the advanced capitalist countries, most such

---

5 'Real Estate Takes Its Place as the Fourth Asset Class', Spring 2015 – at naiop.org.

countries had large rental sectors. But much of this housing was owned by the state, in the form of social/public housing, and, for the most part, the state was actively building its holdings rather than looking to sell them off. Except in rare cases such as Sweden, to which we will turn below, the private rental sector was generally dominated by small 'mom and pop' landlords owning one or at most a handful of dwellings. This 'bittiness' made rental housing inherently unappealing to institutional investors, who, by definition, with millions or billions of dollars to invest, seek opportunities to invest at scale: all other things being equal, the transactional and management costs of making one investment of $100 million will be much lower than when making ten or 100 separate investments. Rental housing was not considered a viable 'asset class' because its ownership was, in most instances, too fragmented; there were very few large portfolios to be bought.

Meanwhile, neither were attractive infrastructure assets widely available for institutional investment. The main reason for this was that most infrastructure was state-owned, and, as with social/public housing, the state in these decades remained committed to retaining ownership. As Phillip O'Neill has explained, assignation to the state of 'the infrastructure property task' within Western political-economic thought is longstanding, dating at least to Adam Smith, who asserted that erecting and maintaining socially vital infrastructures – what he called 'public works' – 'can never be the interest of any individual or small number of individuals'. Infrastructure represented, in short, a classic case of market failure. 'A public acceptance of state responsibility for infrastructure' (including the 'social infrastructure' of health and education), O'Neill writes, 'saw it extended into what we now call a Keynesian fiscal device'.[6]

It is true that private capital's interest in infrastructure provision and ownership has in fact always been more ambiguous than Smith's 'never' allows. Thus, while capital may indeed be wary of financing and holding fixed physical infrastructures – in

---

6 P. M. O'Neill, 'The Financialisation of Infrastructure: The Role of Categorisation and Property Relations', *Cambridge Journal of Regions, Economy and Society* 6 (2013), p. 443.

light, for example, of what David Harvey has described as their particular vulnerability to 'the cold winds of [location specific] devaluation' – capital is, as we shall see, nonetheless deeply attracted to the natural-monopoly characteristics that such infrastructures often enjoy.[7] It is also true that, partly as a consequence of those natural-monopoly advantages, some countries, including the United States, do have a long history of significant levels of private-sector ownership of certain types of important infrastructure.[8] In general, however, core infrastructure assets have historically been publicly owned artefacts, 'funded through public debt and managed by government employees'.[9] And, even where privately owned, they have, like private rental housing, often been assets of such a size as to fall below the radar of scale-oriented institutional financial investors. Privately owned US water systems represent one example, since they have historically been 'quite diminutive, serving small municipalities, unincorporated patches of metropolitan areas, or even single real estate developments'.[10]

But if asset-manager society essentially did not exist prior to the 1990s, the 1970s and 1980s witnessed important stirrings of what would eventually become asset-manager society. Three separate sets of developments were crucial. Certainly, none by itself crystallised asset-manager society, but collectively they rendered it possible, and indeed imminent.

Firstly, beginning in the early 1970s and principally as a result of ad hoc legislative and regulatory shifts, in a few countries – albeit not including the United States – institutional investors did begin to make meaningful investments in real assets of the types we are interested in in this book. In the UK, for example, they started buying farmland, the Finance Act of 1965 having made it much more profitable for them to do so directly as opposed

---

7   D. Harvey, *The Limits to Capital* (Oxford: Blackwell, 1982), p. 378.

8   C. D. Jacobson and J. A. Tarr, 'Ownership and Financing of Infrastructure: Historical Perspectives', World Bank Policy Research Working Paper 1466, June 1995.

9   M. Williams, 'Investments in Infrastructure', August 2017, p. 8 – at cliffwater.com.

10   Jacobson and Tarr, 'Ownership and Financing of Infrastructure', p. 13.

to through investment in property companies, because, unlike the latter, such investors benefited from exemptions or reduced rates of corporation tax on investment income. Approximately 30 per cent of UK agricultural land sold in 1973, for example, was bought by institutional investors, including the Post Office pension scheme.[11] Meanwhile, in the Netherlands, Sweden and Switzerland, institutional investors began buying housing – specifically, multi-family apartment blocks, where the 'bittiness' mentioned above was less of a problem.[12] By 1986, for example, institutional investors owned 8 per cent of Dutch rental-housing stock, while a survey conducted two years later found that over 90 per cent of Swedish pension plans and insurance companies had residential-property holdings of one size or another.[13] As in the case of UK farmland investment, government intervention was typically an important part of the story; changes introduced in the Netherlands in 1968, for instance, enabled inflation-offsetting annual residential rent increases.

Secondly, the 1980s saw the beginning of a broad turning of the tide against the erstwhile hegemony of public ownership of core infrastructures. Led by the administration of Margaret Thatcher in the UK, which pursued the project with an almost evangelical zeal, governments around the world began selling off the physical infrastructures undergirding the delivery of socially vital services, ranging from telecommunications to energy and from transportation to water and sewerage. This, of course, was the beginning of the era we have come to label 'neoliberal', during which the premise that government ownership and operation is inherently inefficient and thus misguided has become nothing

---

11 D. Massey and A. Catalano, *Capital and Land: Landownership by Capital in Great Britain* (London: Edward Arnold, 1978), pp. 127–8.

12 J. Conijn and O. Papa, 'Institutional Investors and Housing in the Netherlands', *Netherlands Journal of Housing and Environmental Research* 3: 2 (1988), pp. 173–81; J. Brzeski, A. Jaffe and S. Lundström, 'Institutional Real Estate Investment Practices: Swedish and United States Experiences', *Journal of Real Estate Research* 8: 3 (1993), pp. 293–323; J. Montezuma and K. Gibb, 'Residential Property as an Institutional Asset: The Swiss and Dutch Cases', *Journal of Property Research* 23: 4 (2006), pp. 323–45.

13 Conijn and Papa, 'Institutional Investors', p. 176; Brzeski, Jaffe and Lundström, 'Institutional Real Estate Investment Practices', p. 303.

less than an article of faith. By the early 1990s, almost all of the UK's physical, state-owned service-delivery infrastructures that could be sold off had been – and thus, although they were not yet owned by asset managers, they were privately owned, and hence potentially acquirable by infrastructure investment funds. Nor, of course, were the relevant privatisations only of infrastructure: in the 1980s, under Right to Buy, around a million social housing units were sold by local authorities in England alone.

And thirdly, the 1980s was the period when asset management really began to come into its own. Institutional investors had been using asset managers on a modest scale since mid-century, but although US assets under management (AUM) by asset managers grew relatively strongly through the 1950s, 1960s and 1970s – at a compound annual rate of 11 per cent (1952–1979) – total AUM did not exceed $100 billion until 1979. It was then that growth went into overdrive. AUM increased at a compound annual rate of no less than 24 per cent between 1979 and 1990, topping $1 trillion as early as 1989.[14]

In short, by the end of the 1980s, the conditions for the realisation of asset-manager society were largely in place. Institutional investors had begun to gain exposure to, and thus some familiarity with, pertinent classes of real assets; ever more such assets were entering into private ownership of one kind or another; and ever more institutional investment was occurring via asset managers, rather than directly. All that was required for asset-manager society to come into being was for these three crucial trends to begin to overlap.

The Establishment of Asset-Manager Society: 1990–2007

Australia

As a tangible, enduring and substantive phenomenon, asset-manager society was born in Australia – it was there that the key trends referred to in the previous section first came together effectively. And, when asset-manager society was born, its

---

14 OECD, 'Institutional Investors' Assets and Liabilities' – at stats.oecd. org.

principal physical locus was infrastructure. Indeed, writing in 2014, Georg Inderst reflected that the Australian financial sector had effectively 'invented infrastructure as an asset class'.[15]

This 'invention' occurred in the early 1990s, and was catalysed by a series of privatisations of public infrastructure initiated by both federal and state governments. Electricity, gas and communications all saw significant ownership transformations, as what Graeme Newell and Hsu Wen Peng later described as 'significantly reduced government spending on infrastructure' led the administrations in question to 'seek alternative funding options for infrastructure development and maintenance'.[16] By 1999, privatisations solely of energy assets (principally electricity networks), and solely by the state of Victoria, had alone raised more than $24 billion.[17] Alongside privatisations, long-term toll-road concessions represented another substantial new opportunity for private-sector investors.

A new breed of asset managers proved to be prodigious buyers, though they were not alone. As Nicole Connolly has observed, infrastructure funds were raised by Australian asset managers in the mid 1990s precisely 'on the back of these privatizations' – which is to say, explicitly to buy the assets that were privatised (or, in the case of concessions, tendered).[18] As Connolly also noted, the first such asset manager to create a dedicated infrastructure fund was Hastings Fund Management. The fund, the Utilities Trust of Australia, had a first close in November 1994. Securing commitments of $115 million from investors including major domestic pension ('superannuation') funds such as the Superannuation Trust of Australia, the fund's first purchase, in November 1995, was a 40 per cent stake in the Sydney Light

15   G. Inderst, 'Pension Fund Investment in Infrastructure: Lessons from Australia and Canada', *Rotman International Journal of Pension Management* 7: 1 (2014), p. 40.

16   G. Newell and H. Wen Peng, 'Assessing the Significance of Motivating Factors and Risk Factors in Infrastructure Funds Management', *Pacific Rim Property Research Journal* 14 (2008), p. 399.

17   M. Skulley, 'Victoria's $1.6 Billion Gas Coup', *Australian Financial Review*, 1 February 1999.

18   N. Connolly, 'Australians and Infrastructure Investments', *Russell Research*, March 2012, p. 2.

Rail project. This was soon followed by smaller stakes in two bigger deals – the $2.4 billion Yallourn power-station privatisation and the $1.8 billion City Link toll way in Melbourne.[19]

Other Australian asset managers responded by swiftly launching their own infrastructure funds. In 1995, the existing $150 million Develop Australia Fund was relaunched as an infrastructure fund under the control of the asset manager Industry Funds Services (one of the forerunners of what is today IFM Investors), and AMP Investments raised capital for two infrastructure funds – the Infrastructure Equity Fund and the Australian Energy Fund. The following year, the firm that would come to dominate Australian infrastructure asset management, namely Macquarie, entered the fray, creating its first infrastructure fund, the Infrastructure Trust of Australia. Fourteen further Macquarie infrastructure funds followed over the next decade, investing in sixty-seven projects across thirteen countries.[20]

Headquartered in Sydney, Macquarie had begun life in the late 1960s as a foreign subsidiary of the UK merchant bank Hill Samuel, only becoming Macquarie – largely locally owned and controlled, and named after Lachlan Macquarie, a Scottish colonial administrator in early-nineteenth-century New South Wales – in the mid 1980s. It was in the second half of that decade that Macquarie first ventured into asset management. The move specifically into infrastructure asset management in 1996 – the same year that Macquarie floated on the Australian stock exchange – was largely the making of the firm.[21] Not until then had Macquarie been, in Gideon Haigh's words, 'other than mediocre as a manager

19　D. Walker, 'Carlton's Other Mr Business', *The Age*, 25 March 1996.

20　A. Capon, 'The Road More Traveled', *Institutional Investor*, 14 February 2005.

21　Although 1996 saw the launch of Macquarie's first infrastructure investment fund, this was not the firm's first significant foray into infrastructure investment per se. Notably, two years previously, it led a consortium that secured the contract to finance, build and operate (under a concession lasting from thirty-six to forty-five years, depending on performance) the 21 kilometre, A$500 million M2 toll road in Sydney, subsequently listing the contract-owning vehicle – the Hills Motorway Group – on the stock exchange. See L. D. Solomon, *The Promise and Perils of Infrastructure Privatization* (New York: Palgrave Macmillan, 2009), pp. 57–62.

of investment monies'. Infrastructure turned Macquarie into a success story – 'perhaps *the* Australian business success story of the past decade', as Haigh wrote in 2007.[22] By the mid 2000s, Macquarie's top executives were consistently earning more than any other businesspeople in the country.

The establishment of an asset-manager society 'prototype' in Australia in the 1990s powerfully illustrated the way in which, on the one hand, investor allocations to certain asset classes, and on the other, the types of funds that asset managers create, always exist in a dynamic, iterative relationship with one another. The very existence of real-asset funds, such as infrastructure funds, both enables and encourages investors such as pension schemes to allocate capital to real assets: such funds' existence sends the message that real assets are a 'thing', and worth considering. In Australia, Hastings's founder, Mike Fitzpatrick, a former star of Australian rules football, was a leading evangelist, determined, in the words of David Walker, to 'sell infrastructure to the industry superannuation funds keen for new ways to invest Australia's compulsory superannuation' – despite the fact that many industry observers 'doubted that infrastructure could become an important or strong-yielding Australian asset class'.[23] Equally, however, demand among institutional investors for ways to invest in real assets clearly encourages asset managers to establish vehicles for that purpose. In the case of 1990s Australia, Fitzpatrick has himself emphasised that, while he certainly played an evangelising role, there was also latent demand: superannuation funds 'had been saying they had a particular interest in infrastructure', he later claimed, and 'no one was really showing them anything that they could invest in'.[24] This, then, was precisely what Fitzpatrick proceeded to do.

Push and pull

Why were Australian pension schemes expressing interest in infrastructure? One reason was that there was an important 'push' factor at work. The early and mid 1990s saw lively and

---

22 Haigh, 'Who's Afraid of Macquarie Bank?'.

23 Walker, 'Carlton's Other Mr Business'.

24 Cited in ibid.

sometimes heated political and public debate in Australia about where superannuation capital was being invested. With government funding for infrastructure development and maintenance in increasingly short supply, some argued that it was incumbent upon superannuation funds to step up to the plate: instead of investing overseas, they should support domestic infrastructure and other areas of national public interest. Investment rules, mandating the channelling of a percentage of superannuation funds into such 'priority' areas, were even proposed, as was a prohibition on overseas investment.[25] Nothing substantive came of these calls for prescriptive asset allocation, but they indelibly coloured the local investment milieu. Writing in November 1994, Barrie Dunstan observed 'considerable pressure [on superannuation funds] from some people in government to consider infrastructure investments'.[26]

Alongside this 'push', however, there was evidently also considerable 'pull'. Infrastructure was increasingly attractive to Australia's institutional investors – and to the asset managers who invested their money – for a number of important reasons, of which five stand out. These factors have in fact underwritten the flourishing of asset-manager society not just in Australia in the 1990s, but around the world and over ensuing decades.

The first such factor concerns the maturity profile of investor liabilities. Key institutional investors such as pension plans and insurance companies hold significant long-term liabilities in the form, respectively, of annuities and expected future payouts to policyholders. In other words, their financial obligations substantially fall due beyond the near or even medium term. This makes long-term assets – those expected to continue to generate income beyond the medium term, and which include not only infrastructure but also real estate – particularly attractive: investors prefer, where they can, to 'match' liability and asset maturities. For example, Robert Bertram – investment

25 J. Hill, 'Institutional Investors and Corporate Governance in Australia', in T. Baums, R. M. Buxbaum and K. J. Hopt, eds, *Institutional Investors and Corporate Governance* (Berlin: Walter de Gruyter, 1994), pp. 591–2.

26 B. Dunstan, 'Infrastructure Lifts Off', *Australian Financial Review* 16 (November 1994).

chief of the Ontario Teachers' Pension Plan, which has long had an above-average allocation to infrastructure – has remarked, 'We began looking for ways to more explicitly link our assets and liabilities in the late 1990s. Infrastructure fit the bill. It's a great asset class for a pension fund with long-term ... liabilities.'[27]

The second key factor is the stability and predictability of the cash-flows generated by many infrastructure investments. 'Their returns are likely to be more stable, and less reliant on economic fortunes than the share prices of major companies', said David Adams, who was responsible for Macquarie's inaugural (1996) infrastructure fund. He continued: 'Infrastructure assets are somewhat insulated, they behave like very defensive stocks. People still pay to go on the roads even in recessions.'[28] Some investors, of course, are not keen on stable and predictable, especially if stability and predictability translate into lower returns. As Marietta Cauchi reported in 2006, average returns on infrastructure assets in the early 2000s were in the 10–12 per cent range (on a project basis), which was 'some way off the 20% and more targeted by private-equity funds'. But infrastructure returns included an annual cash yield of around 6 per cent, which was 'ideal' for certain investors.[29] 'It's a low-volatility, low-risk investment which is very attractive to pension funds that have to make payments out on an annual basis', Deloitte's Gareth Taylor told Cauchi.

One reason that the cash-flows from infrastructure investments tend to be predictable and stable is that society is dependent on infrastructure: as Adams observed, people need to use roads whatever the economic conditions. This goes to the very heart of the nature of asset-manager society: that is, asset managers control infrastructures on which we all fundamentally rely. Jim Craig, who managed Macquarie's first European infrastructure fund, used the word 'essential' to capture this quality of

27   Cited in Capon, 'Road More Traveled'.

28   Cited in K. Maley, 'And the Next Champion Will Be – Infrastructure', *Australian Financial Review*, 9 October 1996.

29   M. Cauchi, 'Infrastructure Gets Hot; Steady Cash the Lure', *Dow Jones International News*, 14 November 2006.

infrastructure assets. (He said this made infrastructure 'unique' – but of course housing, too, is essential.) Infrastructure's essential nature, Craig commented, 'means that it has limited exposure to demand and pricing risk and limited dependence on the economic cycle'.[30] As the UK's National Infrastructure Commission, an executive agency within the government, has observed, the fact that 'demand for essential utilities is not likely to change significantly' means that infrastructure owners can be not just confident but 'certain' that the money they invest 'will be recovered from consumers'.[31]

It is not just the essential nature of infrastructure that engenders cash-flow stability, however. Such stability often also stems from the third factor that makes infrastructure attractive to investors – the monopoly status that it frequently enjoys. Craig referred to this in terms of 'strong competitive position'. Many infrastructure assets and the businesses that hold and operate them have no competition, because introducing duplicated infrastructures – say, a parallel set of water pipes or electricity transmission lines – would be inherently inefficient. In such situations, monopoly is, to use the technical economic term, 'natural', representing the lowest-cost outcome.

And investors like nothing more than monopoly. Cash-flows are stable and predictable because the risk of losing business to a competitor is precisely zero. Allan Moss, who ran Macquarie from 1993 to 2008, liked to advise the managers of his firm's investment funds to seek out assets that were insulated from what he called 'the full rigours of competition'.[32] The UK's privatised regional water and sewerage monopolies, which in due course would in fact become favoured objects of investment for Macquarie and other Australian infrastructure asset managers, represent quintessential examples of such assets, offering investors, in James Meek's evocative terms, 'millions of customers who have no choice of supplier, no choice but to take the water,

---

30 'Macquarie Bank Wins Battle for South East Water', *Dow Jones International News*, 1 October 2003.

31 National Infrastructure Commission, 'Strategic Investment and Public Confidence', October 2019, p. 27 – at nic.org.uk.

32 Cited in Solomon, *Promise and Perils*, p. 51.

and no choice but to pay for it. Millions of captive monthly payments in perpetuity.'[33]

Fourthly, infrastructure can provide investors with protection against inflation risk, inasmuch as the cash-flows generated by infrastructure assets are often either implicitly or explicitly linked to price indices. Tolls on highways, bridges and tunnels, for instance, tend to increase in line with inflation – as indeed do housing rents. And where statutory regulators determine what rates infrastructure owners can charge, inflation is almost always part of the formula. 'Many of our investments are in former government-owned assets where there is an independent regulator', remarked Bertram. 'More often than not, the rate of inflation is a key consideration when that regulator sets prices.'[34]

Fifth and finally, there is a simple risk-diversification angle. Investors are generally not keen on placing all their proverbial eggs in the single basket of securities markets: they prefer to hold some investments that are not strongly correlated with others, meaning that their returns can track different paths, especially in the event of a market downturn. Like hedge funds, both infrastructure and real estate provide such non-correlated diversification. They have, to use the terminology of the trade, low 'beta' – returns are not significantly sensitive to changes in wider market conditions.

The United States and Europe

Meanwhile, as Australian asset managers were busily buying up local infrastructure assets, the first shoots of asset-manager society were also sprouting in the United States. There, though, it was housing, not infrastructure, that asset managers first became interested in. In the late 1980s, the United States experienced a real estate–centred financial crisis that, in many respects, was comparable to the one that engulfed the country in 2007–08. Financial institutions whose core business was making loans for property purchase – the so-called savings and loan (S&L) associations – widely failed, and were taken over by regulators. In

---

33 J. Meek, *Private Island: Why Britain Now Belongs to Someone Else* (London: Verso, 2015), p. 105.

34 Cited in Capon, 'Road More Traveled'.

1989, the government established the Resolution Trust Corporation (RTC) to dispose of their assets, which included repossessed properties as well as delinquent mortgages, and which were available at fire-sale prices.

Among the buyers was the asset manager Blackstone, which teamed up with Goldman Sachs in 1990 to buy a package of multi-family apartment blocks in Arkansas and East Texas. It was a hugely profitable investment for Blackstone, yielding an eye-watering 62 per cent annualised return by the time it exited. Unsurprisingly, Blackstone was keen to make more housing investments, and on a larger scale. But when it floated this idea, it encountered resistance from its limited partners – that is, those whose capital it would be investing. 'I wanted our investors' consent before we committed such a significant portion of their money to this new strategy', Stephen Schwarzman, Blackstone's head, later recalled. 'At our annual investors' meeting, I laid out the opportunity, expecting our limited partners to jump at it. But to my surprise, all except General Motors turned it down.'[35] Their reasoning? It was not that they did not understand Schwarzman's logic. But the S&L debacle still haunted them: 'Even as the real estate market began to grow, investors still felt burned by the crash ... "[We're] loaded to the gills with these terrible real estate deals"', one investor after another told Schwarzman.

Thus, asset managers' investment in US housing grew only slowly and cautiously through the 1990s, as lingering reticence on the part of institutional investors militated against a more rapid expansion of residential portfolios. Most years, new US funds investing mainly or solely in residential assets could literally be counted on one hand. They were generally small, too. The SSR Apartment Value Fund I, established by BlackRock in 1997, to which investors committed $150 million, was one of the very few to raise more than $100 million.

Nevertheless, by the end of the decade, asset-manager investment in US residential property had become somewhat normalised: it was not extensive by any means – but neither was it rare, as it had been at the outset of the decade, when

---

35 S. Schwarzman, *What It Takes: Lessons in the Pursuit of Excellence* (New York: Simon & Schuster, 2019), p. 139.

Blackstone made its move. Aside from Blackstone and Black-Rock, most asset managers that invested in the US multi-family housing market during the 1990s were focused exclusively on real estate, and sometimes exclusively on residential real estate. They included Colony Capital, which, like Blackstone, launched its housing investment business with acquisitions of distressed stock from the RTC. Other prominent players were DLJ Real Estate Capital Partners, the Fifteen Group, IHP Capital Partners, Sentinel Real Estate Corporation, Waterton Associates and Wells Fargo Realty Advisors. Asset managers were particularly active in the New York housing market, with one such firm, the local Praedium Group, having acquired 6,000 multi-family units in the city by 2002.[36]

By this stage, asset managers were also beginning to realise nascent opportunities in US infrastructure. Around a decade after it had done so in Australia, infrastructure finally emerged in the United States as an accepted and recognisable 'asset class'. Perhaps unsurprisingly, one of the most active players in this emerging market space, bringing with it its experience from its domestic market, was Australia's Macquarie. Toll-road concessions, for instance, were among the first fruits to be plucked from the US infrastructure tree; and in 2005, Macquarie funds acquired two: the Chicago Skyway (see Chapter 1) and, for $533 million, an 87 per cent stake in the 22-kilometre Dulles Greenway.[37] As we will see in Chapter 3, however, the development of infrastructure as an asset class in the United States would nevertheless remain patchy and halting for quite some time.

Thus, for all the importance of Australia as the cradle of asset-manager society, and of the United States as a territory where asset managers saw vast long-term potential for real-asset investments, the centre of gravity of asset-manager society during the period under consideration settled decisively elsewhere in the world – namely Europe, including the UK.

Housing represented an important part of the European story. Asset managers began buying up European housing in the

---

36   L. Croghan, 'Praedium's City Holdings Climb on Brooklyn Walk-Ups', *Crain's New York Business*, 25 November 2002.

37   Solomon, *Promise and Perils*, pp. 89–95, 102–3.

second half of the 1990s, and at the centre of the drama was a group of financiers who would end up forming a new asset-management firm, Terra Firma Capital Partners, in 2002. By the time the financial crisis came around in 2007, funds established and managed by Terra Firma owned more than 270,000 dwellings, effectively making it Europe's largest residential landlord. All of these homes had a background in the public sector.

The story is a rather complex one. First, in 1996, an investor consortium called Annington Homes, led by the private-equity Principal Finance Group of the Japanese bank Nomura, acquired 57,400 homes from the UK's Ministry of Defence for £1.7 billion. Four years later, the same Nomura unit, via another company, Deutsche Annington Immobilien GmbH, which it formed and financed in 1997, acquired 64,000 state-owned German railway-worker apartments for €2.1 billion. Then, in 2002, the head of the Principal Finance Group, Guy Hands, and a team of colleagues left Nomura to set up Terra Firma. All the investments that the Group had made since 1995, including both Annington Homes and Deutsche Annington, were transferred into a newly established investment fund called Terra Firma Capital Partners I, which Terra Firma would henceforth manage on behalf of Nomura, the principal equity holder in that fund.

During the next few years, Terra Firma made further small acquisitions of housing in Germany, followed by the biggest acquisition of all in 2005 (see Chapter 1): the €7 billion deal to take control of Viterra, the property subsidiary of the German utility E.ON, which owned and let 150,000 apartments. E.ON had inherited these apartments from one of its predecessors, the originally state-owned energy company VEBA AG, the privatisation of which was completed in 1987. The Viterra deal swelled the Terra Firma housing portfolio to around 230,000 units in Germany and – the UK Annington Homes portfolio having by this time been pruned to around 40,000 units through property disposals – around 270,000 across Germany and the UK combined.

But housing was not the main part of the story of Europe becoming the epicentre of asset-manager society. As in Australia, this story revolved principally around infrastructure. In the late

1990s and into the 2000s in several European territories, asset managers became major – arguably even dominant – players both in investment in existing infrastructures and in the funding and operation of new infrastructures. Let us take those two components of the story in turn.

On occasion, asset managers acquired existing infrastructure assets in Europe directly from governments, just as they had in Australia. In 2005, for example, two Macquarie funds – the Macquarie Infrastructure Group and the Macquarie European Infrastructure Fund – teamed up with Eiffage, a French engineering firm, to acquire the Société des Autoroutes Paris-Rhin-Rhône (APRR), France's second-largest motorway company – with concessions covering 2,205 kilometres of toll road – in which the government was the majority shareholder. With twenty-seven years left to run on the concessions, the deal valued APPR at €7.1 billion, and was financed with around €1.3 billion of investor equity – around €675 million from the Macquarie funds and €635 million from Eiffage – supplemented by €5.8 billion of debt.[38] The deal, in other words, was highly geared.

More commonly, though, asset managers acquired existing European infrastructure assets from private owners. After all, by the late 1990s, when asset managers determinedly turned their attention to the European infrastructure space, governments had already privatised large stocks of infrastructure assets. This was especially true in the UK, which, as we have seen, in the 1980s and early 1990s was indisputably the trailblazer and most committed protagonist of infrastructure privatisation among European governments. Such privatisation had occurred through three main mechanisms: sometimes the state enterprises that owned and operated infrastructure assets were floated on stock markets; sometimes the managers of those state-owned enterprises themselves bought them, relying on external bank debt for funding – a notable example being the buyout of the UK's National Freight Corporation by its senior management team in 1982; and sometimes trade buyers, which is to say companies operating in the business sector in question, bought the

38 'Autoroute Sales Drive €17bn of Loans as French Government Collects EU 15bn', *Euroweek*, 16 December 2005.

enterprises and associated assets. In all three scenarios, asset managers subsequently could – and frequently did – bid to take ownership, either of the infrastructures per se or of the private companies that presently held such assets.

Though it was certainly not alone, Macquarie was once again prominent among asset managers in buying up previously privatised UK infrastructure assets. In 2005, for example, its European Infrastructure Fund led a consortium of investors in buying the Wales and West gas distribution network from National Grid – privatised in 1990 – for £1.2 billion. The following year, Macquarie completed its biggest and most controversial such acquisition. In a deal valued at around £8 billion, the same Macquarie fund led another investor consortium in buying the UK's biggest water company, Thames Water, from the German utility group RWE AG. RWE had itself bought Thames, privatised in 1989, in 2001, after twelve years in which the company had been listed on the London Stock Exchange.

It is also worth noting that, though many of the existing infrastructure assets that asset managers acquired in Europe in the late 1990s and the 2000s were, or had been, state-owned, this was not always the case. Some of the assets that they acquired had always been privately owned. A noteworthy, and again highly controversial, example concerned Blackstone's move into the social infrastructure space in 2004, when, in a deal worth £564 million, it acquired Nursing Home Properties (NHP), the owner of 355 private care homes across the UK. As in so many other cases, the stability and predictability of cash-flows – most residents in the NHP homes had their care paid for by the state through local-authority social-services departments – was a key attraction. Indeed, partly for that reason, such UK care-home chains had by that stage already been a locus of feverish asset-management investment activity for several years. The Four Seasons group had been bought not once but twice by asset managers: first in 1999, by Alchemy Partners; and second in 2004, by which time it owned more than 300 homes, from Alchemy by Allianz Capital Partners.

One of Allianz's rival bidders on the Four Seasons deal was Blackstone itself; but it would be wrong to imagine that only asset managers were in the running to buy existing infrastructure assets in Europe in this period. Alternative buyers came in many shapes and sizes, and one category merits special attention here: institutional investors, such as pension schemes.

As we have seen, some institutional investors began investing directly in real assets, including farmland and housing, prior to the 1980s. It will also be recalled that it was not until the 1980s that institutional investors began routing significant proportions of their overall investment, across all asset classes, through dedicated asset managers; before the 1980s, almost all such investment occurred directly.

When, in the 1990s and 2000s, institutional investors around the world began to allocate growing shares of portfolio investment to housing and infrastructure, some of them continued to invest mainly directly. In other words, institutional investors did not – and today still do not – invest in real assets *only* through asset managers and their pooled funds. Some rapidly became major direct owners themselves of real assets.

Canadian pension schemes were noteworthy examples: such schemes, as Georg Inderst has observed, 'have spearheaded direct investments in infrastructure since the early 2000s'.[39] So distinctive has this approach been that it soon became known as the 'Canadian Model'. According to Preqin, around 50 per cent of Canadian institutional investors with exposure to infrastructure make some direct investments – the highest figure in the world.[40] We have already encountered one important such player – the Ontario Teachers' Pension Plan. Another is the Ontario Municipal Employees Retirement System (OMERS). But the most prolific Canadian institutional investor buying directly into real assets was and remains the Canada Pension Plan Investment Board (CPPIB), which invests the capital held in the national public Canada Pension Plan (CPP). At the time of writing, this capital amounts to around $500 billion, making the CPP one of the world's largest pension funds. CPPIB began buying into European infrastructure in 2006, when it led a consortium in the acquisition of Anglian Water, one of the UK's largest water

39 Inderst, 'Pension Fund Investment in Infrastructure', p. 40.

40 Ibid., p. 44.

companies. Today, CPPIB is the largest shareholder not only in Anglian, but also, among other entities, in Arqiva, the owner of the main UK infrastructure for the transmission of radio and terrestrial television signals. OMERS, meanwhile, is the largest shareholder in Thames Water; Macquarie exited that investment some time ago (see Chapter 4).

Nevertheless – and this is the crucial point – most institutional investors, and especially most pension schemes, continue to rely predominantly on asset managers in order to make investments in real assets. The likes of OMERS and CPPIB are very much exceptions to the rule. According to the OECD, some three-quarters of infrastructure investment by pension plans in terms of investment value is channelled through unlisted investment funds operated by asset managers.[41]

Why should this be the case? To an extent, the tendency for institutional investors mainly to use asset managers to invest in real assets such as infrastructure merely reflects a more general pattern: as we have seen, asset managers today handle the bulk of insurer and pension-fund investments of all types; such out-sourcing is hardly unique to real-asset investments. And yet, some of the reasons why so much institutional investment in real assets occurs through asset managers are specific to this partic-ular asset 'class'. Exploring those reasons is crucial to a proper understanding of asset-manager society and its ascendancy since the 1990s.

In particular, investing in real assets requires greater scale and expertise than investing in financial securities such as equities and bonds; most institutional investors lack both of these attri-butes, and are neither able nor willing to invest in acquiring the latter. As Jennifer Thompson has written, 'direct investing [in real assets] carries greater challenges for investors compared with investing in bonds and equities. Complications stem mainly from the number of parties involved in real-asset projects – lenders, subcontractors, public bodies and private investors.'[42]

---

41 OECD, *Green Infrastructure in the Decade for Delivery: Assessing Institutional Investment* (Paris: OECD, 2020), p. 37.

42 J. Thompson, 'Big Investors Would Like to Bypass Fund Managers', *Financial Times*, 25 September 2017.

Along similar lines, Matti Leppälä, head of PensionsEurope, a trade association for pension schemes, has noted, 'One of the key barriers to pension fund investment in infrastructure is the challenge of assessing and managing risks with which pension funds are not familiar, such as construction risk.'[43]

Very few institutional investors have specialist infrastructure teams. The big asset managers, by contrast, do – and this is a substantial part of the explanation for why pension schemes and similar entities use them. As early as 2005, Macquarie already had over 500 staff working on infrastructure investments, split roughly equally between investment bankers and executives with backgrounds in the infrastructure industry. 'It takes a deal team of 15 to 20 to understand [a target] business', Jim Craig, director of the firm's first European infrastructure fund, said that year, 'and the best due diligence takes time and money.' Few pension schemes are able to afford the latter: Craig reported that Macquarie would often spend up to £3 million just to be in a position to make a bid.[44]

Revealingly, a survey carried out in 2017 by the US asset manager State Street found that more institutional investors would take the direct-investment route than is presently the case were it a viable option for them. Half of the investors surveyed said they would bypass asset managers and invest directly in real assets if they could.[45] But, they could not. Generally, substantive real-asset direct investment is only feasible for the very largest institutional investors with the necessary scale and – partly by dint of that scale – expertise. To be sure, the high-profile Canadian direct investors mentioned above are not all disproportionately large institutions. But by international standards they do tend to be characterised by disproportionately high allocations to 'alternative' assets, including real assets. The share of alternatives in the asset mix of Canada's leading pension plans increased from 10 per cent in 1990 to no less than 33 per

43   Cited in A. Mooney, 'Pension Funds Looking for Infrastructure Investments', *Financial Times*, 9 February 2016.

44   Cited in N. Lockley, 'Macquarie Leads Industry's Charge into Infrastructure', *Financial News*, 6 August 2005.

45   Thompson, 'Big Investors Would Like to Bypass Fund Managers'.

cent in 2014, which is far above international averages.[46] This means that those investors' infrastructure and real-estate teams have substantial sums of capital at their disposal, along with a commensurate ability to shoulder the relevant research and transaction costs.

The final part of the story of Europe becoming the centre of gravity of asset-manager society in the late 1990s and early 2000s involves the growing role of asset managers in funding new, 'greenfield' infrastructures, as opposed to purchasing existing assets. It was in relation to the development of new infrastructure that reductions in government spending on infrastructure in this period were most impactful, and asset managers – marshalling their swelling infrastructure funds and able to multiply their spending power through the aggressive use of leverage – were only too happy to fill the emerging financing void.

By no means all new infrastructure is developed for the state, of course; but much of it is. In Europe in the 1990s and 2000s, this was certainly true, not least in relation to education, health and transportation infrastructure. In that period, new government-commissioned infrastructure development involving private-sector funding typically occurred in Europe through the establishment of public–private partnerships (PPPs – see Chapter 1). PPPs proliferated across much of the continent from the middle of the 1990s, asset managers frequently being centrally involved.[47] But the model achieved its most dramatic growth and penetration in the UK, which consistently accounted for more than half of the European PPP market by both project value and volume; direct government funding was withdrawn more slowly elsewhere. It is thus the UK that is our focus in the short overview of PPPs and asset management that follows.

Recalling our introductory discussion of PPPs, the pertinent point is that the contractor commissioned by the state to build and then operate the infrastructure asset is set up as a Special

---

46 'Alternative Investments – A Proven Path to Higher and Stable Returns', 31 August 2017 – at tridelta.ca.

47 A. Kappeler and M. Nemoz, 'Public–Private Partnerships in Europe – Before and During the Recent Financial Crisis', Economic and Financial Report, No. 2010/04 (July 2010), European Investment Bank.

Purpose Vehicle (SPV) that is often owned by an asset manager. Introduced by the Conservative government in 1992, the UK's PPP system, the Private Finance Initiative (PFI), really took off under New Labour from 1997. Among other things, it was a way for the government to defer payment for new assets by spreading capital costs over the life of the contract, which was usually in the region of twenty-five to thirty years. It was also a way to massage reported levels of public debt: the liability that future payments to the contractor represented did not usually appear on the government's balance sheet.

Schools, hospitals, roads and prisons were the main infrastructures built in the UK under PFI (which became PF2 in 2012 under the Conservative–LibDem Coalition government). By 2017, there were over 700 PFI/PF2 contracts in operation. The assets built under these contracts were worth around £60 billion in total. By that point, public bodies had made around £110 billion in total payments to PFI contractors, and the approximately 700 contracts then in place would see public bodies making further contractual payments of around £200 billion, extending into the 2040s.[48]

From the perspective of the owner of the SPV, the economics of PFI were relatively straightforward. Each year, it would receive its 'unitary' payment from whichever public body it had the contract with. Out of this, it had to meet three main sets of costs. One was debt servicing: typically, most of the money used to finance construction was borrowed. The second was the cost of operating and maintaining the infrastructure. The third was tax. What was left, it kept, and, if it was an asset manager, distributed to fund investors – after the deduction of management and performance fees, of course.

Asset managers swarmed all over the UK PFI market from its very inception, and one was particularly prominent: Innisfree. It was Innisfree that, in 1995 (the year of its incorporation), created the first fund dedicated to investing in PFI projects, for which it raised £85 million. The fund made its maiden investment in 1997, in a waste-to-energy plant in Stoke-on-Trent; later

48 House of Commons Committee of Public Accounts, *Private Finance Initiatives*, 20 June 2018, HC 894, Forty-Sixth Report of Session 2017–19.

the same year, it invested in the UK's first PFI hospital, the £140 million Dartford and Gravesham hospital, in Kent.[49]

Several further Innisfree funds followed. Sometimes they invested at the outset of a PFI project, when construction was beginning; on other occasions, they invested later, when the project was already operational and producing income. Over time, the health sector became Innisfree's main focus, and would herald an important strategic development for the firm: internationalisation. Innisfree funds have invested in PPP health-sector projects in both Canada and Sweden, as well as the UK.[50]

By 2004, Innisfree funds had invested some £268 million in thirty-three UK PFI projects with a combined capital value – including equity and debt – of £4.5 billion. The same year saw a notable change in Innisfree's investment model: henceforth, in a break from its previous practice, the firm would itself commit capital to its funds, equivalent to up to 1 per cent of fund value.[51] Since 2004, Innisfree has continued to dominate PFI/PF2 commissioning. Nearly 15 per cent of all the money that UK public-sector bodies are contracted to pay to contract owners under existing PPP contracts from 2022–23 onwards will be paid to Innisfree funds.[52]

Thus, even where asset managers hold assets under contracts rather than through ownership, the history of asset-manager society indelibly haunts its long-term destiny. Dominant in PFI's past, Innisfree is securely locked into its future. Nowhere is this entrenchment more apparent and material than in a pocket of Merseyside, in north-west England, where Innisfree wholly owns the vehicle that was responsible for one of the country's largest ever healthcare PFI projects: the 2006–09 redevelopment of major hospitals in St Helens and Knowsley. Amounting to some £2.8 billion in total, unitary payments under this scheme will continue until as late as 2047–48, when a final annual payment

49 J. Ford, '£140m Hospital Deal a Shot in the Arm for PFI', *Evening Standard*, 31 July 1997.

50 I will discuss a controversial Swedish example in Chapter 5.

51 A. Felsted, 'How PFI Became a Pension Fund Investment', *Financial Times*, 13 April 2004.

52 'Current Projects', 31 March 2018 – at assets.publishing.service.gov.uk (author analysis).

of £113 million falls due. Of course, Innisfree may have sold its interest by then. But if it does not receive the payment itself, it will decide who does.

After the Financial Crisis: Expansion and Extension

Expansion

Getting an accurate handle on the size and scope of asset-manager society is extremely challenging. One reason for this is a problem of definition: different research organisations measure different things. We will return to this challenge in the following chapter. But one thing that is clear, whichever source one uses, is that, having emerged and consolidated in the Global North between the early 1990s and the mid 2000s, asset-manager society – quantified in terms of the money invested in housing and infrastructure by asset managers – has expanded dramatically since the financial crisis of 2007–09.

In the case of infrastructure, the authors of a recent study of global institutional infrastructure investment between 1990 and 2020 found that the 'vast majority' of investments in infrastructure had been made since 2008.[53] According to Preqin, assets under management (AUM) at unlisted infrastructure funds – the most significant vehicles of institutional investment in infrastructure – increased from $129 billion globally at the end of 2009 to $582 billion by the middle of 2019, implying a compound annual growth rate of not far short of 20 per cent.[54]

Meanwhile, INREV, the European Association for Investors in Non-Listed Real Estate Vehicles, has estimated that global AUM at real-estate investment funds increased from €0.9 trillion in 2009 to €3.3 trillion in 2020 (of which 83 per cent was held in unlisted vehicles), translating into a lower but still very strong compound growth rate of 13 per cent per annum.[55] Of course,

---

53   A. Andonov, R. Kräussl and J. Rauh, 'Institutional Investors and Infrastructure Investing', *Review of Financial Studies* 34 (2021), p. 3887.

54   Preqin, '2020 Preqin Global Infrastructure Report', 4 February 2020, p. 20.

55   'Global Real Estate Investment Managers Reaches AUM of €3.3 trillion', 19 May 2021 – at inrev.org.

real-estate funds invest in commercial as well as residential property, so that this 13 per cent increase does not apply specifically to housing investment. But it is highly likely that the rate of growth in asset managers' housing investment during this period was in fact in excess of 13 per cent, perhaps significantly so.

Consider that, in the years leading up to the global financial crisis, only around one in seven newly launched real-estate investment funds globally focused largely or exclusively on residential assets – the proportion was 14.2 per cent in 2005, for instance. After the financial crisis, this proportion sharply increased, reaching between one-in-four and one-in-five by the mid 2010s (22.2 per cent was the figure for 2015), and subsequently remaining in that range.[56] In other words, real-estate AUM globally have increasingly been steered towards residential assets. Blackstone, which is today the world's largest real-estate investor, is a striking, if extreme example of this shift. In 2009, its funds owned no housing at all; by 2020, housing accounted for perhaps 20 per cent of Blackstone's real-estate portfolio of $300 billion or more.[57]

How might we explain the rapid growth in real-asset investment via asset managers in the period since the financial crisis? Two factors appear to have played an especially important and broad-based role.

The first was a significant shift in the macroeconomic environment. As we have seen, many major institutional investors, with long-term ongoing liabilities to meet, rely on their investments to provide them with steady annual income as well as the possibility of capital gains. This was one of the 'pull' factors, noted above, that first attracted institutional investors (and their asset managers) to real assets in the 1990s – these assets frequently provide just such steady annual cash-flows.

Historically, investments in financial assets generated annual income for investors reasonably reliably. Certainly, dividend yields on equities in the United States and other countries with deep securities markets underwent a secular decline during

---

56   D. Gabor and S. Kohl, 'My Home Is an Asset Class: The Financialization of Housing in Europe', 2021 (pre-publication version).

57   Author calculation, based on company disclosures.

the course of the twentieth century; but investors were largely able to compensate for this by increasing their allocations to bonds, which generate annual interest payments. Across most of the Global North, tight monetary policy helped to keep both nominal and real interest rates relatively high from the beginning of the 1980s all the way up to 2007.

But the financial crisis ushered in a radically different macro-economic era. Western central banks drove down interest rates to close to zero, or even below; and that is where rates remained, by and large, until as recently as 2022. The effect was a dramatic reduction in yields not only on government but also corporate debt. Thus, having come to rely primarily on bonds to earn investment income in the face of the long-term fall in dividend yields, institutional investors were now faced with the novel scenario of not being able to rely on any mainstream financial assets for the generation of recurring annual income at healthy rates of return; US public pension schemes, for example, cut their portfolio allocation to debt securities from around 30 to around 20 per cent between 2009 and 2021.

This largely explains why real assets now came into their own. Read any report on institutional investment in housing, infrastructure or real assets more generally published in the decade following the financial crisis, and the macroeconomic environment invariably features high up on the list of investors' rationales for turning increasingly to these asset classes. In a 2014 survey of institutional investors carried out by the Economist Intelligence Unit on behalf of BlackRock, for example, more than 50 per cent of respondents cited 'Macro environment considerations' among their top three motivations for raising real-asset allocations – the highest share for any factor, in both real-estate and infrastructure investment.[58] This motivating factor was wholly new to the post-crisis period.[59]

---

58 Economist Intelligence Unit, 'The Ascent of Real Assets: Gauging Growth and Goals in Institutional Portfolios', 2015, p. 9 – at impact. economist.com.

59 In Chapter 6, I will consider the question of how the recent rise in inter-est rates, beginning in 2022 in response to a sharp spike in inflation, might affect asset-manager investment in real assets such as housing and infrastructure.

By contrast, the second key factor driving increased rates of growth in investment in real assets – specifically, infrastructure – in the post-crisis period was not entirely new to that period. This was the widespread conviction that there exists what is commonly referred to as an 'infrastructure gap': a gap, that is, between the amount that is being invested in infrastructure construction and renewal and the amount that needs to be invested in it. The idea that such a gap exists is not novel. The US Democratic congressman James Howard, for example, used the term as early as 1985 in arguing that, at prevailing rates of expenditure, the federal government's investment in infrastructure between then and the end of that century would fall short of what was required by \$450 billion.[60]

But if the idea of an infrastructure gap is not new, its profile, currency and impact have positively surged since the financial crisis. If one enters the phrase 'infrastructure gap' in the Factiva search tool, it returns – at the time of writing – around 12,500 hits. What is most striking is the distribution of mentions across time. Prior to the 2000s, there were almost none: a yearly maximum, in 1997, of just twenty-two. 'Infrastructure gap' was simply not part of the mainstream discourse. The following few years saw a modest increase, as the term gained a degree of familiarity; but the number of yearly hits had still only increased to 117 by 2006. Use of the term then leapt, however, with hits reaching over 1,000 per annum by 2014. It was now an established part of the lexicon.

It is hard to say exactly why it is specifically in the past fifteen years or so that a consensus has emerged around the idea that there is an infrastructure gap. There is probably a combination of factors. One is certainly of the view that, more than half a century on, the various vital infrastructures built by the Keynesian state in the aftermath of World War II have been coming to the end of their 'natural' lives. Another contributory factor, undoubtedly, is climate change. As societies have begun in the past two decades to take the reality of climate change more

---

60   D. Farney, 'Congress's Authorization Committee Chairmen Once Dictated Budget; Now, It Dictates to Them', *Wall Street Journal*, 16 April 1985.

seriously, it has become increasingly clear that, even if existing infrastructures are not at the end of their 'natural' lives, they are nonetheless ill-suited to mitigating and adapting to warming: climate change, in short, demands wholesale infrastructure transformation. Finally, there was austerity. As Western governments tightened their fiscal belts in response to the financial crisis, and public infrastructure investment stagnated or declined, the 'infrastructure gap' identified by commentators became not so much a gap as a chasm.

Increasingly persuaded, on the one hand, that an infrastructure gap existed, but hamstrung, on the other hand, by the self-imposed political economy of austerity, Western governments after the financial crisis widely implored the private sector to help plug the gap, and typically saw capital-rich asset managers as the most credible source of finance. In the UK, for example, 2010 saw both the creation within the Treasury of Infrastructure UK – later renamed the Infrastructure and Projects Authority – to shape government policy on infrastructure investment, and the publication of the government's first ever National Infrastructure Plan, described as 'a broad vision of the infrastructure investment required to underpin the UK's growth'. Promoting private-sector investment was an integral component of that plan: the talk was of 'improving private sector investment models', 'encouraging new sources of private capital', and 'unlocking private sector investment in the UK's infrastructure on an unprecedented scale'. Indeed, it was now the government's position that 'infrastructure investment should be made by the private sector *wherever possible*'.[61]

As we shall see in a moment, Western governments have, since around 2010, not only called for increased private-sector infrastructure investment; they have also taken active steps to maximise the likelihood of such investment occurring. But it should be stressed that they have done so under the influence of a constant stream of industry lobbying – not least from asset managers and institutional investors. Those actors have told governments that they will only help plug the growing infrastructure

---

61   HM Treasury and Infrastructure UK, 'National Infrastructure Plan 2010', pp. 3–4, 7, 13 (emphasis added).

gap if the investment conditions are right – and that it is govern-ments' responsibility to put such conditions in place. In 2017, for instance, Larry Fink, head of BlackRock, urged the US adminis-tration of Donald Trump to ensure that publicly commissioned infrastructure projects were brought to market 'in a format appropriate for institutional investment'. What did he mean by 'appropriate'? 'These projects must deliver competitive returns', Fink clarified.[62] Similar arguments have repeatedly been made by trade bodies such as the Global Infrastructure Investor Associa-tion, which, representing the interests of institutional investors, assiduously stresses the alleged benefits of using private finance to deliver infrastructure, and 'work[s] with governments and public bodies to create the right environment to unlock more private capital and increase infrastructure investment'.[63]

To an increasing extent, what Western governments have essentially done since the financial crisis is de-risk private-sector infrastructure investment, in just the manner called for by the likes of Fink. The UK's first National Infrastructure Plan, in 2010, set the tone, the language already being that of 'creating the optimum environment for investment', of 'reducing the level of risk transfer to the private sector', and thus of offering 'rela-tively certain economic returns'. The immediate objective could not have been more transparent: to make UK infrastructure 'an attractive asset class'.[64]

Nothing has changed in the past decade or so. In 2014, the Treasury freely admitted that the UK government paid 'particu-lar regard to the effect on investor confidence' when amending infrastructure-related regulation. So concerned has the govern-ment been not to scare investors away through heavy-handed regulation that it provides guarantees – a total figure of £40 billion was cited in 2014 – if it fears that 'major infrastructure

---

62 Cited in S. Foley, 'Fink Urges US Privatisation Model to Fund Building Drive', *Financial Times*, 10 April 2017.

63 Global Infrastructure Investor Association, 'Closing the Gap: How Private Capital Can Help Deliver Our Future Infrastructure Needs', March 2019, pp. 12–13, 3 – at giia.net.

64 HM Treasury and Infrastructure UK, 'National Infrastructure Plan 2010', October 2010, pp. 11–12, 14–15 – at infrastructure.planninginspectorate.gov.uk.

projects may struggle to access private finance'.[65] Furthermore, when, towards the end of the decade, the National Infrastructure Commission (a sister agency to the Infrastructure and Projects Authority) addressed the matter of a widely reported decline in confidence in the UK's system of infrastructure regulation among the public due to rising costs and poor-quality services, its insistence that public confidence in the system 'must be improved' was justified not for the sake of the public, but rather 'to enable long-term certainty for investors'.[66]

Finally, when the government in 2020 announced the creation of a new, publicly owned UK Infrastructure Bank (UKIB) with public funds at its disposal, it was immediately clear that the ultimate goal was not, in fact, public infrastructure investment as such – still less public ownership of infrastructure. Following the pattern of the past decade, the main role of the bank would instead be 'crowding-in private capital and managing risk', by using cornerstone commitments of public funds 'to attract international investment and unlock capital from institutions including pension funds'.[67] And so it has proved: among UKIB's first deals were sizeable commitments to unlisted infrastructure funds launched by the asset managers NextEnergy Capital (in 2021) and Octopus Investments (2022), designed precisely to catalyse and de-risk matching private-sector funding.

The plan has worked. Governments of the Global North have successfully, if unevenly, de-risked private-sector infrastructure investment – and, as we have seen, the capital has correspondingly flowed in, not least via asset managers' bulging infrastructure funds. That the UK government achieved what it set out to do in this regard was acknowledged by Moody's – the credit-rating agency that is the ultimate arbiter of investment risk. In 2016, the UK's Infrastructure and Projects Authority crowed that Moody's had awarded the country's regulatory

65   HM Treasury, 'Investing in UK Infrastructure', July 2014, pp. 11–12 – at assets.publishing.service.gov.uk.

66   National Infrastructure Commission, 'Strategic Investment and Public Confidence', p. 7.

67   HM Treasury, 'UK Infrastructure Bank: Policy Design', March 2021, pp. 3, 5 – at assets.publishing.service.gov.uk.

regimes for the water, gas and electricity sectors the highest possible score (AAA) – representing the lowest investment risk.
Moody's judged those regimes as 'amongst the most stable and
predictable in the world': an infrastructure investor's 'paradise',
as the *Financial Times* subsequently remarked.[68]

Motivated by concerns about growing infrastructure gaps,
this burgeoning enterprise of state-led de-risking joins the aforementioned transformation in the macroeconomic environment
in substantially explaining the conspicuous growth in real-asset
investment via asset managers in the period since the financial
crisis. They are assuredly not the only relevant factors – but
they are probably the two with the deepest and broadest impact
across both sectors and countries.

Other notable contributory factors have had narrower, sector-
specific impacts. Two of these warrant particular attention. The
first relates to an issue already briefly touched upon: climate
change. As I noted, an increasing amount of the infrastructure
investment now being undertaken has climate mitigation or
adaptation as one objective – none more so than in the case of
renewable-energy generation facilities. At varying speeds and
in different ways, countries are replacing fossil-fuel-fired power
plants with solar and wind farms. This has had significant implications for asset managers.

Owning a coal- or gas-fired plant is not straightforward: the
business is a relatively complex and labour-intensive one. Owning
a solar or wind farm is very different. Once built and operational,
such facilities require very little attention or maintenance, and
they have therefore emerged as a favoured investment object for
asset managers, who acquire them for their income-producing –
not to mention green credential–burnishing – capacity, while
outsourcing the little upkeep required to a local contractor. In
2016, some forty-five per cent of investment firms' infrastructure
deals *of all types* globally were in the renewable-energy sector.

---

68 Respectively: Infrastructure and Projects Authority, 'National Infrastructure Delivery Plan 2016–2021', March 2016, p. 19 – at assets.publishing.
service.gov.uk; J. Ford, 'Lax Regulation Has Turned Britain into a Rentier's
Paradise', *Financial Times*, 1 October 2017.

By 2018, that figure had increased to 57 per cent.[69] By contrast, asset managers have rarely invested in fossil-fuel-fired plants in the same direct fashion (though they may of course own some or all the shares of companies operating such plants). Their direct investments in fossil-fuel infrastructures have tended instead to be in infrastructures of storage, transmission or distribution, rather than energy generation. To be clear, such investments are still happening: in 2020, for example, Brookfield Asset Management and Global Infrastructure Partners led a $10 billion consortium investment in a twenty-year concession for gas pipelines used and owned by the Abu Dhabi National Oil Company, following a similar pipeline deal for $4 billion with the same company the previous year led by two other asset managers, BlackRock and KKR.[70]

The second factor with sector-specific impact involves a textbook case of asset-manager opportunism. The financial crisis lowered the price of some assets so far that asset managers readily shed their historic reservations regarding investment in such assets. The quintessential example here was US single-family housing – that is, standalone homes rather than multi-family apartment blocks. Historically, asset managers and their institutional-investor clients had steered well clear of investing in such housing for rental income, judging that the downsides – disproportionately large acquisition and operating costs relative to the value of the individual asset – far outweighed the upsides.

But the financial crisis changed the calculus.[71] Not only was US single-family housing suddenly cheap, prices having fallen by 50 per cent or more in areas most affected by the subprime debacle and the ensuing surge in foreclosures. Equally importantly, large, cash-rich buyers now had the opportunity both to buy large numbers of dwellings and then to operate them as

69 A. McElhaney, 'Preqin: Infrastructure Fundraising Is on a Tear After a Record 2018', *Institutional Investor*, 7 January 2019.

70 S. Kerr, 'GIP and Brookfield Among Investors in $10bn Abu Dhabi Pipeline Deal', *Financial Times*, 23 June 2020.

71 B. Christophers, 'How and Why US Single-Family Housing Became an Investor Asset Class', *Journal of Urban History*, 8 July 2021 (online early).

rental units, with unprecedented levels of efficiency. The fact that the crisis was geographically concentrated in foreclosure hotspots was critical. Buyers could pick up hundreds of properties in one swoop at weekly or monthly foreclosure auctions, and the clustering of those dwellings in particular neighbourhoods made letting them much less of a logistical challenge than it might otherwise have been.

Furthermore, there was an additional mechanism whereby financial investors could now (indirectly) acquire large stocks of US single-family housing both cheaply and efficiently. The financial crisis saw the aggregation of large numbers of distressed residential mortgages within several different federal-government domains, in particular the Department of Housing and Urban Development (HUD) and the effectively nationalised government-sponsored enterprises (GSEs), Fannie Mae and Freddie Mac. After the crisis, both HUD and the GSEs sold off large numbers of these loans (more than 100,000 in each case) at fire-sale prices, in batches of a scale that only investors such as large asset managers were in a position to acquire. The loans sold by HUD, for instance, were typically priced at discounts of 20–30 per cent on the market value of the underlying property, and 30–50 per cent against the unpaid principal balance.[72] Thus, investors were able to acquire houses by buying these discounted loans, and then foreclosing on the mortgage holder – an opportunity they took up on a large scale.

Accordingly, between 2011 and 2018, the US went from having essentially zero to as many as 300,000 single-family rental homes under the control of large institutional landlords. I will have more to say about the stark costs of this opportunism in Chapter 4. What should already be clear, though, is that, as much as anything else, this represented a transfer of wealth from the powerless to the powerful that was at once straightforward and colossal. Mortgaged homeowners widely lost their homes and wealth; investors acquired those houses on the cheap, then

---

72   B. Greenburg, 'Consolidation After Crisis: How a Few Private Investors Bought Distressed, Federally-Insured Mortgages After the Foreclosure Crisis', *New York University Journal of Legislation and Public Policy* 20 (2017), pp. 887–939.

let them – often to the same group of people – while simultane-
ously enjoying a rapid rebound in asset prices.

This story is of particular interest because of who exactly the
lead investors were. Six entities rapidly emerged as the dominant players in US single-family rental. One of these, American
Homes 4 Rent, was a relatively typical real-estate company – but
the other five were all asset managers, who set about integrating
US single-family housing into asset-manager society for the first
time. It was perhaps as clear a demonstration as we have seen
anywhere of the reality of the contemporary balance of power in
real-asset investment, with asset managers emphatically under-
lining their dominance over not only operating companies such
as American Homes 4 Rent, but also institutional investors,
which typically invest in US single-family housing indirectly via
asset managers rather than directly. Colony Capital, Starwood
Capital and Waypoint Real Estate Group – which by 2015 would
merge their single-family rental assets into a single entity – were
three of the five asset managers to emerge as leaders in the sector.
New York's Pretium Partners was a fourth. The fifth and largest
was Blackstone.

Blackstone funds acquired such housing through both of the
mechanisms outlined above. First, it directly acquired physical properties. Between 2011 and 2017, through a portfolio
company, Invitation Homes, which it created for the purpose,
Blackstone bought around 50,000 US single-family homes at a
cost of more than $10 billion (see Chapter 1). By the time they
exited from Invitation Homes in 2019, Blackstone's funds had
made an estimated profit on their investment of more than $3.5
billion. Second, Blackstone used a company in which it held a
46 per cent stake – Bayview Asset Management – to acquire
homes indirectly. Most notably, Bayview purchased over 30,000
distressed mortgages from HUD (making it easily HUD's biggest
customer), and it subsequently took possession of the borrower's
home in around 60 per cent of cases where the resolution of
those loans was reported.[73]

---

73 B. Christophers, 'The Role of the State in the Transfer of Value from
Main Street to Wall Street: US Single-Family Housing after the Financial Crisis',
Antipode 54 (2022), pp. 130–52.

Extension

It is not only the countries of the Global North, which represent the historic and contemporary heartlands of asset-manager society, that commentators have increasingly identified as suffering from an 'infrastructure gap'. So, too, it is said, do other parts of the world, variously referred to as developing countries, the Global South or – in the language of asset managers – 'emerging markets'. Indeed, in 2017, when the management consultancy McKinsey set about trying to estimate global infrastructure investment requirements in the period to 2035, it concluded that nearly two-thirds of overall investment would be needed in 'emerging economies'. (These included China, which was one of the countries that McKinsey distinguished from 'developed Asia'.) Planned investments generally fell far short of those estimated requirements. According to McKinsey, countries with especially large proportionate gaps between extant spending commitments and estimated need were Brazil, Indonesia and Mexico.[74]

Given the limited fiscal capacity of many governments in the Global South, private-sector investment is widely seen as being even more essential to plugging infrastructure gaps there than it is in the Global North. Calls for private finance capital to respond to this need for investment have escalated markedly in recent times. Much of the solicitation has come from development-oriented organisations such as the United Nations Development Programme (UNDP) and the World Bank, both of which have been publicly making such calls for more than a decade. A key moment came with 2015's Addis Ababa Action Agenda. The third of three UN-hosted international conferences on Financing for Development, the first of which was held in 2002, the Addis Ababa conference and resulting Agenda signalled a decisive shift in development policy towards catalysing specifically private financial investment, and it triggered other influential initiatives such as the World Bank's own Maximizing Finance for Development. So central have development institutions been to the shift in emphasis towards private finance that

74 McKinsey Global Institute, 'Bridging Infrastructure Gaps: Has the World Made Progress?', October 2017, pp. 4, 6 – at mckinsey.com.

many see this shift as evidence of nothing less than a new development paradigm, wherein traditional foreign aid comes to be valued less for its own sake than as a mechanism for crowding-in profit-seeking private capital.

Prior to the 2010s, Western asset managers had a very limited track record of investing in real assets located in the Global South. For one thing, they had no need for 'emerging' markets. From the early 1990s, as they and their institutional-investor clients increasingly turned their attention to real assets, first in Australia and then in Europe and North America, they generally found an abundance of profitable investment opportunities in those core geographic markets. Little of the capital committed to funds remained uninvested 'dry powder'. At the same time, the Global South posed what managers widely saw as excessive investment risk. This purportedly came in many forms, including, as Britta Klagge and Chigozie Neweke-Eze have noted, 'legal and regulatory risks, for example when (domestic) state actors change regulation and remuneration agreements, but also complex bureaucratic procedures and corruption as well as macro-economic risks such as fluctuation of interest-rates, exchange-rates and inflation'.[75]

From the perspective of US and European-based asset managers, the landscape began in some ways to look different in the years following the financial crisis. Partly this was a function of a growing sense of opportunity: the impression was that Global South governments were getting serious about increasing infrastructure investment, and that foreign private finance was welcome. Between 2012 and 2017, for instance, India, according to McKinsey, saw the world's strongest increase in infrastructure spending.[76] Asset managers were keen not to miss out. Moreover, the Global South began to look more attractive partly because the Global North was becoming less so. The historic success of asset managers focused on real assets has inevitably attracted

75   B. Klagge and C. Nweke-Eze, 'Financing Large-Scale Renewable-Energy Projects in Kenya: Investor Types, International Connections, and Financialization', *Geografiska Annaler: Series B* 102: 1 (2020), p. 65.

76   McKinsey Global Institute, 'Bridging Infrastructure Gaps', p. 2.

increasing competition to the field – by 2020 there were reported to be over 700 active infrastructure asset managers and even more real-estate managers – with the result that asset prices have been pushed up, and returns squeezed. Managers have responded to these pressures in a number of ways, of which moving into new geographic markets, characterised by less competition, has been a primary one.

Nevertheless, there was still the perception of excess risk, and so, for a number of years now, Western financial institutions such as asset managers have been vocally advocating the de-risking of real-asset investment opportunities in the Global South, maintaining that such de-risking needs to go above and beyond that undertaken by Global North governments such as the UK's. An early example of such advocacy, as Daniela Gabor has noted, was Deutsche Bank's work in 2010–11 with the UNDP on designing mechanisms for de-risking private-sector investment in Global South renewable-energy assets.[77] Indeed, the UNDP, alongside the World Bank and G20, has been as insistent as the finance sector that attracting external private finance requires wholesale de-risking. The nature and scale of the de-risking that is purported to be necessary has been documented, for instance, in the World Bank's so-called Infrastructure Sector Assessment Programs, which have been produced for countries including Indonesia and Sri Lanka. Likewise, the ways in which barriers to external investment in Global South infrastructure can be lowered is the core theme of the G20's 2018 'Roadmap to Infrastructure as an Asset Class'.

De-risking of infrastructure investment comes in many guises, and has been initiated by a range of different actors. Two of the main categories of risk that it aims to mitigate are construction and demand risk. The former is the risk that a project costs more or takes longer to complete than projected, or that construction to the required standard is simply unsuccessful; the latter is the risk that, once built, a project does not generate the level of revenue anticipated. Governments in the Global

---

77 D. Gabor, 'The Wall Street Consensus', *Development and Change* 52: 3 (2021), pp. 433–4.

South have increasingly sought to offset both sets of risks for international private investors, for instance, in the case of power-generation facilities, by guaranteeing revenue via long-term power-purchase contracts with state-owned utilities. Multilateral institutions have also helped with de-risking. In 2013, for example, the International Finance Corporation (IFC), a sister organisation of the World Bank, initiated a programme designed to steer institutional-investor capital into Global South infrastructure projects. Not only would the IFC co-invest; it would, if its private-sector co-investors incurred losses, absorb some of those losses. By early 2018 the scheme had externally raised $6 billion, of which $3.5 billion had been invested in eighty-seven projects in thirty-nine countries.[78]

Potential investments are not always de-risked to the degree necessary to attract asset managers and other well-capitalised Global North real-asset financial investors. As Klagge and Nweke-Eze have suggested, this especially seems to be the case in sub-Saharan Africa, where continuing low levels of private financial investment suggest that the perceived risks remain too high (and perhaps also the perceived rewards too low), and where, as a result, major infrastructure projects continue to rely disproportionately on the capital of the state, of development finance institutions such as the IFC, and of non-financial private investors (such as energy companies). But it is also sometimes still the case even in countries where, as we shall see, Western asset managers have invested relatively widely. One such country is Brazil. At the time of writing, Brazil is part-way through a major programme of awarding concessions to transportation and sanitation networks in urgent need of investment, but it is struggling to attract foreign capital. The 'ideological radicalism' of the Bolsonaro government, one commentator noted a year before Lula reassumed office, 'often spooks investors'.[79]

Nevertheless, de-risking has been sufficiently widespread, and indeed was already sufficiently well-advanced by the time the

---

78 J. Kynge and O. Ralph, 'World Bank Group Helps Plug Infrastructure Investment Gap', *Financial Times*, 14 March 2018.

79 B. Harris, 'Brazil's Economic Outlook Buoyed by Big-Ticket Investments', *Financial Times*, 4 January 2022.

IFC launched its co-investment programme, that, in 2015, Toby Carroll and Darryl Jarvis could credibly describe 'the escorting of international capital by multilateral development agencies into frontier and emerging market settings' as 'a valued form of development policy, making many (often large) infrastructure projects and other investments proceed with alacrity'.[80]

Asset-manager investment in Global South real assets since around the time of the financial crisis has occurred in three main categories; and the same manager names and countries tend to crop up repeatedly. The first key type of investible asset has proved to be renewable-energy generation infrastructure. In 2018, Sean Kennedy observed that the availability of, most notably, 'cheap land and labour have made many countries in the Global South … lucrative sites for the absorption [in renewable energy projects] of abundant finance capital'.[81] Much of that capital has been invested by asset managers.

Brookfield Asset Management has been one leading player. Historically, its main renewables assets were in hydroelectricity. In 2007, for instance, it spent $288 million to acquire a 156 MW hydro facility in Brazil.[82] But as, over the past decade, the wider renewables market has shifted more towards solar and wind, Brookfield has moved along with it. Arguably its most notable deal in this space outside the Global North came in 2017, when it acquired TerraForm Global for $787 million, plus the assumption of $455 million in net debt. TerraForm Global owned and operated, or had contracts to buy, a portfolio of thirty-one wind and solar parks with a combined capacity of 952 MW, spread across Brazil, India, China, South Africa, Thailand, Malaysia and Uruguay.[83] In recent years, India has become an

80   T. Carroll and D. Jarvis, 'Introduction: Financialisation and Development in Asia Under Late Capitalism', in T. Carroll and D. Jarvis, eds, *Financialisation and Development in Asia* (London: Routledge, 2015), p. 6.

81   S. Kennedy, 'Indonesia's Energy Transition and Its Contradictions: Emerging Geographies of Energy and Finance', *Energy Research & Social Science* 41 (2018), p. 232.

82   'Brookfield Asset Management to Acquire Hydroelectric Facility in Brazil', *ENP Newswire*, 21 December 2007.

83   'Brookfield to Acquire TerraForm Global', 7 March 2017 – at globe newswire.com.

especially popular territory for renewables investment by asset managers; in 2020, for example, Global Infrastructure Partners paid around $230 million to buy the 306 MW solar portfolio of RattanIndia Power.

Africa has received less of this type of investment, but it has not been entirely overlooked. A noteworthy investor there has been Meridiam, a French asset manager specialising in infrastructure investment. The Meridiam Infrastructure Africa Fund was launched in 2014 and, when the fund was closed to new investors in 2019, it had raised €546 million, 70 per cent of which came from private institutions such as pension plans and insurers, with the remaining 30 per cent provided mainly by development-finance institutions. Among the fund's investments have been four solar power plants in Senegal, with a combined generating capacity of 140 MW. Notably, two of these plants represented case studies in de-risking, realised as they were through the World Bank's Scaling Solar programme, which aims to promote private investment in renewable energy in emerging markets. Debt financing for the two plants in question was provided by the IFC, the European Investment Bank, and the French development finance institution Proparco. In addition, the Multilateral Investment Guarantee Agency, a member (like the IFC) of the World Bank Group, issued €6.9 million in guarantees, 'providing protection against non-commercial risks for a duration of up to 15 years'.[84]

Alongside renewable energy, a second principal object of real-asset investment in the Global South by asset managers has been road concessions. Again, Meridiam has blazed a trail in Africa – participating in a consortium that in 2020 was awarded the $1.5 billion, thirty-year concession to Kenya's Nairobi–Nakuru–Mau Summit motorway; but, again, most of the investment activity has been in South America and southern Asia. In the former, Brookfield has led the way once more, forming a joint venture in 2012 with Abertis Infraestructuras, a Spanish toll-road management company, to take ownership of Arteris, one of the largest owners and operators of toll-road concessions in Brazil.

84 'Two PV Plants Bring Clean Energy to Senegal', *Renewable Energy Magazine*, 2 June 2021.

Today, Brookfield controls some 3,700 kilometres of Brazilian toll roads.[85]

Brookfield's first investment in Indian infrastructure was in the same sector: in 2015, it acquired from Gammon Infrastructure Projects six road concessions, of which two were toll-based and four were based on annuities from India's National Highways Authority. Meanwhile, one of Brookfield's main competitors in international infrastructure investment, the Australian asset manager Macquarie, had entered the Indian road-concession market three years previously, and today its funds collectively constitute the largest international investor in Indian highways. KKR, which, like Brookfield, controls a diversified mix of toll and annuity roads in the country, in its case running to more than 900 kilometres across eleven states, is another significant investor in Indian highway assets.[86]

The third and final key category of real asset to have attracted major Western asset managers to the Global South is farmland. Here, too, Brookfield is a very important actor. In 2020, it reported that its Brazilian assets included 269,000 hectares of agricultural property.[87] This does not make it the biggest investor in Brazilian farmland among international asset managers, however. The largest is the US-based asset manager Nuveen, which invests in farmland through the specialist management vehicle Westchester Group Investment Management. At the end of 2019, Nuveen–Westchester, which also holds farmland in Chile and eastern Europe (Poland and Romania), owned around 350,000 hectares of Brazilian agricultural real estate, with an estimated value of nearly $2 billion, having increased its Brazilian holdings by approximately 50,000 hectares within the previous two years alone.[88] The country in which Nuveen–Westchester owns most farmland, incidentally, is Australia, where it has holdings of around 360,000 hectares. Its landholdings

85 'Brookfield Case Study', 22 June 2020, Brazil–Canada New Energy Investment Forum 2020, p. 4 – at clientesinterativa.com.br.

86 'Ontario Teachers' to Invest $175m in KKR's Road Platform in India', 20 April 2022 – at realassets.ipe.com.

87 'Brookfield Case Study'.

88 Westchester, '2020 Farmland Report', p. 4 – at faculty-senate.uiowa.edu.

thus neatly link Global South countries such as Brazil, where asset-manager society is a relatively new phenomenon, with the country – Australia – where, some three decades ago, asset-manager society was born.

For all the inroads that asset managers have latterly made into real-asset investment in the Global South, this chapter has shown that the history of asset-manager society is predominantly a Global North history, at least in terms of where capital has been invested. Nowhere in the Global South do we see anything approaching the broad and deep colonisation of housing and infrastructure markets by asset managers that we find today in parts of the Global North. Will this geographical imbalance persist? Chapter 6 will peer into the metaphorical crystal ball on this question. But one thing should already be evident: if asset managers fail to cultivate asset-manager society more fully in the Global South, it will not have been for want of trying to capture such opportunities as present themselves.

As well as the fact that asset managers are opportunistic and increasingly deep-pocketed investors, we know now why they regard housing and infrastructure as attractive asset classes, and why such attractiveness has generally increased historically: the 'investibility' of housing and infrastructure on a scale and producing returns that asset managers consider viable has been far from consistent over time, or indeed across space. Governments have played a particularly pivotal role in fashioning the terms – and often even the possibility – of such investibility. We also know why, when pension schemes and insurance companies have invested in these asset classes, they have usually done so specifically via external asset managers. In short, we know where, when, why and how the phenomenon of asset-manager society came into being.

3

Mapping Asset-Manager Society

Windows on the World

Ever since it came into being, asset-manager society has been controversial. The critiques have ranged widely across economic, social and political matters. One of the earliest broadsides from within the financial world came in the mid 2000s, and targeted Australia's Macquarie. 'Modern finance is notable for three negative features', wrote Edward Chancellor, a former Wall Street merchant banker. 'Excessive fees, excessive leverage and excessive complexity. Macquarie seems to have these in more extraordinary degree than most.'[1] More recently, critics have tended to hail from outside the world of finance, in these cases railing against asset managers' perceived profiteering and degraded housing and infrastructure services.

What is particularly interesting in this regard is the consistency of response, which has typically amounted to a rebuttal along the following blunt lines: *Get your facts straight*. After Chancellor's attack, for example, Macquarie issued a contestatory 'fact sheet' that ran to no less than three pages. A decade later, when critics representing the United Nations launched a volley against Blackstone in relation to the allegedly harmful social consequences of its post–financial crisis investment in

---

1 Cited in G. Haigh, 'Who's Afraid of Macquarie Bank?', 4 July 2007 – at themonthly.com.au.

housing, the firm responded with a withering diatribe accusing the critics of a litany of 'significant factual errors'.[2]

This history of critique and counter-critique prompts two immediate remarks. On the one hand, one can empathise with the likes of Blackstone and Macquarie. Clearly, it is important to try to get one's facts right. This is true, needless to say, whatever one happens to be writing about. Moreover, the world of asset management is indeed frequently subject to mischaracterisation within both the media and the academy.

On the other hand, however, there is something brazen about asset managers of the type discussed in this book crying foul. For one thing, just because some facts are wrong, that does not necessarily mean the critique elaborated around them is also wrong: highlighting factual errors in response can be a diversionary tactic. More importantly, we have to recognise that there is a good reason why critics' facts are sometimes wrong. The world of real-asset asset management is cloaked in secrecy. Shadowy at the best of times, it remains largely hidden behind a wall of non-disclosure: even firms that are publicly listed tend to have few if any obligations to say much about how things work at the investment coalface. Even asset managers' clients often complain that they do not quite know – because they are not adequately told – what they are getting into when they commit capital to unlisted investment funds.[3] And they know a good deal more than everybody else.

Our exploration thus far of the basic parameters of asset-manager society (Chapter 1) and of the course of its development in recent decades (Chapter 2) has offered a series of 'snapshots' of the phenomenon. What we do not yet have, however, is a sense of the fuller picture those snapshots add up to. Or, to use a different metaphor, some of the key pieces of the jigsaw puzzle have been identified, but we do not yet know where those pieces fit or what the overall puzzle looks like.

Developing such an overall picture is the aim of this chapter. In the early years of the third decade of the twenty-first century,

---

2 The letter is available in pdf form at ohchr.org.

3 See, for example, J. Cumbo, '"Absolute Transparency" Needed on Private Market Fees, BlackRock Says', *Financial Times*, 30 May 2022.

what, broadly, does asset-manager society consist of? And why does the map of actually-existing asset-manager society take the form that it does?

Mapping this territory is indispensable to any proper evaluation of asset-manager society. One cannot draw reasoned conclusions about the phenomenon unless one knows basic things, such as what assets are principally owned, where and by whom, how they generate income, and where the capital used to acquire them originated. But this chapter is also intended as a critique of the very informational vacuum that makes the identification of asset managers' much-lauded 'facts' so difficult in the first place.

Researching and writing about asset-manager society is sometimes much more like detective work than it should be. The fact (one of the few we *can* be sure of) that so little is publicly visible about unlisted infrastructure and real-estate funds – what assets they own, who ultimately makes money from them, and in what exact proportions – is surely a political problem as much as it is an empirical one. After all, the assets that interest us are ones that hundreds of millions of people intimately rely upon to live their everyday lives. In owning and operating such assets, asset managers increasingly take on the role of quasi-governments (albeit unelected ones), and no democratic government could reasonably expect its assets and operations to be so free of scrutiny as real-asset asset managers' presently are. Should we not be told much, much more about these things?

In any event, in the pages that follow I argue that we can best get a grip on contemporary asset-manager society by considering it through three distinct but connected lenses, or windows. In the first section, asset-manager society is considered from the perspective of the particular physical things that asset managers invest in, and that society relies upon. What types of infrastructure and housing have most substantially come under asset-manager ownership? In which market segments, by contrast, do asset managers have only a limited presence? How can we account for such differences? And how – through what investment structures and methods, and under what contractual conditions – do asset managers invest in assets of these various types?

The second section explores asset-manager society geographically, considering various dimensions of its spatiality, including not just where in the world asset managers principally control real assets, but where the money they invest comes from.

In the third and final section, the chapter turns to the major commercial players in asset-manager society. As we have seen, hundreds of asset managers are active in the infrastructure and housing investment sectors. Nevertheless, the Pareto principle – otherwise known as the 80/20 rule – very much applies here: a small number of extremely large and influential asset managers play a disproportionately significant role, accounting for the lion's share of real-asset investment. Given their outsized influence, understanding how these industry leaders operate provides an invaluable window on asset-manager society more broadly. Three such managers are profiled: one (Blackstone) is a major actor in investment in housing; the second (Macquarie) is a major actor in infrastructure investment; and the last (Brookfield) is a major player in both. As we shall see, while all three are asset managers, they are in reality very different animals.

Assets

Housing

If there is one type of asset that epitomises the physical substance of asset-manager society, then arguably it is housing. Completely essential to healthy social reproduction, housing has long been the locus of legally protected monetary payments from users (tenants) to owners (landlords). Thus, whereas assets coming under the control of private asset managers may have represented an unforeseeable and radical departure from historical norms in the cases of, say, hospitals or schools, the transition was considerably less radical with respect to housing: the move from property company to private-equity company was, in reality, a relatively small one. Housing fits asset-manager society hand-in-glove.

Most housing owned by asset managers is so-called multi-family housing, which essentially means tenanted apartment blocks. As we saw in Chapter 2, there is in some countries a relatively long history of institutional investors such as pension funds owning such housing, and in all those countries – most notably the Netherlands, Sweden and Switzerland – asset managers have joined the ranks of major institutional owners during the past decade. But asset managers in recent times have also invested substantially in multi-family housing in countries lacking histories of substantive financial-investor housing ownership. Today, they own large swathes of such housing not only in numerous other European countries (including France, Germany, Ireland, Spain and the UK) but also in North America (both Canada and the United States) and Asia (including China and Japan).

Blackstone and Brookfield, as I will explore below, are two major international investors in multi-family housing. But these are not the only significant asset managers operating in this space. Two others with large international multi-family portfolios are Greystar Investment Management and PGIM Real Estate, both US firms. As of 2021, the former, through a series of funds such as Greystar Equity Partners X (which was closed in 2019 with aggregate equity commitments of around $2 billion), owned a multi-family portfolio containing over 100,000 units located predominantly in the United States and Europe, in which over $30 billion of limited-partner capital was invested.[4] At the same date, PGIM's multi-family portfolio was slightly smaller, containing around 90,000 apartments.[5] But it was no less international, comprising income-generating assets in countries including Japan and the UK in addition to the United States itself.

As we have seen, asset-manager ownership of standalone, detached, 'single-family' homes is much less common than multi-family ownership. Only in the United States is there today a significant asset-manager presence in the single-family rental sector. In other countries where asset managers own single-family homes, as Blackstone does via Sage Housing in the UK, their participation is much more limited. When Blackstone and other asset managers began buying up large numbers of US

---

4   Greystar, 'Rental Housing Investment Management Solutions' – at greystar.com.

5   PGIM Real Estate – at pgim.com.

single-family units for rental after the global financial crisis, the *Wall Street Journal* spoke of 'the final frontier in real estate for institutional investors' having been tamed.[6] But if the frontier has indeed been tamed in the United States – the fragmented nature of single-family housing had long deterred large investors of all kinds, leaving the market mainly to small landlords – it has still not been meaningfully tamed elsewhere.

In this respect, however, single-family housing stands essentially alone among the various main categories of residential accommodation. Just as multi-family housing has widely come under asset-manager ownership, so too, increasingly, have student housing, senior housing, and even manufactured-housing (i.e., mobile home) communities. In fact, one of these, senior housing, is identified by PGIM Real Estate as being on its short list of 'specialized investment strategies': the firm has invested some $4 billion internationally in more than 20,000 units since, in 1998, establishing a senior-housing investment platform – structured around a series of dedicated Senior Housing Partnership funds.[7] Often labelled 'care homes', senior housing represents social infrastructure (see below) as well as residential real estate. Among the countries where PGIM has invested in senior housing is the UK, where in 2020 it was estimated that asset managers controlled some 13 per cent of the care home sector, equating to 56,700 beds.[8]

Student housing represents another highly favoured asset-manager investment. In 2017, for example, three major managers – AXA Investment Managers, CBRE Global Investment Partners and Greystar – teamed up to buy Resa, Spain's largest student accommodation provider, with nearly 10,000 student beds in nineteen cities. Greystar is in fact one of the world's largest owners of student housing, with substantial assets in, among other places, the Netherlands and the UK, as well as Spain, which were collectively valued in 2021 at around

6 R. Dezember, 'Blackstone Moves Out of Rental-Home Wager with a Big Gain', *Wall Street Journal*, 21 November 2019.

7 'Senior Housing' – at pgim.com.

8 E. Mendonça and S. Bucak, 'PE-Owned UK Care Homes under the Spotlight Amid Coronavirus Pandemic', *Private Equity News*, 23 March 2020.

$10 billion. Another major owner is Blackstone. Its 2020 purchase of the UK's iQ Student Accommodation for £4.7 billion was the country's largest-ever private property deal of any kind; two years later, it spent more than twice that amount, some $13 billion, in acquiring American Campus Communities in the United States.

Finally, in recent years asset managers have also begun to invest in manufactured-housing communities, especially in the United States. Typically, mobile homes themselves are owned by their occupants – but they do not own the land on which their homes are located. They rent their sites from the community owner, to whom they also pay fees for shared amenities, services and utilities. The ownership and operation of such manufactured-housing communities is a business that asset managers have widely entered. Apollo Global Management, Blackstone and the Carlyle Group are all significant investors in this space. By 2020, for example, Blackstone's portfolio of US manufactured-housing assets – held through the Blackstone Real Estate Income Trust (BREIT) – had grown to over 7,000 sites, spread across more than forty communities.[9]

In all cases, what the asset manager is investing in when buying housing is the predictable and reliable rental income it generates, plus any potential for capital gain. In this regard, manufactured housing is emblematic, as the rents it generates are among the most reliable and predictable of all. Even if mobile homes can be moved (and often they cannot), the moving costs are prohibitive. Tenants are, in other words, largely stuck, with no choice but to continue to pay rent. Frank Rolfe, a legendary investor in the sector through his company RV Horizons, expressed this captivity best, famously saying that a mobile-home park 'is like a Waffle House where the customers are chained to their booths'.[10]

---

9   Blackstone, 'BREIT marketing deck', October 2020, pp. 30–1 – at breit
.com. BREIT is a non-traded real-estate investment trust, which is effectively
an unlisted investment fund (open-ended, in this case) accessible to a wider
range of investors.

10   Cited in, for example, P. Whorisky, 'A Billion-Dollar Empire Made of
Mobile Homes', *Washington Post*, 14 February 2019.

How much housing in the aggregate, across all the sub-sectors mentioned above, do asset managers own and control? There are no reported figures, but we can hazard a rough estimate based on the holdings today of two leading managers. France's AXA has a global housing portfolio reportedly valued at around $27 billion.[11] Blackstone's global real-estate portfolio is valued at approximately $550 billion.[12] Somewhere around 20–25 per cent of this seemingly represents Blackstone's residential assets – thus, $110–140 billion.[13] Meanwhile, INREV estimates that AXA and Blackstone's shares of all global real estate controlled by asset managers presently stand at around 2.5 and 10 per cent, respectively.[14] Assuming the same percentages for their respective shares specifically of residential real estate controlled by asset managers suggests a total global stock of asset-manager-owned housing worth around $1.1 trillion using the AXA data, or $1.1–1.4 trillion using the Blackstone data. Thus, something over $1 trillion would appear to be a reasonable estimate.

Farmland

Quite unlike housing as a physical phenomenon, farmland is in fact quite similar to housing as a financial phenomenon. For an investor-owner who does not also farm/occupy the land/house, the two types of asset generate the same type of income: rent. The two are also comparable insofar as each is a relatively *illiquid* asset type, meaning it is generally not readily exchangeable for cash. (This is true of infrastructure, too.) Finally, farmland, in many countries, has a particular similarity specifically to single-family housing. That is, it is 'bitty', fragmented: each asset – a

---

11   'AXA IM Alts Expands Global Residential Portfolio with Japan, US Deals', 24 May 2022 – at realassets.ipe.com.

12   Blackstone, 'Real Estate' – at blackstone.com (as at mid 2022).

13   In April 2020, Blackstone reported that approximately 80 per cent of its real-estate portfolio comprised logistics, residential and office properties. It further said that logistics accounted for 'over one-third' of the portfolio. If we assume that logistics represents 35 per cent, then residential and office property combined represents approximately 45 per cent. This is the basis of my estimation that residential likely accounted for between 20 and 25 per cent. See Blackstone, 'First Quarter 2020 Investor Call', 23 April 2020.

14   'Global Real Estate Assets Under Management Reaches €4.1tn in 2021', 18 May 2022 – at creherald.com.

single house or a single farm – tends to be relatively small, seen from the perspective of firms seeking to invest billions of dollars. 'You don't find farms in fifty-, seventy-, hundred-million-dollar pieces like you do office buildings', one asset manager told the sociologist Madeleine Fairbairn.[15] In England, for example, the average farm size is just eighty-seven hectares.[16] With English farmland valued at an average of about £16,000 per hectare, this implies an average value per farmland property of about £1.4 million – an expensive house, admittedly, but a house nonetheless, not an apartment block.

This bittiness is one reason why asset managers and other financial investors have rarely invested in farmland in the past. Another reason is that the landscape for such investors, in Gregory Meyer's words, has long been 'rutted with restrictions'. 'Several US states including Iowa, the biggest corn grower, have long prohibited corporate ownership of farms', Meyer explained. Restrictions have also applied in other territories: 'Investors in many parts of the world may lease, but not own land.'[17] Much of this restrictiveness comes down to the fact that farmland ownership is often politically and socially sensitive, which means that the perceived suitability and even morality of farmland investments by financial investors is almost always contested.[18]

However, just as the financial crisis changed the calculus – the perceived risks and rewards – of investment in housing for many asset managers, so it also changed the calculus of farmland investment. Some of the reasons for this were the same: farmland, like foreclosed housing, was cheap – and the collapse of interest rates made all assets that reliably generated recurring income appear attractive. Yet there were also more specific reasons why the way farmland was viewed changed, and asset

---

15 M. Fairbairn, *Fields of Gold: Financing the Global Land Rush* (Ithaca: Cornell University Press, 2020), p. 40.

16 Department for Environment, Food and Rural Affairs Statistics, 'England Regional Profiles', March 2021, p. 6 – at gov.uk.

17 G. Meyer, 'Investors Grab Golden Opportunity to Plough Funds into Farmland', *Financial Times*, 3 March 2016.

18 S. Ouma, 'This Can('t) Be an Asset Class: The World of Money Management, "Society", and the Contested Morality of Farmland Investments', *Environment and Planning A: Economy and Space* 52: 1 (2020), pp. 66–87.

managers widely began to consider it a viable asset class. The years 2007–08 saw not just a financial crisis, but a food-price crisis, when, as Meyer observed, 'grain shortages led to panic buying and investors piled into agricultural enterprises'. Moreover, heightened awareness of growing global pressure on land resources in the context of the climate crisis was increasingly casting a new light on the intrinsic value of land. After all, the uniqueness of land as an asset type is that, as Mark Twain is alleged to have quipped, 'they ain't making any more of it'.

Having expanded strongly since the financial and food-price crises of 2007–08, asset-manager investment in farmland is dominated by a handful of big players, several of which we have already encountered in earlier chapters: Brookfield, Macquarie, Manulife and Nuveen. Two other asset managers with substantial farmland assets, in each case valued at more than $1 billion, are Canada's Fiera Comox and Switzerland's UBS Asset Management. All six of these managers own hundreds of thousands of hectares, distributed across various territories, but with a particular focus on Australia, Brazil and North America.

To the extent that farmland investment by asset managers has extended into other, 'emerging' markets, it has often been smaller, niche managers that have led the way. Fairbairn has highlighted three examples from three very different parts of the world: acquisitions of farmland in Eastern Europe, Russia and Ukraine by the US-headquartered NCH Capital; acquisitions in Africa by the UK-based Emergent Asset Management; and acquisitions in Southeast Asia by Australia's Duxton Asset Management.[19]

Perhaps unsurprisingly given the relatively recent emergence of this asset class, it remains small relative to both real-asset investment more generally and the volume of land potentially available for purchase. Thus, while the $22 billion collectively raised by over one hundred agriculture- and farmland-focused funds between 2006 and 2016 may sound like a lot, consider that a single Global Infrastructure Partners general infrastructure fund – Fund IV – raised the exact same amount in 2019.[20]

19 Fairbairn, *Fields of Gold*, p. 47.

20 Respectively: ibid, p. 43; J. Stutts, 'GIP Smashes Records with $22bn

Meanwhile, Jose Minaya, who heads up Nuveen, estimated in 2016 that, despite the post–financial crisis boom, less than 1 per cent of 'institutional quality' farmland around the world was at that stage in the hands of financial investors. 'You are in the very early stages of this', he said.[21] To Minaya's peers in the asset management world, this would doubtless have sounded like a promise. To others, perhaps, it would have sounded like a warning.

Energy

Asset managers' energy infrastructure investments come in various forms, from fossil-fuel-based to renewables, and occupy all parts of the supply chain, including power generation and transmission and fuel distribution and storage. Such investments are integral to contemporary asset-manager society. Not only is social life utterly dependent on energy infrastructures, but energy represents the largest infrastructure-investment sector for asset managers. Some 56 per cent of approximately 82,000 total institutional investments in infrastructure identified by Preqin globally between 1990 and 2020 – of which over 97 per cent occurred via managed funds rather than directly – were in energy assets (see Figure 3.1).[22] By the latter year, asset managers domiciled in OECD and G20 countries held direct energy-infrastructure investments – that is, investments in infrastructure per se, as opposed to shareholdings in corporations that themselves held infrastructure – worth \$263 billion: more than the amount of investment in any other infrastructure sector.[23]

Historically, what has arguably been the most significant form of energy infrastructure has in fact existed largely outside

---

Fund IV Final Close', *Infrastructure Investor*, 12 December 2019.

21 Cited in Meyer, 'Investors Grab Golden Opportunity'.

22 To be clear, these numbers refer to unique 'investor-deal' events. If, for example, a pension scheme independently and directly acquires a wind farm, that represents one investment (i.e., one investor-deal). But if an investment fund containing capital pooled from ten partners acquires a wind farm, that represents ten investments (ten investor-deal events), since ten parties have effectively (if indirectly) invested in the farm.

23 OECD, *Green Infrastructure in the Decade for Delivery: Assessing Institutional Investment* (Paris: OECD Publishing, 2020), p. 41.

Figure 3.1

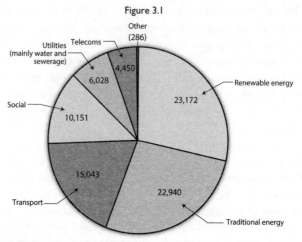

Number of institutional-investor investments in infrastructure globally, by asset type, 1990–2020

Source: Andonov, Kräussl and Rauh, 'Institutional Investors and Infrastructure Investing', *Review of Financial Studies* 34 (2021), p. 3890.

the ambit of asset-manager society: that is, the infrastructure of fossil-fuel extraction. Drilling rigs have always been owned predominantly by oil and gas companies or their contractors, whether in the private or public sector. Certainly, asset managers have long invested in oil and gas companies such as the Western 'majors' by buying their shares; but, other than in the case of private-equity-based ownership of entire companies, such investments do not confer the control over physical assets that is characteristic of asset-manager society (see Chapter 1).[24]

To the extent that asset managers control major fossil-fuel energy infrastructures, these therefore tend to be infrastructures not of extraction, but rather of other kinds. One is fuel distribution. In 2019, for instance, Brookfield, in its largest ever transaction in India, paid $1.9 billion for a 1,500 kilometre pipeline distributing millions of cubic metres of natural gas each day from the KG Basin off India's east coast to fast-growing centres of energy demand in the west of the country. A second kind is fuel storage, which is an area where Global Infrastructure

---

24   On this issue, see B. Christophers, 'The End of Carbon Capitalism (as We Knew It)', *Critical Historical Studies* 8: 2 (2021), pp. 239–69.

Partners has traditionally been very active. In 2007, for example, it acquired a major liquefied petroleum gas storage facility in Visakhapatnam, India. A third, much less common, kind is coal- or gas-fired power plants, one example being the $335 million purchase of a 1,000 MW gas-fired plant in Texas by Energy Capital Partners in 2011. Finally, to the degree that electricity continues to be generated from fossil-fuel sources, a fourth significant type of fossil-fuel infrastructure widely owned by asset managers is electricity transmission networks. In 2006, for instance, Brookfield led a consortium that paid $1.55 billion for Chile's main power grid, comprising over 8,000 kilometres of transmission lines.

By contrast, the most important type of renewable-energy infrastructure, namely renewables-based power plants, is, as we have seen, often owned directly by asset managers – and this is increasingly the case. Investment funds have been prolific buyers of wind farms, solar farms, and to a lesser extent hydroelectric plants, in both the Global North and South. This is clearly important for several reasons, not the least of which is that it means the transition from fossil fuels to renewables also represents a transition to asset-manager society. Asset managers are slowly but surely displacing oil and gas companies in the custodianship of the core of the world's energy infrastructure. Writing these words in 2022, when Russia's invasion of Ukraine has thrust questions of energy security and cost into the spotlight, underlines the significance of this ongoing but seldom-discussed transition in infrastructure ownership.

The year 2017 had something of a symbolic importance in this regard: it was the first year in which institutional investors committed more capital to asset managers' renewable-energy funds than to their conventional-energy counterparts.[25] In turn, of the $263 billion of energy infrastructure investments held by OECD/G20-based asset managers in 2020, fully $171 billion represented renewables investments.

What type of income do these various energy infrastructure investments generate for asset managers and their investor

25 Preqin, 'Conventional and Renewable Energy', June 2017 – at preqin. com.

clients? Unlike housing and (tenanted) farmland, where there is a simple answer (rent), incomes in the energy sector take several forms. Owners of power plants, whether fossil-fuel- or renewables-based, are paid for the electricity they produce, either in wholesale markets or under long-term bilateral power-purchase agreements with customers such as electricity retailers or industrial consumers. Owners of transmission, distribution and storage infrastructures, on the other hand, typically receive payments – often volume-based – from the companies that rely on access to those infrastructures in order to deliver their power or fuel to the market.

Transportation

Transportation assets come second behind energy assets in terms of the scale of asset-manager infrastructural investment (Figure 3.1). Given this book's focus on asset-manager society – and thus on those infrastructures in which daily life is most deeply and directly embedded – our interest is mainly in transportation infrastructures that people use frequently and widely, such as rail infrastructures (track and rolling stock), roads, bridges, parking facilities and, increasingly, electric-vehicle charging networks. But transportation infrastructures in which asset managers commonly invest also include airports and seaports.

Whereas, in many countries, there is a long history of private ownership of energy infrastructures such as power plants and pipelines, private investment in transportation infrastructures tends to be a phenomenon strictly of more recent heritage, often dating to the privatisation programmes of recent decades. Historically, such infrastructures were predominantly publicly owned and funded.

Sometimes, private investment in existing, formerly public transportation assets has entailed outright ownership transfer – as, for example, with many airports and seaports. Often, however, such investment has occurred through concessions. Even if many such concessions convey rights tantamount to ownership, insofar as they confer both complete operating control and claims on all revenues over the (sometimes very long) concession term, ultimate ownership remains with the state, which has been reluctant to relinquish its roads and bridges entirely. Similarly, new roads and other such transportation assets tend still to be built for the state, and the asset that the private sector invests in is not the road itself, but the contract – frequently in the form of a public–private partnership (PPP) – to build and operate the road, and the right to receive future payments stipulated by that contract.

Thus, today, while asset managers do own transportation infrastructures, they more commonly own transportation-infrastructure concessions and PPP contracts. Among quotidian transportation infrastructures, the two in which asset managers have invested most widely are parking facilities and roads. We can usefully explore the nature of such investments by briefly considering sample assets held by Macquarie, a frequent and large-scale investor in both types.

Parking facilities typically constitute a fairly straightforward investment, entitling the asset manager to receive fees and fines. One of Macquarie's main current holdings in the parking sector is Empark, based in Spain but operating long-term parking concessions internationally, which Macquarie acquired in 2017 in a deal valuing the concessionaire – with 535,000 parking spaces held through more than 400 contracts – at around €1 billion.

Road investments, meanwhile, remunerate the asset manager in one of two main ways. The first is tolls; as we saw in Chapters 1 and 2, Macquarie has invested substantially in toll-road concessions in countries including France, India and the United States. The second is so-called availability payments (also referred to as annuities), where the public body that tenders a road contract commits to making regular payments to the contractor subject to various performance requirements being met – principally the road being 'available for use' and in good condition. In 2010, for example, for around $125 million, Macquarie's Mexican Infrastructure Fund acquired a twenty-year contract granted by the Mexican state of Durango to maintain ten toll-free stretches of highway, generating monthly availability payments funded out of the state's federal tax participations.

Rail infrastructure investment by asset managers is less common, but certainly not unknown. Indeed, Macquarie itself has inevitably been an active player. For instance, in 2012, it formed Macquarie European Rail by buying from the UK's Lloyds Banking Group three portfolios of rolling stock leased to UK and European passenger and freight operators. Macquarie exited this investment in 2020. But the business of owning and leasing train rolling stock remains one, especially in the UK, in which asset managers play a prominent role: two of the UK's three leading rolling-stock companies are currently owned by investment consortia controlled by asset managers.

Telecoms

As an investment object, telecoms infrastructure assets are very much like the energy transmission and distribution infrastructures described earlier: typically, corporate customers make payments to the asset owner in order to access and use infrastructure that enables them to provide particular products or services to consumers. Telecoms infrastructures have been present in the portfolios of asset managers since the early 2000s, but the 'data revolution' of the past decade or so has substantially increased both demand for such infrastructures and, consequently, asset managers' appetite for holding them.

Three types of telecoms infrastructure, all fundamental to enabling services on which large parts of society have come to rely, have received the lion's share of asset-manager investment. The first, and, until recently, consistently the biggest locus of investment, has been wireless communication infrastructure, especially cell towers, which are used by providers of telephony and data services. The second is fibre-optic networks, which are increasingly used to provide the same services (plus television), but on a 'wired' rather than wireless basis. The third and final type, where growth has recently been most heavily concentrated, is data centres, which for asset managers also represent a form of real-estate investment, inasmuch as they are essentially buildings used to house computer systems – and which today, in the era of cloud computing and server farms, are often vast in scale.

Three notable recent deals can serve as illustrative examples of investments in each of these sub-sectors. First, in 2019, for $3.6 billion, Brookfield acquired a vast portfolio of some 130,000 operational telecom towers in India from Reliance Industries, a major multinational conglomerate headquartered in Mumbai. The value of the portfolio to Brookfield lay largely in the future revenues guaranteed by a thirty-year contract with Reliance's own market-leading mobile operator, Jio. But Brookfield also saw significant growth prospects, and it invested in the expectation of being able to exploit these. For one thing, at the time of the deal, the Reliance towers carried only Jio's equipment, even though most were capable of accommodating multiple operator-tenants. Furthermore, another 45,000 towers forming part of the acquired portfolio were under development.

A second notable deal occurred the following year, when Macquarie trumped a series of bids by Brookfield for Cincinnati Bell. This company provides high-speed data, video and voice services to both consumer and business customers in a number of regional US markets. But Macquarie was clear that the business's principal value lay in the infrastructures through which those services are delivered – principally, an approximately 20,000 route-kilometre fibre-optic network in Greater Cincinnati and a roughly 8,000 route-kilometre fibre-optic network in Hawaii. The deal valued Cincinnati Bell at around $2.9 billion.

Thirdly, in 2021 Blackstone agreed to buy the US-based QTS Realty Trust, in a transaction valued at about $10 billion. QTS is the owner and operator of approximately 8 million square feet of data-centre space in twenty-eight locations across North America and Europe, used for the purposes of data storage and processing by over 1,000 customers including software and social-media companies – Twitter, for instance, is one large customer – as well as government entities. As befits the fact that QTS is at once a real-estate and an infrastructure business, the deal to buy it was a joint investment by Blackstone's perpetual infrastructure fund, Blackstone Infrastructure Partners, and its real-estate investment trust, BREIT – thus, in the case of the latter, adding data centres to a portfolio predominantly made up of multi-family housing and mobile-home communities.

Water

Another type of physical infrastructure that is increasingly widely controlled by asset managers is that of water supply. Two structural features of such control are worth highlighting here. First, where asset managers control water-supply networks, they often also control sewage-treatment networks, insofar as it is common in many countries for the ownership and operation of regionally specific mains and sewers to be consolidated. Second, control of the infrastructure is typically also coupled with responsibility for actual service provision: in most territories where asset managers are substantially active in water-infrastructure ownership, the decoupling of service provision from infrastructure control – whereby an entity supplies water and/or sewerage services using a network owned by a third party – is the exception rather than the rule.

While the incorporation of water-supply infrastructures into asset-manager society is accelerating, it remains a relatively circumscribed phenomenon: for now, at least, ownership of such infrastructures by asset managers is much less common than asset-manager ownership of energy, transportation or telecoms infrastructures. There are good reasons for this. As a 2020 OECD report on institutional investment in infrastructure pointed out, a series of factors frequently serve to limit 'the attractiveness of the [water] sector's risk-return profile for private investors compared to other infrastructure sectors'. One is the difficulty of raising tariffs: 'the water sector generally has a poor record of cost recovery, with tariffs often too low to fully cover operational and maintenance costs, and rarely covering capital costs. Many jurisdictions lack an independent regulator for tariff setting and concerns regarding affordability often keep tariffs below cost reflective levels'. Another related difficulty is that of enforcing user payment, including through service termination: 'Given the essential nature of water supply services, operators typically cannot disrupt services in the case of non-payment.'[26]

The main exception to this pattern of guardedness has been the UK. English and Welsh water and sanitation services and the infrastructures enabling their provision were privatised in 1989. Although asset managers were not initially active participants (except as minority shareholders in the ten publicly

---

26   OECD, *Green Infrastructure*, p. 50.

listed water and sewerage companies created by privatisation), they have assumed a considerably more central role over the intervening three decades. If, in other territories, asset managers and other private financial investors have been wary of the water sector in view of the difficulty of raising tariffs, the relative ease of doing so in England and Wales courtesy of an accommodating regulatory regime helps, by contrast, to explain private-sector investment enthusiasm: the three decades since privatisation have witnessed significant and consistent increases in real water rates.

As we have seen, a seminal moment in terms of asset-manager participation in the UK water sector came in 2006, when Macquarie led an investor consortium in buying the country's biggest water company, Thames Water, from the German utility group RWE. While Thames has since changed hands, and now has a pension fund as its main owner, plenty of other English and Welsh water (or water and sewerage) companies are today controlled by asset managers. At least three – Bristol Water, South East Water and Southern Water – are majority-owned by individual asset-management firms, in the shape respectively of iCON Infrastructure, Morrison & Co and Macquarie. And at least two other water companies are owned by investment consortia that are themselves controlled by asset managers: Affinity Water (whose main shareholders are the asset managers Allianz Capital Partners, InfraRed Capital Partners and DIF) and Yorkshire Water (whose controlling shareholders are GIC Special Investments, Corsair Infrastructure Management and Deutsche Asset Management).

Meanwhile, an example of a country in which asset managers play a more limited role in water-supply infrastructure ownership, but where recent years have nonetheless seen a significant expansion of that role, is the United States. As Elizabeth Douglass has noted, neglected water and sanitation infrastructures – usually owned by municipalities – are seen by many in the United States as a 'national plague'. With such infrastructures needing more than an estimated $1 trillion of investment over the next twenty years, and with federal funding for them having fallen by three-quarters in real terms since 1977, an investment gap has opened up into which asset managers, among others, have gladly stepped.[27]

Again, we have already encountered one example – the Carlsbad desalination plant in California (see Chapter 1), which is owned by Aberdeen Standard Investments and supplies water to the San Diego region. And Aberdeen is far from being alone. Indeed, asset managers' entry into the US water sector, particularly since the 2007–09 financial crisis, has been sufficiently notable to attract the attention of the mainstream press. In 2016, for instance, the *New York Times* identified a series of other asset managers that had latterly taken control of municipal waterworks through either outright ownership or long-term concessions, including Alinda Capital Partners, Carlyle Group, KKR and Table Rock Capital. Such acquisitions represented, the *Times* suggested, 'the leading edge of the [asset management] industry's profound expansion into [US] public services' more widely.[28] I will examine this phenomenon in more detail in Chapter 4.

Social

Social infrastructure is the final significant physical component of asset-manager society. This category comprises long-term physical structures that house and facilitate social services of some kind, the most important being schools and other educational institutions, hospitals and other healthcare facilities, and prisons and courthouses. From this list, the bulk of investment by asset managers and other institutional investors has historically occurred in schools and hospitals. Sometimes another asset type is included on this list: care homes. As I indicated earlier, however, these are just as often grouped together with other types of residential property.

Social services have an intimate connection with government. Certainly, in many countries educational and health services are widely provided and funded privately, with the state in many such instances playing at most a regulatory role. But where that

---

27 E. Douglass, 'Towns Sell Their Public Water Systems – and Often Regret it', 8 July 2017 – at mcgrawcenter.org.

28 D. Ivory, B. Protess and G. Palmer, 'In American Towns, Private Profits from Public Works', *New York Times*, 24 December 2016.

is the case, the term 'social services' is arguably a misnomer: the services are basically private ones. Thus, in the present context at least, 'social services' are understood to be services over which government – at either national or local level – has a significant degree of control and responsibility. It may not provide the services itself; they may be contracted out. But it decides who provides them, and on what terms. More pointedly for us, the state decides how the physical infrastructure underpinning the provision of those services is financed, developed, owned and managed.

In recent decades, as we began to see in earlier chapters, governments in many countries have increasingly allowed for a growing role for private-sector actors in the control and operation of social infrastructure. Generally, they have done so through long-term contracts of some description, whereby infrastructure investment conveys ownership (or rights equivalent to ownership) for a certain period, but where control ultimately returns to the state. Public–private partnerships (PPPs – see Chapters 1 and 2) represent the most common contractual form for such investment in social infrastructure. Indeed, alongside transportation (especially road projects), social infrastructure has long represented the primary 'stuff' of PPPs. The owner of the PPP contract is remunerated via what are essentially availability payments from the relevant public body, often – but certainly not always – linked to performance criteria.

Asset managers and other major financial investors are attracted to social infrastructure for many of the same reasons they are attracted to other types of infrastructure: the ability to match asset and liability maturities; cash-flow stability and predictability; hedging of inflation risk. In common with, for example, renewable-energy infrastructures, social infrastructures also possess a further attractive quality: the benefit to their provider of being seen to be 'doing good', the importance of which has increased in line with the investment community's growing attention to environmental, social and governance (ESG) concerns. As Georg Inderst has written, 'Social infrastructure facilities help governments provide essential services to the community and improve living standards. Such assets tend to have a high ESG score and can improve sustainability rankings of asset owners' and managers' portfolios.'[29]

But social infrastructure is also seen to come with special risks. Again, Inderst is an instructive guide:

> Political risk is inherent in [social] infrastructure investment … National policies can change. Hospitals, schools, kindergartens etc. are typically heavily regulated with frequent adjustments. Re-regulation is likely in this field, and feared by investors. Contract renegotiations are a difficult territory in theory and practice. There is also 'social risk' when a project is opposed by pressure groups or the media. Recent examples are public opposition to private equity/infrastructure funds' involvement in prisons, hospitals and care centers.[30]

If investment in general comes with health warnings (the ubiquitous 'the value of investments can go down as well as up…'), such warnings are especially apt in a space – the broadly defined 'social' sphere – where, for many people, the presence of speculative investment capital has always been particularly unwelcome.

Partly as a result, this has never been one of the larger segments of the institutional infrastructure investment space. It lags well behind energy and transportation, for example (Figure 3.1). Of the several thousand yearly global infrastructure investments by asset managers and other financial investors registered by Preqin between 2011 and 2019, an average of just 12 per cent were in the social sector.[31] And that proportion is even lower when the market is measured in terms of investment value rather than numbers of transactions, because social infrastructure investments tend to be much smaller than investments in other types of infrastructure asset. 'The average deal size in social infrastructure fluctuates between \$100–200m, well below the average size of economic infrastructure projects (now over \$500m)', writes Inderst. 'The median UK Private Finance Initiative project

29   G. Inderst, 'Social Infrastructure Finance and Institutional Investors: A Global Perspective', MPRA Paper No. 103006, October 2020, p. 34 – at mpra. ub.uni-muenchen.de.

30   Ibid., p. 24.

31   Ibid., p. 28.

value was less than £50m.'[32] Thus, whereas social infrastructure accounted on average for 12 per cent of annual infrastructure deal volume over the past decade, its share of overall infrastructure investment value was only about 5 per cent.[33]

As a result, the world's biggest asset managers in the real-asset milieu – the Blackstones, Brookfields and Macquaries – tend not to be very active in social infrastructure investment. With bigger funds, capitalised to the tune of billions rather than hundreds of millions of dollars, such firms consider most social-infrastructure investments to be too small. This leaves the field largely to smaller, often specialist players. For example, asset managers that have launched and invested dedicated social-infrastructure funds in recent years include, among others, Germany's AviaRent Invest, the US firms Franklin Templeton and Harrison Street, and the UK's Newcore Capital Management.

As the historic heartland of PPP (with its Private Finance Initiative), the UK has also historically been the heartland of private social-infrastructure investment. And in terms of the main market actors, the UK has long been typical: the most active social-infrastructure asset managers in the country are indeed small specialists, not the large generalists. Here, the most important name is not Newcore but Innisfree (see Chapter 2). At the time of writing, Innisfree has twenty-six active health-sector infrastructure investments with a combined capital value of £10.8 billion, and seventeen active education-sector infrastructure investments – encompassing some 260 UK schools – with a combined capital value of £1.5 billion, making it the social-infrastructure asset manager par excellence.[34]

Geographies

In addressing asset-manager society geographically, there are three principal categories of place to consider. The first concerns the sources of the capital that managers invest: Where in the

32   Ibid., p. 22.

33   Ibid., p. 28.

34   Innisfree, Health and Education Portfolios – at innisfree.co.uk.

world does all the money come from? The second concerns the managers themselves: Where are these managers based? Which is to say: Where is all the money that is ultimately invested in housing and infrastructure institutionally aggregated? And third: Where is the money invested? In which countries' infrastructures and residential property?

What follows is necessarily expressed in broad brush-strokes. As I have emphasised, the world of asset management is a secretive, closely held one, and discerning its spatial contours is far from straightforward. Nevertheless, it is possible to make some key observations. I will deal with infrastructure and housing separately, because there are notable differences between the two.

Infrastructure

Inevitably, the sources of capital for infrastructure investment by asset managers largely mirror the sources of capital for such managers' investment more generally. The latter map is dominated by North America (especially the United States) and Europe: of the estimated $103 trillion in capital managed globally by asset managers in 2020, over 70 per cent represented the capital of investors based in North America ($49 trillion, of which $45 trillion was from the United States) and Europe ($26 billion); the 'developed' Asia-Pacific (Japan and Australia), with $9 trillion, and the 'developing' Asia-Pacific, with $14 trillion, accounted for most of the rest. Only around 3 per cent came from investors based in Latin America, Africa and the Middle East.[35] If the ultimate owners of asset-manager society are the investors, such as pension schemes, whose money it is that managers invest, then that society is owned overwhelmingly in the West.[36]

But the infrastructure map is not exactly the same as this more general map. For one thing, investors in different regions have different appetites for and degrees of exposure to different asset classes: some have significant proportional allocations to infrastructure; some have only relatively modest ones. Thus, in researching this geographical question in 2016, Preqin found

---

35 BCG, 'The $100 Trillion Machine', July 2021, p. 4 – at bcg.com.

36 See Chapter 5.

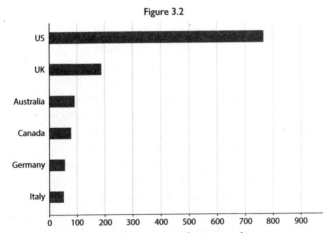

Figure 3.2

Number of unique institutional investors in infrastructure, by country, 1990–2020 (showing only countries with fifty or more such investors)

Source: Andonov, Kräussl and Rauh, 'Institutional Investors and Infrastructure Investing' – 'Internet Appendix', p. 5.

that, of the seventy-five institutional investors it identified globally each with more than $1 billion allocated to infrastructure, the highest number were, in fact, based in Australia – the historic birthplace of asset-manager society, as we have seen – followed by the United States and Canada.[37] To complicate the picture further, however, much of the Canadian institutional capital identified by Preqin circulates independently of asset-manager society: as we saw in Chapter 2, Canadian institutional investors are notable for investing in infrastructure directly (rather than via asset managers) to a much greater extent than investors elsewhere.

In summary, we can say that the bulk of the institutional money invested in infrastructure by asset managers comes from US, European and Asia-Pacific investors, but with investors in some countries – notably Australia – playing a much more significant role than they do within the asset-management world more generally. In total, the Preqin database identifies 1,861 institutional investors globally that invested in infrastructure – via asset managers and/or directly – between 1990 and 2020.

37 Preqin, 'The $1bn Club: Largest Infrastructure Fund Managers and Investors', August 2016, p. 4 – at preqin.com.

They hailed from sixty-nine countries, but, as Figure 3.2 shows, only six countries provided fifty or more such investors; indeed, as many as two-thirds of the sixty-nine countries provided ten or fewer infrastructure investors.[38]

A comparable geographical picture applies, secondly, to the locations of infrastructure asset managers themselves: most are based in North America, Europe and the Asia-Pacific region. But asset managers outside North Ameirca play a far more significant role in infrastructure investment than they do (as we shall see) in real-estate investment, or in investment in general across all asset classes. At 42 per cent, the proportion of global infrastructure assets under management (AUM) held by asset managers based in North America in 2020 was only slightly ahead of the proportion (35 per cent) held by European-based managers; meanwhile, Asia-Pacific managers held 20 per cent.[39]

Similarly, the 2016 research by Preqin mentioned above found that, of eighty-four asset managers that had raised at least $1 billion for infrastructure investment during the previous decade, roughly equal proportions were headquartered in Europe (39 per cent) and North America (38 per cent). Asia – notably South Korea – was home to the next-largest share. Within Europe, the UK dominated, being home to a third of the managers in question. But while, on Preqin's count, Europe marginally beat out North America in terms of numbers of large managers, it remained in its shadow when it came to hosting the very biggest managers. Of the ten largest infrastructure asset managers by capital raised, Preqin reported that no fewer than eight were based in North America, of which seven were in the United States and one, Brookfield Asset Management, was in Canada. A ninth, KB Asset Management, was Korean. Only one of the top ten – albeit the biggest of all, Macquarie Infrastructure and Real Assets (MIRA) – was identified as being Europe-based, specifically in the UK. But even MIRA is not really European: it is part of the Macquarie Group, which is of course Australian.

38   A. Andonov, R. Kräussl and J. Rauh, 'Institutional Investors and Infrastructure Investing: Internet Appendix', 20 April 2021, p. 5 – at oup.com.

39   BCG, 'The $100 Trillion Machine', p. 18.

Finally, what of actual investment? Where is the lived substance of the infrastructural component of asset-manager society – that is, the physical, invested assets – geographically concentrated? Again, the headline answer is: mainly in Europe and North America, with Asia following. Yet in this case the concentration is less pronounced, and is consistently declining. The reason for this is straightforward: asset managers based in North America and Europe widely, and increasingly, invest in infrastructure assets in the 'emerging' markets of Africa, Latin America and 'developing' Asia, as well as in their home territories; meanwhile, there is essentially no flow in the opposite direction. Thus, even as more than 70 per cent of the money managed globally by asset managers originates in North America and Europe, the same two regions today receive less than 50 per cent of private financial infrastructure investment, while the share going to Latin America and Africa – perhaps 10 per cent – far exceeds their combined contribution of investment capital.[40]

As we saw in Chapter 2, Europe, much more than the United States, has traditionally been the heartland of physical infrastructure investment by asset managers, alongside trailblazing Australia. As James McBride and Anshu Siripurapu, among many others, have noted, the United States, for a variety of reasons, largely lacks 'a culture of private ownership of major infrastructure' – such infrastructure is ordinarily owned instead by the state, whether federally or municipally.[41] In Europe and Australia, by contrast, widespread infrastructure privatisation from the 1980s opened the door to ownership by asset managers and other private financial investors – not least in the UK, where between 2010 and 2015 over 1,000 infrastructure deals were completed, which was more than the next ten European countries combined.[42] Within Europe, France and Germany were in second and third place, respectively.

40 M. Williams, 'Investments in Infrastructure', August 2017, p. 11 – at cliffwater.com.

41 J. McBride and A. Siripurapu, 'The State of US Infrastructure', 8 November 2021 – at cfr.org.

42 Preqin, 'European Infrastructure', November 2015, p. 3 – at preqin.com.

But in recent years the United States has closed the gap on Europe, as the prevailing philosophy about 'how to build and maintain America's stuff' has, as Brian Alexander has observed, shifted 'profoundly'.[43] I will have more to say about that shift in Chapter 6, but the key factors are these: everyone recognises the yawning national infrastructure gap; and a growing role for private investment capital is increasingly widely accepted, whether for principled or pragmatic reasons. In any event, by 2014, infrastructure funds in the market with a primary focus on North America, for the first time had a larger capital-raising target than those focused on Europe.[44] By 2017, North America–focused infrastructure funds also boasted both greater invested-and-unrealised asset value and more dry powder than Europe-focused funds.[45]

Asia lags behind North America and Europe, in third place – as it does on both originated investment capital and asset manager location. But there is one large and very important difference between the nature of the infrastructure investments made in Asia and those that predominate in Europe and the United States, as Patrick Adefuye notes: 'Many infrastructure projects in Asia are greenfield developments of new assets, rather than the acquisition of existing assets at the secondary stage or the rejuvenation of brownfield assets. This reflects that the region has greater demand for new infrastructure capabilities than its more developed counterparts, like Europe, where three-quarters of deals are for existing revenue-producing assets.'[46] In other words, the money that asset managers put into infrastructure deals in Asia frequently goes to building new assets, while in Europe most deals finance asset retrofitting or even simple title transfer. This indicates a very different investment economy. Asset managers and their institutional investors frequently wax

---

43 B. Alexander, 'Privatization Is Changing America's Relationship with Its Physical Stuff', *Atlantic*, 12 July 2017.

44 Preqin and Ferguson Partners, 'Infrastructure Industry Themes', February 2014, p. 6 – at preqin.com.

45 PriceWaterhouseCoopers, 'Investing in the ASEAN Infrastructure Asset Class', 2018, p. 16 – at pwc.com.

46 P. Adefuye, 'Are Infrastructure Deals in Asia Running out of Steam?', 1 May 2019 – at preqin.com.

lyrical about their role in helping build the world's crucial infrastructures – 'providing infrastructure that improves national, regional and local economies', in the words of the Global Infrastructure Investor Association.[47] While this has never been what they principally do, in Asia, at least, the reality does appear to bear a somewhat greater resemblance to the rhetoric.

Of course, Asia is a huge and extraordinarily heterogeneous place. By no means have asset managers invested in Asian infrastructure evenly across the region. It is worth noting that China, despite its size, is not the principal territorial locus of private financial infrastructure investment, because the country's vast infrastructure expansion of recent decades has been predominantly led and funded by the state.[48] Thus, the number of private financial infrastructure investments in China between 2005 and 2018 as identified by Preqin (992) was dwarfed by the number over the same period in India (2,278), which has been comfortably the leading Asian market for such investment.

'India not only boasts a booming economy', observes Adefuye, 'but is making a large-scale, rapid shift from an agrarian economy to an industrial one. As such, its large population and rapid development have created a huge need for infrastructure, while its unindustrialized history means it does not have large networks of pre-existing assets.' Nor – unlike China – does India have a heavily interventionist state. The result is that most of the new infrastructure sprouting up around the country is privately financed and owned, affording a prominent role to asset managers. And while there are certainly local infrastructure asset managers of note – Mumbai's IDFC Alternatives is one – the reality is that it is Western asset managers that largely control India's burgeoning portfolio of privately owned infrastructures. Two of the three managers profiled below, Brookfield and Macquarie, are hugely significant players.

---

47 Global Infrastructure Investor Association, 'Closing the Gap: How Private Capital Can Help Deliver Our Future Infrastructure Needs', March 2019, p. 4 – at giia.net.

48 I. T. Liu and A. D. Dixon, 'What Does the State Do in China's State-Led Infrastructure Financialisation?', *Journal of Economic Geography* 22: 5 (2022), 963–88.

Housing

If the above sketch more or less captures the key geographies of asset managers' infrastructure investment – where the money comes from, where it is institutionally aggregated, and where it is put to work on the ground – it is somewhat harder to provide a comparable sketch for their housing investment. Publicly reported data pertaining to such geographies tend to refer to real-estate investment at the aggregate level – combining residential with all types of commercial-property investment – and these data can therefore tell us little about the patterns of investment in housing specifically.

The question of where exactly the capital that asset managers invest in housing comes from is the hardest to answer. To the extent that researchers have satisfactorily addressed this question, the answer seems to be that the relevant map matches quite closely the picture for asset management in general: in other words, the capital originates in North America/Europe/other regions in approximate 50/25/25 per cent shares. Daniela Gabor and Sebastian Kohl, for example, have found that the dominance of North American institutional capital very much applies to contemporary asset-manager investment specifically in European housing. 'The most important drivers of the financialization of European housing', Gabor and Kohl write, 'are US pension funds and insurance companies', whose holdings of European real estate that include housing are invested primarily via asset managers, and which in 2021 amounted to more than double the equivalent holdings of European-based pension schemes and insurance companies.[49]

What is clearer still, secondly, is that North American–based managers thoroughly dominate the international landscape of asset-manager housing investment, and to a materially greater extent than they do infrastructure investment. This is partly a reflection of the historical geography of physical investment opportunities. Save for exceptional cases like Germany, where around the turn of the millennium asset managers found

---

49 D. Gabor and S. Kohl, 'My Home Is an Asset Class: The Financialization of Housing in Europe', January 2022, p. 33 – at greens-efa.eu (hereafter cited as 'GK2').

themselves able to buy formerly publicly owned housing on a substantial scale, openings outside North America were until recently relatively few and far between. Housing investment by asset managers accordingly lacks the type of long and substantial track record of investment in non-US assets with which we are so familiar – in the shape of Australia and Europe, and especially the UK – in the infrastructure space. Indeed, the asset managers that bought large quantities of German housing in the early 2000s were themselves primarily US-based firms.

Certainly, there are today European-based asset managers with extremely significant residential real-estate holdings concentrated in multi-family housing, student housing and care homes. Among the most prominent are two based in France (AXA Investment Managers and Amundi), two in Germany (Allianz Real Estate and Patrizia) and one in the UK (Round Hill Capital). While most of the housing that these managers own is itself also located in Europe, AXA and Round Hill, in particular, have pursued significant territorial expansion. AXA's acquisition of two multi-family assets in Tokyo in May 2022, for example, was its fifteenth separate purchase of Japanese residential property in just twelve months, adding to a global housing portfolio now spread across fifteen different countries.[50] This makes AXA one of the most geographically diversified owners of residential property in the world.

Nevertheless, the contemporary universe of major housing asset managers is very much a North American, and more narrowly US-based, universe. As of mid 2021, Preqin reported some 1,720 active real-estate investment funds globally which invested exclusively or primarily in housing. Of these, no fewer than two-thirds (1,154) were managed by asset managers headquartered in the United States.[51] No other country hosted more than 100 of

---

50 'AXA IM Alts Expands Global Residential Portfolio'.

51 D. Gabor and S. Kohl, 'My Home Is an Asset Class: The Financialization of Housing in Europe', 2021, pre-publication version (hereafter cited as 'GK1'.) Note that this data point corresponds closely to reported figures for geographic shares of real-estate AUM more widely: BCG estimated that, in 2020, 69 per cent of real-estate AUM were held by asset managers headquartered in North America, ahead of managers based in Europe (18 per cent) and the Asia-Pacific region (12 per cent). See BCG, '$100 Trillion Machine', p. 18.

the funds in question: the second to fourth spots were occupied by the UK (whose resident managers ran eighty-nine residential-focused funds), Germany (seventy-seven funds) and Canada (sixty-two funds). One of the leading US-based housing asset managers, Blackstone, is profiled below. Other major US asset managers with significant housing assets include, in no particular order, Lone Star Funds, Carlyle Group, Greystar Investment Management, CBRE Global Investors, Goldman Sachs Asset Management, Starwood Capital Group and PGIM Real Estate.

Lastly, North America also geographically dominates asset managers' actual physical housing investment. Of the 1,720 active residential-focused investment funds globally in 2021, 70 per cent (1,200) invested primarily or solely in North America.[52] This is both a Canadian and US story, but, again, principally a US one. Not only do asset managers own substantially more multi-family housing in the United States than in Canada, with one recent estimate suggesting that, by 2021, their cumulative multi-family holdings in the former exceeded 1 million units.[53] In the United States, asset managers also widely own assets in four other sub-classes of residential property – senior housing (i.e., care homes), student housing, manufactured-housing communities, and single-family rental housing.

Indeed, two of these four sub-classes are more or less uniquely US phenomena. Asset managers do not own manufactured-housing communities or single-family rental housing on anything other than a very marginal scale anywhere else in the world. Manufactured housing, for its part, is simply not common outside the United States, although Australia, Israel and the UK, among others, do all have variants of it. Meanwhile, it took the materialisation in the United States of an unusual and propitious set of circumstances in the wake of the global financial crisis to persuade asset managers finally to make a move into single-family housing investment, which they had previously avoided (see Chapter 2).

---

52   GK1.

53   H. Vogell, 'When Private Equity Becomes Your Landlord', 7 February 2022 – at propublica.org.

Beyond North America, while asset managers have invested substantially in multi-family housing in Asia, and especially Japan, Europe nonetheless represents the principal focus of their housing investment. Approximately 300 of the 1,720 residential funds active globally in 2021 were focused on Europe – more than twice the number (126) focused on Asia.[54] Student housing, care homes and multi-family housing have all widely come under asset-manager ownership across Europe in the past decade or so, in countries ranging from the Czech Republic to the UK, France, Denmark, Ireland and the Netherlands. As Gabor and Kohl, among others, have observed, this development has seen a clutch of prominent European cities including Amsterdam, Berlin and London emerge as housing investment hotspots.[55]

Where multi-family housing, the biggest investment sub-class, is concerned, perhaps the most noteworthy European territory in terms of developments of the past decade is Spain. As in the United States, homeowners in Spain came under intense pressure as a result of the global financial crisis, as housing market values slumped and unemployment soared. Many lost their homes to foreclosure, and Spain's lenders – themselves battling to remain solvent – sold large numbers of these foreclosed homes to US-based asset managers. Moreover, again repeating the US pattern, those managers also acquired large numbers of homes by purchasing portfolios of delinquent mortgages and carrying out selective foreclosures themselves. One of the biggest investors in Spanish housing among US asset managers has been Blackstone.[56]

Gabor and Kohl provide an instructive example of a particular investment fund that in several respects neatly encapsulates

---

54   GK1.

55   GK2, pp. 35–7; B. Christophers, 'Mind the Rent Gap: Blackstone, Housing Investment and the Reordering of Urban Rent Surfaces', *Urban Studies* 59 (2022), pp. 698–716.

56   See, for example, M. Janoschka, G. Alexandri, H. Ramos and S. Vives-Miró, 'Tracing the Socio-Spatial Logics of Transnational Landlords' Real Estate Investment: Blackstone in Madrid', *European Urban and Regional Studies* 27: 2 (2020), pp. 125–41; I. Yrigoy, 'The Political Economy of Rental Housing in Spain: The dialectics of Exploitation(s) and Regulations', *New Political Economy* 26 (2021), pp. 186–202.

the nature of much asset-manager-led investment in European housing in recent times. Launched in 2019 and closed to new investors in 2021, by the end of the latter year the $2.3 billion fund had completed four residential purchases. These were in Germany and Spain – perhaps the two most important contemporary European markets for such investment. But the fund, like so many others, was not European-managed: its manager was the US-based asset manager KKR. And KKR Real Estate Partners II Europe, as the fund was called, had raised capital, it appeared, largely within the United States, its principal known investors being five New York City public pension schemes and the state of Maine's Public Employees Retirement System.[57] Such, in short, is the shape of a quintessential vehicle of investment in European housing in the early 2020s.

While much of the housing latterly acquired by asset managers in Germany, Spain and other European countries remains under their ownership at the time of writing, this pattern does not hold everywhere. In some countries, asset managers have bought large stocks of housing only to sell it later, taking advantage of inflated asset values to realise capital gains for themselves and their limited partners. In fact, this is part and parcel of the typical cycle of the real-asset asset-management business: that is, buy *and sell* (see Chapter 4).

A company of significant interest in this respect is Germany's Vonovia. Vonovia is noteworthy for our purposes not because it is an asset manager – it is not one – but because much of the housing in its huge European portfolio was previously owned by asset managers – principally in Germany, where many of its approximately 350,000 residential units were inherited from Terra Firma and the Fortress Investment Group, but also in Sweden, where it acquired a substantial housing portfolio from Blackstone in 2019. Of course, this is not a uniquely European dynamic: in the United States, Blackstone built a large portfolio of single-family rental dwellings through its portfolio company Invitation Homes between 2011 and 2017, only to then begin the process of exiting the investment (see Chapter 2). The point

---

57   GK2, p. 43.

is that, at a certain moment in time, it may not appear that a particular home – or school building, water treatment plant or wind farm – is part of asset-manager society. But it may recently have been, and may still bear the asset manager's indelible imprint.

Before moving on to a selection of the key actors in asset-manager society, one final observation concerning that society's geographical configuration is important. The fact that asset managers themselves may be based in, say, New York, London or Paris, does not mean that the all-important funds that they use to pool together limited-partner capital and make portfolio investments occupy the same location. Over the years, significant competition has arisen between national and subnational territorial jurisdictions as to which can offer asset managers the most beneficial – in other words, feeble – combination of tax and regulation for the legal domicile of their funds. Where exactly managers choose to establish investment funds ultimately depends on many factors, including the range of jurisdictions from which the limited partners in those funds originate.

The upshot of this is that the past few decades have seen the emergence of a far-flung network of key domiciliary nodes where much of the back-office administration of managers' myriad funds occurs; this network is now a crucial part of the institutional plumbing of asset-manager society. The likes of Bermuda and the Channel Islands are part of it, but the bulk of funds established by North American and European asset managers to invest in infrastructure or housing tend today to be domiciled in either the US state of Delaware, the Cayman Islands or Luxembourg – or in some combination of these. Asset-manager society is thus deeply embedded – financially and legally, if not physically – in the shadowy spatial world of tax havens and 'offshore'. I will explore some of the implications of this in Chapter 5.

Firms

Blackstone

The Blackstone Group is the world's largest 'alternative' asset manager, which is to say the largest manager ranked by investment in asset classes other than publicly listed securities.

Headquartered in New York, Blackstone is intimately associated with the man who has run it since cofounding it in 1985 – Stephen Schwarzman, the 'Black' (*schwarz* in German) in the firm's name. Now a billionaire many times over, Schwarzman has built a business that, by the time of writing, had grown assets under management to approaching $1 trillion. Blackstone is an institutional linchpin of global asset-manager society.

For its first two decades, Blackstone was impenetrable to outside observers, as it was a private partnership with very limited reporting requirements. To a degree that changed in 2007, when the firm took the major step of listing on the New York Stock Exchange. Notably, it did so as a publicly traded partnership, in which investors bought and sold units rather than shares. Twelve years later, the firm undertook its most recent significant structural transformation, converting from a partnership into a corporation in order to increase the range and number of investors able to invest in it.

Blackstone has had something of a stop-start history of investment in infrastructure. It originally established an infrastructure investment platform in 2008, poaching two directors from Macquarie to run the launch and operation of its debut infrastructure fund. But the fund underperformed – raising only $450 million against a target of $2 billion – and in 2011 the same directors left to set up their own firm, Stonepeak Infrastructure Partners. An infrastructure investment business was relaunched at Blackstone in 2017 with a new flagship fund (Blackstone Infrastructure Partners); but the firm remains a neophyte and relative minnow in the space compared with the likes of Brookfield, Macquarie and Global Infrastructure Partners. Even Stonepeak has considerably greater infrastructure assets under management, with approximately $53 billion compared to Blackstone's $31 billion.

Instead, Blackstone is relevant to our story principally as a housing investor. It is frequently identified as the world's leading overall real-estate owner – it owns vast quantities of office and logistics (i.e., warehouse) properties, alongside smaller hotel and retail property portfolios – and it is certainly one of the world's biggest owners of housing. It enjoys this status, moreover, despite having exited from Invitation Homes, which, by the time Blackstone sold its final shares in 2019, owned some 80,000 single-family homes across the United States.

Remarkably, all the housing in Blackstone's current portfolio was acquired during the relatively short period since the global financial crisis. It did own some housing in the mid 2000s, its main such asset being the approximately 31,000 German units it acquired for €1.4 billion from WCM Beteiligungs- und Grundbesitz-AG in 2004, in what at the time was the country's biggest ever sale of housing to a non-domestic buyer by a private owner. But, around 2006, Blackstone correctly sensed approaching trouble in global housing markets, and took the decision to sell all its existing residential property holdings. The units in Germany were offloaded in March 2007 to two London-based asset managers, and at a considerable profit.

Since 2011, Blackstone has embarked on a vast, transnational programme of housing acquisition arguably without parallel in history. It has bought substantial stocks of housing to rent out – encompassing the full menu of single-family housing, multi-family housing, care homes, manufactured housing, and student housing – in at least eleven countries: the United States and Canada in North America; Japan in Asia; and, in Europe, the Czech Republic, Denmark, Germany, Ireland, the Netherlands, Spain, Sweden and the UK. It is important to emphasise the words 'at least'. It is entirely possible that Blackstone has also acquired housing elsewhere: it is under no obligation to report publicly all the investments its funds make. The acquisitions that have occurred in the eleven countries mentioned above are those that are discoverable in the public domain and through publicly available sources.

In broad terms, this investment has been of two main strategic types. The first, chronologically speaking, was investment in market distress. The financial crisis of 2007–09 caused turmoil in global housing markets and markets for housing finance, and Blackstone strategically targeted residential property assets that became 'distressed' as a result, implying both that sellers were forced to sell and that – partly as a consequence – the assets were available for below market value. Blackstone picked up distressed housing assets in countries ranging from Germany to Ireland, but it was in two other countries that it pursued this strategy most extensively and most profitably – Spain, where significant market distress lingered until at least the mid 2010s, and the United States. In both of these countries, Blackstone was able to acquire large numbers of cheap assets, in the shape of both homes themselves and mortgages that, in many cases, enabled it to take control of the homes to which the mortgages applied (see Chapter 2).

Investing in market distress is a relatively straightforward strategy: buying cheap, waiting for asset markets to recover, and then selling – as Blackstone did in the United States by cashing out of Invitation Homes between 2017 and 2019. Blackstone's other principal strategy for investing in housing, however, has been more sophisticated, and also more varied. In this case, it has invested not in under-priced assets, and thus in the potential for price recovery, so much as in the ability to raise rents. Where, it has asked, has it been possible to buy housing and then grow the ongoing rental income that such housing generates? Perhaps the point is so obvious that it need not be made – but raising rents creates value for landlords not just directly, in the form of the extra cash income earned, but also indirectly, to the extent that it increases the perceived value of the asset to other investors, and thereby affords the possibility of realising capital gains through disposal.

Identifying a range of local conditions occasioning opportunities to achieve rental growth, Blackstone has in recent years pursued this housing investment strategy in countries including Denmark, the Netherlands and Sweden. In some countries and cities, the feature of greatest interest to Blackstone has been supply shortages. Where demand for rental housing is strong but the ability of supply to respond to that demand is constrained for one reason or another, rents, Blackstone has wagered, are liable to rise. This logic has underpinned its recent investments in housing in Amsterdam, for instance. In other places, it has been a coincidence of rundown housing stock with accommodating rent regulation that has appealed. If landlords are permitted to raise rents substantially after undertaking renovations, investing in the rehabilitation of rental-housing stock in areas of buoyant demand can be a highly profitable approach. Blackstone has pursued this approach in, for example, Copenhagen and Stockholm (see Chapter 4).

The combined result of these various investment strategies has been a burgeoning housing investment portfolio to rival that of any other asset manager, or indeed property company. In mid 2019, the firm reported that it owned more than 300,000 residential units around the world. It subsequently stopped disclosing its unit holdings, but one recent independent report stated that, in 2020, Blackstone owned some 117,000 units just in Europe, of which approximately 40,000 were in Spain.[58] As we have seen, our best estimate is that Blackstone funds today control housing globally worth more than $100 billion. Indeed, it bought housing assets worth in excess of $20 billion in the period of the coronavirus pandemic alone.[59]

Another result of Blackstone's rapid assembly of a formidable global housing portfolio, however, has been a torrent of criticism. Fairly or not, Blackstone has over the past decade become a lightning rod for a wider critique of the growing participation of financial investment institutions of various kinds in home ownership. Those who have attacked the firm's practices in this space include a range of high-profile individuals, such as the prime minister of Denmark and the US senator Elizabeth Warren. Arguably the most stinging criticism was levelled by the UN 'rapporteurs' Surya Deva and Leilani Farha, who in 2019 wrote an open letter to Schwarzman alleging that Blackstone's housing investments were 'inconsistent with international human rights law and norms' and 'had deleterious effects on the enjoyment of the right to housing'.[60] In Chapter 4, I will consider some of the main grounds for this criticism.

---

58 Ibid., pp. 47, 55.

59 M. Vandevelde, 'Blackstone Dealt Legal Setback after $5bn Low-Income Housing Deal', *Financial Times*, 29 June 2022.

60 S. Deva and L. Farha, 'Dear Mr Schwarzman', 22 March 2019 – at ohchr.org.

Brookfield

If one company more than any other represents the corporate embodiment of asset-manager society, then Canada's Brookfield Asset Management is undoubtedly that company. Like Blackstone, it is a massive owner of housing. But it is also a massive owner of the various other physical infrastructures that undergird contemporary social and economic life. Of a similar size to Blackstone – its assets under management are slightly smaller, at around $700 billion in mid 2022 – it is likewise a publicly listed corporation with an expansive international reach in terms of both where it has offices and where it makes investments. As Mark Vandevelde correctly noted in a 2020 profile of the firm in the *Financial Times*, Brookfield 'receives less scrutiny or attention than rivals of similar size'.[61] But there is no good reason why that should be the case.

Part of the reason for this lack of attention, perhaps, is Brookfield's organisational complexity. Vandevelde wrote that 'when the Brookfield group buys an asset, the money usually comes from one of the investment funds it runs for outside investors'. And in that, of course, Brookfield is comparable to all other real-asset asset managers: using funds to invest the money of outside investors (their limited partners) is, by definition, what such managers do. But this is about as far as the comparison goes. In organisational terms, beyond this basic equivalence, Brookfield departs substantially from asset managers with altogether simpler corporate structures, Blackstone included. Brookfield, as Vandevelde remarked, arguably has 'one of the world's most complicated corporate structures', so much so that 'what exactly Brookfield is, and how it operates, is maddeningly difficult to ascertain'.

At the risk of oversimplifying, this, at the time of writing, is broadly how things work. The key to understanding Brookfield is to recognise that it is a collection of institutional entities. At the top of the pyramid is Brookfield Asset Management itself ('Brookfield', for short, or BAM). Below it are what it calls its 'affiliates'. There are five of these, but only three are relevant

---

for our purposes: Brookfield Property Partners (which specialises in real estate), Brookfield Renewable Partners (renewable energy assets) and Brookfield Infrastructure Partners (other infrastructure assets). The last two are listed firms – publicly traded partnerships, like Blackstone used to be – in their own right. Until recently, Brookfield Property Partners was also one such, but in 2021 BAM acquired all units it did not own, thus making it a wholly owned subsidiary.

BAM is the largest single shareholder in each of its affiliates. In turn, when BAM establishes investment funds to make asset purchases – in, say, the renewables space – its affiliates are typically the largest providers of capital to those funds, which of course also raise money from external limited partners. Thus, to take an instructive example, when Brookfield established a new infrastructure fund, Brookfield Infrastructure Fund IV, in 2019–20, its affiliates Brookfield Renewable Partners and Brookfield Infrastructure Partners committed a combined \$5 billion to the fund; meanwhile, some 170 external limited partners committed a further \$15 billion.[62]

What makes the picture particularly complicated, however, are two wrinkles in this core operating model. First, BAM's limited partners are able to invest not only through BAM's funds but also in its affiliates, thereby generating management fees (and so-called 'incentive distributions') for BAM, since it is the general partner of each affiliate. Second, some BAM investments are made directly, using its own balance sheet, which is to say neither via funds nor via its affiliates – and the latter also sometimes make investments directly rather than through commitments to Brookfield funds. Needless to say, the resulting overall picture represents a considerable headache for would-be analysts of the empire. In the case of real-estate investments, for example, while most are held within Brookfield's investment funds, some are held on its own (BAM) balance sheet, and some on the balance sheet of Brookfield Property Partners.

In terms of residential property assets specifically, Brookfield – understood in its totality – is just as diversified as Blackstone.

62　Brookfield Asset Management, 'Brookfield Closes US\$20 Billion Global Infrastructure Fund', 7 February 2020 – at bam.brookfield.com.

It owns manufactured housing, student housing, care homes and multi-family housing. It has also recently made a belated move into single-family housing, establishing a dedicated fund – Brookfield Single Family Rental – for this purpose in 2020, and acquiring a controlling interest in Conrex, owner of approximately 10,000 rental homes across the US Midwest and Southeast, in the same year. But, while equally diverse, Brookfield's housing portfolio is smaller than Blackstone's: it owns only around 50,000 multi-family units, for example, compared to Blackstone's hundreds of thousands. Brookfield's residential portfolio is also much more tightly confined to North America. Only rarely has it bought housing further afield, entering the UK student housing market in 2016, for instance, through the acquisition from Avenue Capital of a thirteen-property portfolio containing around 5,700 beds; and entering the Australian senior housing market in 2020 with the purchase of Aveo Group and its approximately ninety 'retirement villages', housing around 12,000 residents.

In infrastructure, though, Brookfield is much bigger and more international. Although it does not have meaningful investments to speak of in either the water or social infrastructure sectors, it is substantially active in all of the other sectors profiled earlier in this chapter. In transportation, it owns, inter alia, some 32,000 kilometres of rail network in Australia, Brazil and North America, and around 4,000 kilometres of toll roads in countries including Brazil, Chile and India. In telecoms, its reported assets include fifty-two data centres, around 20,000 kilometres of fibre backbone – including networks in France and the UK – and over 180,000 cell-tower sites spread across six countries.[63] Plus, as we saw in Chapter 2, Brookfield owns hundreds of thousands of hectares of farmland, including around 270,000 hectares in Brazil alone.

Last but not least, Brookfield controls vast energy assets. Some of this represents fossil-fuel infrastructure (principally, 16,500 kilometres of natural gas pipelines and 600 billion cubic feet of natural gas storage) and some is energy-source-neutral (for example, 2,000 kilometres of electricity transmission lines in Texas). But the bulk, and certainly an ever-increasing proportion, is in renewables. With a reported $58 billion of assets under management in renewable power, Brookfield today ranks as one of the world's largest owners of renewables assets of any kind, with nearly 6,000 generating facilities and some 21 GW of cumulative generating capacity. The largest share of this capacity is in hydropower, with facilities in both North and South America, the latter including a large plant in Colombia, acquired in 2016. The next-largest share is in wind, with facilities controlled in four continents: both Americas, Europe and the Asia-Pacific. Smaller still, but again spread across the same four continents, is Brookfield's solar-farm portfolio.

Macquarie

The last real-asset manager profiled here is a different type of entity again. While both Blackstone and Brookfield are asset managers more or less *tout court*, Macquarie is not. The Macquarie Group is a highly diversified financial services company headquartered in Australia, which offers a full suite of retail, commercial and investment banking products. But our interest is only in one of its divisions: Macquarie Asset Management. In fact, we are actually interested in only one of this division's three legs: namely, Macquarie Infrastructure and Real Assets (MIRA), whose name more or less speaks for itself.

While MIRA does invest in real estate, this has historically been only a marginal part of its business. As of 2018, real estate accounted for only 3 per cent of its assets by value.[64] Housing, in turn, accounted for only a small fraction of that 3 per cent – logistics has been Macquarie's main thematic focus within real estate. In short, MIRA invests in infrastructure – the sinews of society's physical fabric. It is consistently ranked as the largest infrastructure owner globally among financial investment institutions, its infrastructure AUM now exceeding A$200 billion.[65]

---

64 'Macquarie Infrastructure and Real Assets, Credentials, 31 March 2018', p. 17 – at macquarie.com.

65 'Macquarie Group, Management Discussion and Analysis, Year Ended 31 March 2022', p. 80 – at macquarie.com.

Every single day, the firm reckons, over 100 million people around the world rely on the infrastructures that it owns to go about their everyday lives. Much of asset-manager society, in other words, is Macquarie's society.

Like other infrastructure asset managers, MIRA invests mainly through unlisted funds. Over the past decade or so, it has typically been actively managing around thirty active funds of this kind at any one time. These generally have a geographic focus (for example, the Macquarie Mexican Infrastructure Fund), a strategic–thematic focus (the Macquarie Supercore Infrastructure Fund, which is open-ended, invests only in regulated assets, and targets yield more than capital returns), or both (the Korea Private Concession Fund).

Much more than most of its peers, however, Macquarie also has longstanding and extensive experience of operating listed funds, even if these have increasingly been in the minority among its infrastructure funds. Indeed, its inaugural infrastructure fund, 1996's Infrastructure Trust of Australia, was itself listed. One of the things that is significant about this is that, unlike the likes of Blackstone, Macquarie therefore has large numbers of retail fund investors: if the latter generally do not have the financial wherewithal to invest in unlisted funds, listed vehicles are a different matter. At the time of writing, there are three active MIRA-managed listed funds – the Macquarie Infrastructure Corporation, which is US-listed and invests in US infrastructure; the Macquarie Korea Infrastructure Fund, which is South Korea–listed and owns infrastructure in that country, including a large portfolio of toll roads; and FIBRA Macquarie Mexico, which is a Mexico-listed real-estate investment trust that invests in Mexican commercial property.

In line with the majority of real-asset asset managers, MIRA–Macquarie generally invests some of its own capital in its managed funds – listed and unlisted – alongside the capital of its limited partners. But limited-partner money nonetheless consistently represents the lion's share of committed capital – again, as in the case of most other asset managers. As of 2018, this proportion was as high as 98 per cent in MIRA's case. Of a total of $A86.2 billion of equity capital held in MIRA funds collectively at that point, some $A84.3 billion represented the capital of external investors. Macquarie Group ($A1.6 billion) and its employees ($A0.3 billion) provided the other 2 per cent of equity.[66]

Meanwhile, another respect in which Macquarie looks quite different from Blackstone and Brookfield is in its geographical footprint – unsurprisingly, perhaps, given its Antipodean origins. Certainly, it has substantial assets in the Americas, which represent 22 per cent of its portfolio value at the time of writing.[67] But much of this value is in Latin American assets, such as Brazilian farmland, Peruvian commercial real estate, and cell towers and other infrastructure in Mexico. MIRA's North American assets, which are predominantly in the United States, do not stand comparison with those of its two North America–based rivals profiled above.

Where Macquarie is relatively stronger, though, is in Europe and the Asia-Pacific region. The former, with the UK in a prominent position (Macquarie has bought more than £50bn of UK infrastructure assets since 2005), accounts for around half of MIRA's portfolio value.[68] Indeed, there are very few countries in Western and Central Europe where MIRA does not presently have substantial infrastructure investments – seemingly only Norway, Portugal and Switzerland. And from its historic and contemporary base in Australia, Macquarie has long enjoyed considerable competitive advantages over its North American rivals when it comes to exploiting Asia-Pacific investment opportunities. MIRA's infrastructure assets in that region are today worth more than its assets in the Americas, and include investments in Australia, China, India, Japan, the Philippines, Singapore and South Korea. Globally, MIRA now controls infrastructures in approximately thirty countries.

As well as being highly geographically dispersed, those infrastructures are also perhaps as sectorally diversified as any other

---

66 'Macquarie Infrastructure and Real Assets, Credentials', p. 11.

67 'Putting the World's Long Term Savings to Work' – at mirafunds.com.

68 The UK figure is from G. Plimmer, 'Southern Water Sewage Dumps Show Scale of Clean-Up Job for Australian Owner', *Financial Times*, 19 September 2022.

major asset manager's real-asset portfolio. To begin with, MIRA has significant investments in all of the infrastructure sectors covered by Brookfield, from rail and toll roads to fibre networks and data centres; and while it is smaller in some such areas (owning 'just' 13 GW of green power-generation capacity, compared to Brookfield's 21 GW), it is much bigger in others (its sprawling farmland estate, in Brazil and – principally – Australia, extends to some 4.7 million hectares, producing red meat, grains and oil seeds). Indeed, the two firms are direct, long-time rivals, and frequently face off as competing bidders when major infrastructure investment opportunities come to market.

In addition to the sectors addressed by Brookfield, however, Macquarie is also active in others. It is a longstanding investor, for example, in the water sector, currently owning water (and in some cases wastewater) infrastructures in Australia, China, the UK and the United States. Another area where Brookfield is not active but Macquarie has been so is airports. Today, it has substantial stakes, and in some cases controlling interests, in smallish regional airports in Australia, India and the UK. But the firm's biggest airport deals, for now at least, are behind it: in 2013, it sold its final remaining stake in Sydney Airport, having controlled the ninety-nine-year concession to that asset for much of the period since it was granted by the government in 2002; and in 2019, it exited a major fifteen-year investment in Brussels Airport.

Lastly, albeit more peripherally, Macquarie has also dipped its toe into the ownership of social infrastructure. In 2020, for example, Macquarie European Infrastructure Fund 6 took control of the large Viamed Salud network of healthcare facilities in Spain, spread across nine cities and comprising nine acute-care hospitals, three convalescence centres, fifteen outpatient clinics, and one specialist aged-care facility.

In any event, no map of asset-manager society, historically or in the present, would be complete without according a prominent place to the Macquarie Group and MIRA.

Our overall cartography has shown that, together with Blackstone, Brookfield and a series of other major Western asset managers, using capital supplied by institutional investors located predominantly in North America and Europe, Macquarie has increasingly come to own many of the fixed physical building-blocks essential to contemporary social life – especially, but not exclusively, in the West itself. Housing, energy and transportation systems, in particular, have widely come under asset-manager control. We have seen hints of what this means both for asset managers themselves and for those relying on access to managers' proprietary assets in order to get by. A fuller reckoning of that question is the subject of the remaining chapters.

4

The Costs

Troubled Waters

In December 2012, a joint venture between the US asset manager KKR (with a 90 per cent stake) and the private water company Suez (with 10 per cent) paid $150 million for a forty-year concession to run the municipal waterworks of the port city of Bayonne in New Jersey. In addition to making this upfront payment, the joint venture committed to investing $157 million in the ageing municipal water infrastructure over the life of the contract. For forty years, then, payments for water supply made by Bayonne's households and businesses would remunerate not the local public authority, but principally an asset manager headquartered across the Hudson River in New York City.

The 2012 agreement was greeted with considerable fanfare. Ratepayers would see an initial 8.5 per cent increase in their water and sewerage charges, but thereafter the picture was rosier: the city officials who signed the deal promised a subsequent four-year rate freeze.[1] Expressing its 'commitment to maintain continuous investment into the system', KKR was lauded for its 'long-term vision'.[2] And the expectation was that, while the deal would certainly make profits for KKR, these would be relatively modest in scale. 'Infrastructure investments of such kind usually deliver internal rates of return of a little over 10 per cent', observed Greg Roumeliotis in reporting on the deal

---

[1] D. Ivory, B. Protess and G. Palmer, 'In American Towns, Private Profits from Public Works', *New York Times*, 24 December 2016.

[2] 'United Water and KKR Sign Unique Utility Partnership with City of Bayonne, NJ', 20 December 2012 – at businesswire.com.

for Reuters, 'lower than those typically seen in the buyouts of companies'.[3]

But the reality turned out to be very different. Ratepayers got burned. It transpired that the deal had guaranteed KKR and Suez a minimum amount of annual revenue, and thus, paradoxically, the less water that residents used, the more – per litre – they paid for it. The city had also sweetened the deal for the investors by absorbing the risk of unforeseen capital investment. In 2016, the combination of low water usage and 'unexpected repairs' (paid for by the city) saw rates leap by 13.25 per cent.[4] Flush with that increase, KKR – its putative 'long-term' vision now notably absent – began shopping its majority stake late the same year. In January 2018, it achieved the exit it was looking for, selling its position to another asset manager, Argo Infrastructure Partners. Its five-year investment in Bayonne's waterworks concession earned KKR a chunky internal rate of return (IRR) of some 36 per cent.[5]

KKR was not the only major asset manager that invested in US municipal water assets in those years. In 2011, for example, using its Carlyle Infrastructure Partners fund, the Carlyle Group paid approximately $100 million for a package of three western water systems, two in California and one in Montana. It, too, exited profitably within five years, selling the three systems to Canada's Algonquin Power and Utilities for $250 million in January 2016. And it, too, attracted significant criticism, not least in Montana, where in 2014 the city of Missoula sued under eminent domain laws to take its water system back under public control, 'claiming Carlyle skimped on upkeep and repairs while enriching itself'.[6] In August 2016, by which time the water-works belonged to Algonquin, Montana's Supreme Court ruled in Missoula's favour, and the following June, at a compensatory cost of $84 million, the city retook ownership.

3 G. Roumeliotis, 'KKR Joins Private Equity Charge in US Water', 20 December 2012 – at reuters.com.

4 R. Dezember and H. Gillers, 'KKR Seeks Buyer for Water Ventures', *Wall Street Journal*, 22 December 2016.

5 A. Vitelli, 'KKR Makes Splash with US Water PPP Exits', 26 January 2018 – at infrastructureinvestor.com.

6 Dezember and Gillers, 'KKR Seeks Buyer for Water Ventures'.

Under a new local municipal leadership, Bayonne has also recently explored retaking control of its water infrastructure from asset managers' hands. But with the cost of buying itself out of the remaining three decades of the forty-year waterworks concession contract estimated at over $300 million, it simply cannot afford to. By mid 2021, frustration among Bayonne's ratepayers and municipal leaders with the millstone that the 2012 water contract represented had, it was reported, 'reached a boiling point'.[7]

Utopia or Dystopia?

The champions of asset-manager society are terrific and tenacious salesmen and women. Whenever a deal to take control of a key piece of infrastructure or a residential property asset is struck, the same claims about why this is a good thing – a social and economic utopia, no less – are invariably rolled out. These claims fall into two main categories.

First, certain claims highlight why asset-manager society is good for ordinary people in their capacity as individual investors. The thrust of this discourse is that the money that asset managers invest in housing and infrastructure is the money predominantly of ordinary citizens, in the form of individual retirement savings held in pension plans. Asset managers 'do good' because they perform a valuable service on behalf of those ordinary savers, taking their capital and helping it to grow through dedicated, disciplined and expert investment practices. For now, we will park these particular claims: Chapter 5 represents a critical interrogation of them.

The second type of claim highlights why asset-manager society is good both for ordinary people in their capacity as users of infrastructure and housing, and for the governments that these users democratically elect, which historically have often themselves played important roles in infrastructure and housing provision. These claims are more varied and elaborate,

7 P. D'Auria, 'Frustration over Bayonne's Water Contract Has Reached a Boiling Point', 18 June 2021 – at nj.com.

but essentially boil down to the postulate that private-sector actors in general, and asset managers in particular, are simply better owners and custodians of housing and infrastructure than the public sector can ever be, which means that asset-manager ownership is good both for users and – to the extent that it relieves them of responsibilities for which they are inherently ill-suited – also for public authorities. It is explicitly claims of this second kind to which this chapter responds.

All manner of examples of the latter type of discourse can be found in the burgeoning annals of asset-manager society. For illustrative purposes, let us take the assertions of the Global Infrastructure Investor Association (GIIA), a leading trade association for institutional investors in infrastructure and their asset managers. In its 2019 report on the role of private capital in delivering the world's infrastructure needs, the GIIA offered a prototypical enumeration of the various purported benefits to users and governments of society's essential physical systems being financed and owned privately rather than publicly. Such benefits, it averred, are principally fourfold.

First, it said, private ownership maximises infrastructure investment and service quality because public-sector operators 'are prone to underinvest' and thereby to create 'a poor experience for consumers'. Second, private ownership is more reliable, allegedly delivering new infrastructure 'more often on time and on budget' than public ownership, and with a lower risk of project cancellation. Third, private ownership is cheaper, both for users of infrastructure (because it entails 'greater efficiency' of operation) and for governments choosing between in-sourcing and outsourcing of asset build and operation (because outsourcing 'results in lower overall life cycle costs', thus reducing the cost of public procurement). Last, but definitely not least, private ownership, according to the GIIA, reduces risk to the state and, behind the state, taxpayers, insofar as key risks – 'design and construction costs, delays, volatile market demand, and operation and maintenance costs' – are 'transferred to the private sector'.[8]

---

8 Global Infrastructure Investor Association, 'Closing the Gap: How Private Capital Can Help Deliver Our Future Infrastructure Needs', March 2019, pp. 12–13 – at giia.net.

The specific words in this case were the GIIA's, but more or less the same combination of factors has repeatedly been invoked in legitimating the rise of asset-manager society – in positing it as an unequivocally *good thing* for citizen-users and their governments – for three decades now, and throughout the world.

Quite clearly, however, stories like the one that has seeped out of Bayonne in New Jersey since KKR arrived in town a decade ago jar dramatically with these celebratory claims. To say the very least, the GIIA's list of benefits – ostensible reliability, quality, cheapness and so forth – would raise quizzical eyebrows among the residents of Bayonne and their representatives in local government.

Thus, the vital question, surely, is this: Is the story of Bayonne (and indeed that of Missoula, Montana) an exception? Is this in fact just a local aberration from a more positive norm, one cleaving more closely to – if not quite matching – the utopian vision articulated by the GIIA?

The answer, this chapter shows, is no. Bayonne, I will argue, *is the norm*. The costs incurred by residents and by the state in Bayonne and Missoula because of their water-supply systems coming under the control of asset managers – costs ranging from 'skimped' investment to increased user rates and heightened risk – are the costs associated with asset-manager society more generally. And, crucially, such costs are not accidental. Rather, they are the more or less inevitable upshot of core features of the model by which asset-manager society operates. They are, in short, a feature, not a bug.

Hence, far from being some kind of utopia, asset-manager society for those living in it – those, lest we forget, such as the tenants of Summer House on the island of Alameda, whom we encountered briefly in the Introduction – is much more akin to a dystopia.

This chapter will build out this argument in stages, considering in turn the different key types of cost associated with asset-manager society. Along the way, I will draw on scholarship that helps us to understand these costs, and I will also consider what other scholars have perceived to be the main downsides of asset managers owning housing and infrastructure. What follows is definitely not the first such critique; but a central part of the argument to be made is that the core thrust of existing critiques – which typically appear under the banner of so-called 'financialisation' – is both insufficient and largely off the mark. A fuller, more nuanced critique is required.

Asset-manager ownership of infrastructure and housing, we shall see, does not in fact reduce risks to governments and taxpayers; it exacerbates them. It does not relieve and liberate governments, giving them freedom of action; it tends instead to constrain them and the futures that they endeavour to fashion. And asset-manager society definitely does not maximise investment and service quality over the long term; for a variety of reasons, but especially due to an impetus to rapid turnover of assets – with waterworks passing from KKR to Argo, and housing from Fifteen Group to Kennedy Wilson to Blackstone – it is in fact a locus precisely of short-termism, with all the implications for asset custodianship that such an ethos implies.

Terrific and tenacious salesmen and women the champions of asset-manager society may be. But, in the final reckoning, their product is snake-oil, and their utopia a pure moonshine.

'Risk Capital'

Asset unbundling and de-risking

To understand why the costs of asset-manager society are onerous and are shouldered by citizens and the state, we need to begin with the political economy of the mechanisms by which 'real assets' such as housing and infrastructures of energy, water, transportation, and so on, come to be owned by asset managers in the first place.

Here, an indispensable reference point is Stephen Graham and Simon Marvin's seminal 2001 account of what they called 'splintering urbanism'.[9] The late part of the twentieth century saw the beginning of a widespread process – ongoing today – of

---

9 S. Graham and S. Marvin, *Splintering Urbanism: Networked Infrastructures, Technological Mobilities and the Urban Condition* (London: Routledge, 2001).

'unbundling' of previously integrated infrastructure networks; Graham and Marvin were especially interested in urban infrastructure networks (hence, splintering *urbanism*); but the process they described has a more general application. Integrated infrastructure systems, Graham and Marvin showed, began to be disaggregated 'vertically'. A prime example would be power networks, which were increasingly unbundled into separate generation, transmission and distribution 'assets'. Such systems were also disaggregated sectorally (for example, into mobile versus landline telecommunications assets) and geographically. The overall result was, and continues to be, a disparate patchwork of economically, if not always physically, discrete infrastructures of social reproduction.

Driving this trend were a variety of underlying factors. Ideals of comprehensive and 'rational' joined-up urban planning were being eroded. At the same time, there was a mounting of forces in favour of privatisation – sometimes internally among a country's elite institutions, such as in the UK, but at other times compelled by external institutions such as the International Monetary Fund and its favoured regime of 'structural adjustment'.

If changes in planning orthodoxy enabled asset splintering, privatisation effectively required it. It did so, observed Graham and Marvin, because governments found the private sector reluctant to invest in 'large-scale, comprehensive and "bundled" networks' but much more willing to put capital into their unbundled components. Concerned to isolate the respective risk and return profiles of different network elements, investors sought out 'individual revenue and profitability streams for particular infrastructural developments, within tight definitions of accounting that minimise[d] social or geographical cross-subsidies'.[10] Each local, unbundled system element – an electricity distribution network here, a toll road or housing complex there – was effectively posited as a unique set of 'investment qualities'.[11]

But, of course, not all such discrete, local investment propositions would prove attractive to private capital. Without the

10 Ibid., p. 97.

11 P. O'Brien, P. O'Neill and A. Pike, 'Funding, Financing and Governing Urban Infrastructures', *Urban Studies* 56 (2019), p. 1299.

'social or geographical cross-subsidies' mentioned above, investors could not see how some assets, in some places, could be
made to pay. More fundamentally still, the spatial fixity that is
characteristic of all the physical systems we are concerned with
in this book – be they houses or farmland or schools – is itself
a risk from the investor's perspective, even if an asset happens
to look 'investible' at a particular moment in time. Capitalism
is nothing if not geographically unstable. Infrastructural investments, however, are immovable. As David Harvey observed in
The Limits to Capital, 'Production, labour power and commerce
do not necessarily follow the paths beaten out by infrastructural investments.' Being embedded in or on the land, real assets
are 'particularly vulnerable to the cold winds of devaluation'.
All other things being equal, therefore, capitalists are typically
unwilling to invest in such assets 'without protection against the
risk of location specific devaluation'.[12] Manifesting as 'market
failure', this intrinsic unwillingness substantially explains why
historically it typically fell to the state to finance and produce
the assets in question, as Adam Smith went to some lengths to
explain in *The Wealth of Nations*.

There has therefore long been a clear underlying tendency
for asset-manager society to develop in geographically uneven
ways. For all the above reasons, asset managers – and indeed
other private-sector investors in real assets – are inevitably geographically selective, choosing to cherry-pick the 'best' assets in
the 'best' locations while underinvesting in those where financial returns appear to be less reliable and predictable. Indeed,
Graham and Marvin saw this as one of the most important
consequences of splintering urbanism, leading to an inexorable
erosion of the status of infrastructures and the services associated with them as 'quasi-public goods to be consumed by all'.[13]

A revealing analysis of such selectivity in action has been
provided by Matti Siemiatcki, in a study of around 1,000 urban
transportation public–private partnerships (PPPs) in some seventy
countries. Promoted as a means of expanding geographies of

---

12   D. Harvey, *The Limits to Capital* (Oxford: Blackwell, 1982), pp. 409,
378.

13   Graham and Marvin, *Splintering Urbanism*, p. 102.

infrastructural provision to underserviced locations against a background of historically uneven patterns of state-financed infrastructure investment, PPPs, at least in the transportation sector, have in fact done nothing of the sort, tending instead to reinforce or even exacerbate existing spatial inequalities of provision. Urban transportation PPPs came to be 'concentrated in the largest and wealthiest cities in a small number of countries'. Siemiatcki found this outcome easy to explain: different projects proposed by governments had widely varying levels of attractiveness to private investors, and investors had, 'unsurprisingly, selected the most profitable projects with the lowest risks'.[14]

This geographical political economy, then, helps to account in more substantive and analytical fashion for the state practices of asset 'de-risking' that first appeared in our discussion in Chapter 2. All real assets are vulnerable to the 'location specific devaluation' described by Harvey, some being much more vulnerable than others, and hence governments have in many cases stepped in to alleviate the risks that private investors – among which asset managers are increasingly prominent – refuse to take on.

Building on the work of Graham and Marvin, other scholars have explained just how profound a transformation of the built environment this de-risking entails. In essence, core physical frameworks of social life continue to be reconfigured *specifically to generate dependable financial returns for investors*. Phillip O'Neill, for example, has highlighted the 'key truth' that 'the private infrastructure investor seeks an urban configuration through which the infrastructure investment can become profitable'; hence, local-government policy becomes, in the words of Peter O'Brien and colleagues, a matter of 'translating urban infrastructure into assets matching the needs of institutional investors globally'.[15] The only certainty in all of this is that,

---

14 M. Siemiatycki, 'Urban Transportation Public–Private Partnerships: Drivers of Uneven Development?', *Environment and Planning A* 43 (2011), pp. 1707, 1720.

15 Respectively: P. O'Neill, 'The Financialisation of Urban Infrastructure: A Framework of Analysis', *Urban Studies* 56 (2019), p. 1321; O'Brien, O'Neill and Pike, 'Funding, Financing and Governing', p. 1293.

whatever lengths governments go to in order to de-risk real-asset investment opportunities, the retort from the private sector will always be that they need to go further. 'The constraining factor around infrastructure investment', one UK-based adviser to the institutional-investment community claimed in 2016, after years of aggressive de-risking by the UK government, 'is not institutional investor willingness to invest, but rather a lack of appropriate, well-structured projects.'[16]

Michael Pryke and John Allen have examined a notable and instructive example of real assets that might otherwise have been considered too risky, being structured specifically with a view to rendering them investible by finance capital. It is an example we encountered already: the Carlsbad desalination plant in Southern California (see Chapter 1). The original owner of the plant, before it was sold to Aberdeen Standard Investments in 2019, was a joint-venture vehicle established by two of the world's leading infrastructure asset managers, Brookfield Asset Management and Stonepeak Infrastructure Partners, which financed the investment with a combination of equity raised principally from limited partners, and securitised debt. A Water Purchase Agreement was signed with the San Diego County Water Authority in 2012, under which the authority agreed to purchase a stated volume of water at a set unit price over a thirty-year period, 'regardless of whether the water [was] needed or not by the residents of San Diego'.[17]

What particularly intrigued Pryke and Allen was how that unit price of water was set. It turned out that it was based not on the market for water so much as on the market for money, being 'structured financially by Stonepeak to meet the projected equity return and bond interest rates over the lifetime of the project'. In other words, Carlsbad 'was "engineered" to meet the future financial yields of equity and bond investors across the globe': over half the contracted household water price

16   Cited in A. Mooney, 'Pension Funds Looking for Infrastructure Investments', *Financial Times*, 9 February 2016.

17   M. Pryke and J. Allen, 'Financialising Urban Water Infrastructure: Extracting Local Value, Distributing Value Globally', *Urban Studies* 56 (2019), p. 1340.

represented investors' capital costs.[18] In asset-manager society, in short, the perceived 'need' to provide investors with predictable, regular income is elevated alongside, and sometimes clearly placed above, the actual need of users for ease and affordability of asset access and use.

As should be clear enough by now, the central concern animating the de-risking impulse is demand risk: that is, the risk that demand for the services associated with a particular physical asset does not meet expectations, and that, as a result, ownership of that asset does not generate the expected level of revenue. In turn, the central mechanism whereby the reconfiguration of real assets to meet investor requirements addresses such demand risk is the incorporation of some kind of revenue guarantee. Our primary examples thus far have been in the US water sector – namely, the minimum annual revenue that Bayonne pledged to KKR and the fixed volumes and unit prices that San Diego pledged to Stonepeak–Brookfield – but the phenomenon is in fact increasingly generalised across the various sectors and territories in which real-asset asset managers invest.

The UK's Private Finance Initiative (PFI), for example, has become notorious for the cast-iron revenue guarantees that it grants to asset managers, thus mitigating all demand risk. As we saw in Chapter 1, PFI projects are structured in such a way as to trigger guaranteed annual 'unitary payments' to the private owner of the PFI contract over the course of the contract life. These payments are made irrespective of the level and nature of actual usage of whatever the physical asset is that the government has procured through the contract – for instance a school, a road or a hospital.

From a different part of the world, consider a particularly striking institutional exemplar: the Macquarie Korea Infrastructure Fund, which the Australian asset manager Macquarie established in 2002 to invest in Korean infrastructural assets. By 2010, the fund had made fourteen concession-based investments, thirteen of which (twelve toll roads and a subway line in Seoul) were operational, and one of which (port facilities in

---

18 Ibid.

Busan) remained in construction. Of these fourteen, all but one (the port) was supported by a minimum-revenue guarantee from the Korean state, with a threshold – that is, the percentage of projected annual concession revenue protected by the guarantee – typically being in the 80–90 per cent range.[19]

Nor, it should be noted, are such revenue protections available only on infrastructure investments. They are increasingly a feature of state-sponsored, private-sector housing investment too – not least in the growing build-to-rent (BTR) market, into which asset managers have recently swarmed like bees to the proverbial honeypot. In 2017, for instance, the Scottish government launched a Rental Income Guarantee Scheme to boost new construction of private rented housing, guaranteeing 50 per cent of any gap between actual and projected rental incomes in order to 'provide greater certainty of rental income to investors and landlords'.[20] One asset manager to have responded to the government's initiative is Edmond de Rothschild Real Estate Investment Management, which in 2021 used its Residential Investment Fund UK to finance the development of 114 BTR apartments in Glasgow.[21] Meanwhile, south of the border, the UK government has made available to BTR investors (including asset managers) valuable 'inverse' forms of revenue guarantee by diluting any requirements – such as to provide affordable housing – that might impinge upon an investor's ability to maximise income.[22]

The costs of de-risking

There are two main significant sets of implications to the de-risking phenomenon, the first of which is relatively obvious, the second rather less so. Firstly, insofar as risk – and especially demand risk – is deflected away from the private-sector investor,

19 Macquarie Group, 'Macquarie Korea Infrastructure Fund: General Presentation', May 2010, pp. 15–16, 28 – copy available from author.

20 'New Scheme to Boost Investment in Housing', 12 October 2017 – at gov.scot.

21 IPE Staff, 'Edmond de Rothschild's UK Fund Buys Scottish BTR project', 8 December 2021 – at realassets.ipe.com.

22 R. Goulding, A. Leaver and J. Silver, 'From Homes to Assets: Transcalar Territorial Networks and the Financialisation of Build to Rent in Greater Manchester', forthcoming in *Environment and Planning A: Economy and Space*.

someone other than that investor ends up paying when things do not go as expected or hoped – which, needless to say, they often do not. Typically, it is the state, and behind the state the taxpayer, that absorbs the real costs of de-risking, which is to say that the risk is *socialized*: when Harvey's 'cold winds of devaluation' cut into real-asset values, it is the public sector that ends up catching a chill.

Those costs should not be underestimated. 'The fiscal costs of demand de-risking can be significant', Daniela Gabor has observed; asset privatisations such as PPPs 'can easily turn into budgetary timebombs'.[23] Gabor herself cited numerous examples of such timebombs. One concerned the Sankofa gas development off the coast of Ghana, a PPP between the Ghanaian government and private-sector investors. Under a 'take or pay' clause in the contract, the publicly owned Ghana National Petroleum Corporation must purchase a predetermined quantity of gas irrespective of whether it is able to use it. In 2019 alone, the government's bill for 'unused gas' was $250 million, the result of a combination of lack of demand and delays in building the infrastructure needed to offtake Sankofa's gas. The contract has become a considerable 'fiscal burden' for the country.[24]

The Ghana example, to be clear, does not in fact involve asset managers: the private-sector investors in the Sankofa contract are both energy companies, in the shape of Italy's Eni and the Dutch Vitol. Nevertheless, countless examples of states de-risking investments made specifically by asset managers, and then subsequently suffering comparable fiscal consequences, can be cited.

To take one among numerous possibilities from the dismal PFI landscape, in 2019 it came to light that one of three custodial suites built and operated for Sussex Police under a thirty-year PFI contract signed in 2001 was no longer being used.[25] But

23   D. Gabor, 'The Wall Street Consensus', *Development and Change* 52: 3 (2021), p. 442. See also N. Hildyard, *Licensed Larceny: Infrastructure, Financial Extraction and the Global South* (Manchester: Manchester University Press, 2016).

24   'Ghana's Sankofa Gas Project – Backed by World Bank – Brings Fiscal Pain', 7 April 2020 – at brettonwoodsproject.org.

25   I. Cipirska, 'The Lost Billions PFI Scandal', 16 October 2019 – at portsmouth.co.uk.

this would have no impact on the level of payments (amounting to over £150 million) that the police force would be required to make over the remaining twelve years of the contract to Infrared Capital Partners, which was the asset manager that owned both the contracting body – Sussex Custodial Services – and, for the term of the contract, the custodial facilities themselves.

Meanwhile, at least one of the investments by Macquarie's Korea Infrastructure Fund (MKIF) mentioned above has seen substantive activation of the minimum-revenue guarantees provided by the Korean state. This involved Metro Line 9, the country's first private metro-rail investment project under a PPP scheme, for which in 2005 a consortium led by MKIF and Hyundai was awarded a thirty-year concession, the first fifteen years of which was supported by a revenue guarantee from the Seoul Metropolitan Government (SMG). In the event, ridership fell well below the projections contained in the agreement, requiring SMG to pay more than $150 million to the investor consortium between 2009 (when the line opened) and 2013, putting SMG finances under significant stress.[26]

The case aroused heated local debate, finally coming to a head when MKIF tried to push through a plan to raise fares by nearly 50 per cent. SMG baulked; MKIF filed suit in a local court; and, in May 2013, the court ruled in SMG's favour. This prompted both MKIF and Hyundai to sell their stakes, for a combined sum of around $700 million, in October of that year, thereby earning a healthy profit on their eight-year investment. For its part, SMG, furious that the likes of MKIF had been (in the words of a *Korea Times* reporter) 'gaining excessive profits without any risks', called time on the incorporation of revenue guarantees in any concessions that it might grant in future.[27]

A more widely reported example is that of the long-term parking concessions granted by the City of Chicago in the 2000s. In 2006, the asset manager Morgan Stanley Infrastructure Partners (MSIP) paid $563 million for a ninety-nine-year concession

26 J. Lu, J. Chao and J. Sheppard, 'Government Guarantees for Mobilizing Private Investment in Infrastructure', 2019, p. 33 – at ppp.worldbank.org.

27 N. Hyun-woo, 'Macquarie Pulls Out of Subway Business', *Korea Times*, 24 October 2013.

to run the city's underground parking garages. Two years later, the city signed a seventy-five-year concession to its 36,000-strong street-parking meter system, for which an investor consortium led by MSIP (with a 50.01 per cent stake) paid $1.15 billion. Under both deals, the bulk of the risk was absorbed by the city, with all manner of clauses inserted in the concession contracts to protect the 'interests' of the investors. Among the most significant were 'adverse action' and non-compete clauses. I will consider the former as they applied to the parking-meter concession and the latter in relation to the garages concession, although in reality both types of clauses were included in both agreements.

Under the parking-meter deal, the city would be liable to pay so-called true-up penalties to MSIP and its partners in the event of 'adverse actions' such as the temporary removal of any parking meters from service – due to street closures, for example. It turned out that adverse actions – as defined by the contract – were commonplace. In 2012 alone, Stephanie Farmer has reported, the investor consortium charged the city $61 million in true-up revenue for the use of parking spots by non-paying (for example, disabled) motorists, and for street closures due to construction works, festivals and other events. This total penalty, remarkably, was nearly three times the annual sum ($22 million) that the city had earned from the meter system just six years earlier – when it was still in public ownership. In other words, from the city's perspective, the concession deal had in one fell swoop transformed the meter system from 'a revenue-generating source ... into an annual budgetary expenditure'.[28]

Meanwhile, under the garages deal, a non-compete clause obliged the city to protect the monopoly rights and market share of MSIP by not permitting the opening of new parking facilities within wide areas around the garages covered by the concession; the clause allowed MSIP to extract compensation from the city if it did grant such permission. Just three years after the award of the concession, in 2009, the city council approved a parking garage just one block from one of the concessioned lots.

28 S. Farmer, 'Cities as Risk Managers: The Impact of Chicago's Parking Meter P3 on Municipal Governance and Transportation Planning', *Environment and Planning A* 46 (2014), p. 2168.

Unsurprisingly, MSIP sued. The case went to an independent arbitrator, who in 2013 ruled that the city had breached the contract and would have to pay up. The city's lawyers tried to fight the decision – suing in county then state court to overturn the arbitrator's ruling – but failed. In 2015, by which time Morgan Stanley had sold the concession to a consortium of new financial investors, the city settled, at a cost of more than $62 million. The words of Justice James R. Epstein of the Illinois Appellate Court are worth noting. The court could not side with the city, he ruled, 'irrespective of the unfortunate impact upon taxpayers'.[29]

The cases of Sussex, Seoul and Chicago (not to mention Bayonne and Carlsbad) are important and instructive for any number of reasons. Perhaps their greatest significance in relation to our understanding of the political economy of real-asset investment, however, is to encourage us to bury one of the most pervasive and pernicious myths about asset managers, and indeed other major investors in 'alternative' assets. This is the widespread belief that, collectively, such investors represent a prototypical form of 'risk capital', deserving large rewards specifically for taking on large risks that other investors are unwilling to bear. We need to abandon this myth because the de-risking widely implemented by governments in order to render real assets investible by such actors makes a mockery of the very idea.

Clearly, there is risk involved when asset managers invest in real assets, but states tend systematically to arrogate that risk to *themselves* when configuring such assets to appeal to the investors in question. The reality is that asset managers actively resist the assumption of risk. Interestingly, none does so more vigorously than what is perhaps the most storied 'risk capitalist' of them all: Blackstone. In his memoirs, the firm's long-time chief executive, Stephen Schwarzman, writes repeatedly about his aversion to risk, providing numerous examples of how the firm avoids it and, in the process, rolls that risk over to others.[30] Third parties have corroborated such aversion. Describing the

29 D. Mihalopoulos, 'City Hall's $62 Million Blunder', *Chicago Sun-Times*, 22 May 2015.

30 S. Schwarzman, *What It Takes: Lessons in the Pursuit of Excellence* (New York: Simon & Schuster, 2019).

dictum that 'one must risk money to make money' as the 'rudi-mentary rule of investing', David Carey and John Morris, in their book about Blackstone, cited a former partner of the firm as saying that Schwarzman 'had a hard time coping with' that rule. For such a successful investor, Schwarzman's risk aversion, the source said, 'was really extraordinary'.[31] But what we have seen here is that such aversion is in fact not extraordinary at all. Aversion to and avoidance of risk by asset managers is embed-ded in the very institutional landscape of real-asset investment.[32]

The second important set of implications of asset de-risking is less directly financial, and more to do with governments' freedom of movement to plan and shape the built environment in an orderly, coherent and socially beneficial fashion. Config-uring assets such as transportation networks or energy systems in such a way as to ensure a steady flow of income for private investors is always a matter of physical as well as financial re-arrangement. These are, after all, *real* assets, and their ability to generate cash predictably can depend on all manner of physical manipulations, from restricting rights of way over the land used by solar farms or wind parks to controlling access to tolled bridges or roads. The physical manipulations required to render 'bankable' a particular asset in a particular geographical location can potentially be as impactful for the state's ongoing planning capacity as the financial manipulations discussed above often are for its ongoing fiscal capacity. This is a distinct but often no less significant 'cost'.

The geographer Phillip O'Neill has observed that this is espe-cially true in dense urban landscapes, which is where joined-up state planning of the built environment is arguably most important, and which is certainly where most asset-manager investment in real assets tends to be concentrated. O'Neill cites Allen Scott and Michael Storper's vivid conceptualisation of

31 D. Carey and J. E. Morris, *King of Capital: The Remarkable Rise, Fall, and Rise Again of Steve Schwarzman and Blackstone* (New York: Crown Business, 2010), pp. 70–1.

32 For more on this, see B. Christophers, 'The Risk Myth: Blackstone, Housing, and Rentier Capitalism', in M. Hyötyläinen and R. Beauregard, eds, *The Political Economy of Land: Rent, Financialization and Resistance* (New York: Routledge, 2022).

cities as 'complex congeries of human activities', and argues that isolating a particular urban infrastructural item such as a parking garage, apartment block or tunnel as an economically discrete investment asset – which Graham and Marvin would no doubt regard as a quintessential act of urban 'splintering' – is itself always also 'a pivotal act of urban planning'.[33] The reason for this is that housing and assorted infrastructure networks variously frame and facilitate the myriad 'daily flows and rhythms' that constitute urban social life. Thus, to manipulate the former in any substantive way is inevitably also to shape the latter: that is, it is to govern and plan those flows and rhythms.

O'Neill writes: 'Negotiating private finance into urban infrastructure is necessarily a negotiation of what flows will be invested in and propagated and what flows are minimised or shut down.' Crucially, this negotiation has enduring, knock-on effects, because it will of course 'impact on spatial organisation and governance for long time periods'.[34] If privatisation of, say, a road-bridge represents an overt act of planning in the present, it also shapes what the state can hope to achieve by way of planning in the future. It opens up some opportunities while constraining others.

With its infrastructure concessions, Chicago represents an illuminating example of this. Farmer has demonstrated that the parking-meter deal, in particular, substantially diminished local state capacity for effective planning. As she says, parking meters are 'but one component of Chicago's interconnected street-level transportation network'.[35] Such interconnectivity means that binding contractual arrangements and obligations relating to one network component (the parking-meter system) cannot but have implications for what can and cannot be planned for, and achieved through, other components. The key limiting factor in the Chicago parking-meter case, Farmer suggests, has been the true-up penalties mentioned above, which must be paid to MSIP and its investment partners if existing meters are removed from the system and replacements of equal value are not provided elsewhere.

---

33 O'Neill, 'Financialisation of Urban Infrastructure', p. 1321.

34 Ibid.

35 Farmer, 'Cities as Risk Managers', p. 2168.

Consider the impact on bus rapid transit (BRT), which the Chicago Transit Authority first introduced in 2012, with an eventual target of twenty routes. The city's BRT systems use dedicated traffic lanes designed for curb-side boarding. But BRT planners, Farmer found, had to take 'great pains' to avoid true-up penalties. For example, planning the first two routes required finding comparable replacement parking spaces for 116 existing spaces that needed to be removed. Meanwhile, another way in which the concession contract created headaches for BRT planners was by reducing their flexibility 'to realign routes even temporarily for rush hour, such as temporarily removing a lane of parking in order to create a dedicated bus lane during rush hour to speed the flow of traffic'. All told, 'concerns for efficient traffic management' with respect to bus transit repeatedly had to be sacrificed to 'protecting MSIP from demand and revenue risk'.[36]

The parking-meter concession likewise hampered planning of the city's growing network of bicycle lanes. Planners needed to find comparable replacement parking spaces for those that had to be removed from the system in order to avoid blindspots where car drivers could not see approaching cyclists. The removal of meters and the identification of replacement locations was similarly necessitated by the city's determination to provide on-street bicycle 'corrals', in which cyclists could park their bikes (designed not just to make cycling more convenient, but to protect pavement space for pedestrians). 'If we didn't have this [parking meter] deal, they could remove the parking meter space and get it done today', a bike-network planner told Farmer. 'It is so easy to accomplish this but our hands are tied.'[37]

More generally, the parking-meter concession motivated street-management planning decisions that increasingly went against the public interest. For one thing, the recurring need to take existing parking spaces out of the system for one reason or another led the city to create a bank of replacement meters that could be called upon when required. It did this by converting curb-side spaces zoned for other uses, including for instance loading zones in front of then-vacant storefronts – 'despite

36 Ibid., p. 2169.
37 Ibid., p. 2170.

the fact that the storefront may be rented out in the future'.[38] Furthermore, on some streets with parking meters, the city removed an existing ban on rush-hour parking that was designed to speed up rush-hour traffic.

In short, Farmer concluded, the deal with Morgan Stanley created a local state that, in the short, medium and long term, was substantially hamstrung in its ability to plan for a liveable city. This was primarily because 'strong risk protections for the concessionaire resulted in a loss of autonomy over the public right of way'. By dint of that loss of autonomy and of the stipulations contained in the concession contract, Chicago's transportation-planning policies were gradually but perceptibly 'remade to serve financial investors' exchange values rather than prioritizing social use values'. Or, as one planner pithily put it: 'the city gave up the freedom of future management options'.[39]

Financialisation?

Asset managers invest in housing and other infrastructural assets to make money for their external investor partners and for themselves. Granted, there are, as we saw in Chapter 2, a series of rationales specifically for real-asset investment that are peculiar to this asset class, including its perceived capacity to provide a hedge against inflation, and the fact that returns are not necessarily correlated with returns on equities and bonds. Nevertheless, the principal reason for asset managers to invest in real assets is the exact same reason that they invest in any other type of asset – to generate investment returns for their clients.

In fact, generating investment returns is an even stronger motivation in alternative asset management than it is in the asset management business more generally. The explanation for this has to do with fee structures and business models. In the 'mainstream' asset-management business of investment in cash, bonds and public equities, performance-based fees generally play only

---

38 Ibid.
39 Ibid., pp. 2168, 2170.

a limited role. Either there are no such fees at all, as for instance in the case of index-tracking funds, which have become increasingly dominant in recent times, or the fees tend to be relatively low. Instead, the mainstream asset manager's remuneration consists largely of management fees, which are based not on the performance of investments, but typically on the amount of capital that has been committed by the client.

Of course, a mainstream asset manager does nonetheless care about investment performance: if returns consistently underperform, clients will ultimately take their money elsewhere, and management fees will suffer. But an alternative asset manager cares about investment performance in a much more immediate and fundamental sense. This is because performance fees represent a far more significant element of an alternative asset manager's business model, and – assuming the model's successful implementation – they account correspondingly for a far greater proportion of such a manager's overall revenues. Whereas the likes of BlackRock, State Street and Vanguard – the 'Big Three' index-fund managers – are predominantly passive investors, rarely charging performance fees, unlisted real-asset funds (together with hedge funds and private-equity funds) are all actively managed, and substantial performance fees are invariably charged.

Compare, by way of illustration, BlackRock and Blackstone. At BlackRock, for which alternatives represented at the time less than 3 per cent of assets under management, performance fees generated only 3 per cent of revenues in 2019.[40] At Blackstone, for which alternatives represented 100 per cent of assets under management, performance fees generated fully 40 per cent of revenues in the same year.[41] Both are asset managers, but in reality they mostly operate in different businesses.

All of which is to say that, for the companies whose businesses we are primarily concerned with – the Blackstones, Brookfields and Macquaries – investment performance is paramount, as

40   BlackRock, Inc., *Annual Report for the Fiscal Year Ended December 31, 2019*, pp. 2, 20.

41   Blackstone Group Inc., *Annual Report for the Fiscal Year Ended December 31, 2019*, p. 142.

indeed it also is, of course, for BlackRock's own (proportionately small) real-assets arm. Maximising returns on investment is the absolute *sine qua non*. Whatever aspect of asset managers' real-asset investment operations one might hold up for consideration, this ineluctable commercial imperative should never be far from one's mind: asset managers hold real assets in order to make profits from them.

As asset managers' ownership of housing and various other indispensable infrastructures has expanded in recent years, and especially since the financial crisis, criticism of such ownership, perhaps unsurprisingly, has mounted. Loosely grouped together under the umbrella term of 'financialisation' (there are now bur-geoning scholarly sub-literatures on financialisation in relation to both housing and infrastructure), the gist of these critiques has been that alternative asset managers' naked profit-maximisation agenda is ill-suited to the stewardship of physical systems that play such obviously important functions in social life and the processes of its reproduction.

The specific charge that is made against asset managers and other financial institutions is that they represent financialised owner-operators of real assets. For example, in the paradigmatic case of housing, the planning scholar Martine August has cate-gorised 'real estate investment trusts, private equity funds, asset management companies, and pension funds' as 'financialized landlords', thereby differentiating these financial institutions from what she calls 'non-financialized' corporate landlords.[42] 'Financialized landlord' is an increasingly commonplace label in the critical literature on financial-institutional investment in residential property.[43]

What do August and others mean when they say that asset managers and other financial institutions that invest in real assets are financialised actors? The literature contains both relatively

---

42 M. August, 'The Financialization of Canadian Multi-Family Rental Housing: From Trailer to Tower', *Journal of Urban Affairs* 42 (2020), p. 976.

43 Among other examples, see R. Rolnik, *Urban Warfare: Housing Under the Empire of Finance* (London: Verso, 2019); A. Walks and S. Soederberg, 'The New Urban Displacements? Finance-Led Capitalism, Austerity, and Rental Housing Dynamics', *Urban Geography* 42 (2021), pp. 571–82.

loose and more conceptually precise definitions. In attacking financialised landlords for running their businesses on the basis of 'financial logics, metrics, and priorities', August's own critique is an example of the former.[44] 'Financialized landlords', she says, 'extract needlessly high rents, systematically transferring income from working people to wealthy fund managers and investors.'[45]

The more precise definition is that a financialised owner-operator treats housing or infrastructure *like a financial asset*, thus 'financialising' it, too. But what exactly does treating a house or item of infrastructure 'like' a financial asset entail? Here, the venerable political-economic categories of exchange value and use value come into play. The uniqueness of financial assets as such is that they have only exchange value, and no use value. Hence, to financialise (or treat as financial) a non-financial asset is to deny or disregard its use value – a house's value as shelter, for instance – by wholly subordinating such value to the asset's value-in-exchange. In practice, critics argue, this means that asset managers and other 'financialised' owner-operators come to treat housing and infrastructure as 'just another asset class' – which is to say, precisely akin to actual financial assets such as stocks or bonds. This claim has been explicitly made for both built real-estate and farmland, for example.[46]

As a critique of asset managers and their growing real-asset holdings, however, 'financialisation' (at least conceptualised thus) is ultimately wrongheaded, and altogether too blunt. This is not because asset managers do not prioritise exchange value or are not single-minded profit-maximisers: they very clearly do, and

44   August, 'Financialization of Canadian Multi-Family Rental Housing', p. 990.

45   M. August, 'The Big Debate: Can Landlords Afford to Forgive Rent During the Pandemic?', 28 April 2020 – at thestar.com.

46   See, respectively, J. Van Loon and M. Aalbers, 'How Real Estate Became "Just Another Asset Class": The Financialization of the Investment Strategies of Dutch Institutional Investors', *European Planning Studies* 25: 2 (2017), pp. 221–40; M. Fairbairn, '"Just Another Asset Class"?: Neoliberalism, Finance, and the Construction of Farmland Investment', in S. Wolf and A. Bonanno, eds, *The Neoliberal Regime in the Agri-Food Sector* (New York: Routledge, 2014), pp. 257–74.

are. Nor is it to imply that such profit maximisation is not ill-suited to the sphere of social reproduction; it certainly is. As the UN's rapporteurs scolded Blackstone (see Chapter 3), and as Daniela Gabor and Sebastian Kohl have recently argued, it is extremely hard to regard the 'mandates and risk/return requirements' of institutional investors and their asset managers as being compatible with 'the delivery of housing as a human right'.[47] Rather, the critique of 'financialisation' is a non-starter for our purposes because of the ill-founded distinction that it draws between asset managers (and other financial institutions) on the one hand and other private-sector real-asset owners on the other.

To assert that what is particular about so-called 'financialised landlords' is their privileging of 'financial logics, metrics, and priorities' and their attendant extraction of 'needlessly high rents' is, by definition, to suggest that other, ostensibly 'non-financialised' landlords are *not* financially motivated, profit-seeking actors with broadly the same inclination to treat housing as a financial asset, and thereby seek to maximise rental income. But property companies like Germany's Vonovia, the world's largest owner of residential property, are hardly charities – they, too, are capitalist institutions, red in tooth and claw. Indeed, for all the warm-and-fuzzy mythology invested in the hoary figure of the small-time 'mom-and-pop landlord', there is no compelling a priori reason to suppose that such a landlord is any less focused on profit maximisation than Vonovia, or an asset manager such as Blackstone. If being a 'financialised landlord' truly involves observing financial logics and chasing exchange value, what non-charitable, non-philanthropic, non-state landlord is not financialised?

Insofar as our interest in this book is in examining the specific implications of asset managers being the owners of housing and other vital infrastructures of social reproduction, we need to think more carefully about what, if anything, meaningfully distinguishes asset managers from other types of private owner of such assets. After all, plenty has previously been written from a critical perspective about the privatisation of infrastructure and housing, and about why it matters if such assets are owned

47 D. Gabor and S. Kohl, 'My Home Is an Asset Class: The Financialization of Housing in Europe', January 2022, p. 73 – at greens-efa.eu.

privately rather than publicly. The very last thing we need is yet another vanilla critique of housing or infrastructure privatisation per se. None of what has been said in the preceding paragraphs is intended to suggest that no meaningful differences exist between ownership by asset managers and other types of private ownership. But, to the extent that such a difference does exist, the prioritisation and application of 'financial', profit-maximising logics surely cannot be it.

On the Lives of Real-Asset Funds

The KKR investment with which I opened this chapter saw the US asset manager acquire a forty-year concession to run the municipal waterworks of Bayonne, New Jersey, only to sell out a little over five years later. Having been applauded for its 'long-term vision' upon making the investment – forty years is indeed a long time – the firm was widely criticised for taking the money and running upon exiting, seemingly prematurely, with a significant profit. Yet the reality is that, once invested, KKR did not have much of a choice. Strictly speaking, it, or at least the fund it had used to make the investment, *could* not hold the Bayonne concession for the duration.

That fund was KKR's first dedicated infrastructure vehicle – namely, KKR Global Infrastructure Investors I, which was formed in 2011 with approximately $1 billion in limited-partner commitments. This was a closed-end fund, meaning that it had a limited lifespan (ten years), and that all assets in which the fund invested would have to be sold prior to the fund being wound up and its proceeds being shared between the fund partners. In other words, whether the managers of the fund wanted to hold onto the Bayonne concession was neither here nor there. Sale within a matter of years was preordained.[48] All that was uncertain was when exactly it would take place, to whom and at what price.[49]

48 Sometimes the life of closed-end funds is extended by one or two years, thus lengthening the period during which assets can be held and options for their disposal explored.

49 Of course, KKR could have held on to the asset by using another of

On the face of it, it is perplexing that asset managers such as KKR should invest in physical systems like infrastructure and housing using fixed-term, closed-end funds. Infrastructure and housing are primary examples of what are referred to by investors as 'long-dated' assets, where it is known that revenue streams will predictably recur until well into the future (forty years in the case of the Bayonne concession), and perhaps even in perpetuity. Not only that, but this particular temporal characteristic is repeatedly cited precisely as one of the main reasons why institutional investors such as pension schemes and insurance companies seek exposure to real-asset investments in the first place (see Chapter 2). That is, they want to hold assets with a maturity profile to match that of their main (long-term) liabilities.

The paradox appears stark. If investors are genuinely investing in assets like real estate and infrastructure for the long term, why would they do so via asset-management vehicles that not only encourage but necessitate liquidation in the short, or at most medium term? Or, as Zak Bentley has put it, perhaps rhetorically: 'are relatively short-term [closed-end fund] structures really the best way to maximise investments in long-dated assets?' The question seems an obvious one to ask. 'Why', wondered one fund manager whom Bentley consulted, 'would you structure something where you've got a limited-life exposure to an asset class that is long-life or perpetual in nature?'[50]

Given this seemingly incongruous scheme of things, it may be helpful to understand how and why it originally came about. Perhaps the keyword in this respect is *familiarity*. When alternative asset managers set about establishing real-estate and infrastructure funds in the 1990s and 2000s, and began reaching out to their existing institutional-investor clients to secure capital commitments to these new funds, they wanted it to appear much

its funds to acquire it when the KKR Global Infrastructure Investors I vehicle sold out. Such intra-group, inter-fund transactions do happen, but they are very rare, not least because they raise extremely complex – and potentially highly conflictual – issues around transfer pricing, with the limited partners in the respective funds having diametrically opposed interests on this score.

50   Z. Bentley, 'Is It Time to Take a Closer Look at Long-Term Funds?', 2 April 2020 – at infrastructureinvestor.com.

like business-as-usual rather than as a step into the unknown – a smooth rather than abrupt transition. What they principally offered their clients at that time was private-equity investment, and hence private equity – with its distinctive closed-end fund structures and 'two and twenty' fee structure (see Chapter 1) – became the default model.

The distinctive fund and fee structures of private equity were what their clients were familiar with. One veteran of the early era of infrastructure asset management explained the logic in the following terms: 'We tried to make our fund structure as much like private equity as possible, in order to minimise any obstacles to prospective investors.' Another confirmed: 'You're already trying to do something new, which is raise a first-time fund. Do you make it even more complex and introduce a different structure than people are used to? You probably don't.'[51]

Interestingly, some institutional investors baulked: it simply did not make sense to them to invest in infrastructure (and real estate) via short-term, closed-end funds, if long-term returns were what they were looking for. Foremost among these naysayers were the big Canadian pension schemes mentioned in Chapter 2, such as the Canada Pension Plan Investment Board and the Ontario Municipal Employees Retirement System. As we saw in that chapter, these funds are famous for having pioneered direct infrastructure investing (the so-called 'Canadian Model'), effectively cutting out the asset-manager intermediary. The overwhelming dominance of closed-end structures among the new infrastructure funds being launched by asset managers in the 2000s played a significant role in the Canadians' strategic thinking.[52] 'One of the reasons Canadians became direct investors', Thierry Déau of the French asset manager Meridiam Infrastructure, has observed, 'is because they couldn't find long-term funds', and long-term investment was explicitly their objective.[53]

---

51   Cited in ibid.

52   M. Torrance, 'The Power of Governance in Financial Relationships: Governing Tensions in Exotic Infrastructure Territory', *Growth and Change* 38 (2007), p. 682.

53   Cited in Bentley, 'Is It Time to Take a Closer Look?'.

Nevertheless, the Canadians were very much in the minority in electing to invest principally directly. As they moved into real estate and infrastructure, most institutional investors accommodated asset managers' familiar closed-end model, however incongruous it may have seemed in this new, unfamiliar context.

Notably, asset managers investing widely in infrastructure and housing have in more recent years increasingly talked about a change of approach. When one reads the contemporary financial or trade press, one cannot fail to come across examples of asset managers extolling newly launched open-ended real-estate or infrastructure funds that are more explicitly suited to the realisation of long-term investment goals. These funds, with no set lifespan, are typically referred to as 'permanent' or 'perpetual' capital vehicles, and tend to be associated with the enactment of so-called 'core' as opposed to 'opportunistic' investment strategies (see Chapter 1). Their introduction represents, at least in part, a response from the real-asset asset-management sector to the charge that fixed-term closed-end funds reflect and reinforce a short-termist, even mercenary investment mentality.

Consider, for instance, the following fine words from 2021, spoken by one manager of a large open-ended infrastructure fund:

> The power of our permanent capital model is that we can think about things like a strategic rather than a financial investor. What that allows us to do is to stick with high-conviction themes and to really think about what a business could become in 10, 15, 20 years from now versus just what will it be over the next three-to-five years. That's just a very different mindset and a very different lens.[54]

The manager in this case happened to be Sean Klimczak, global head of infrastructure at Blackstone. But, with its evocation of a different, strategic, long-term mindset, it could just as well have been someone from any number of other asset-management firms that have latterly joined the 'permanent capital' bandwagon.

---

54   Z. Bentley and B. Alves, 'Blackstone: "Permanent Capital Allows Us to Think Like a Strategic"', 1 September 2021 – at infrastructureinvestor.com.

To sound a note of scepticism here is certainly not to suggest that such permanent-capital vehicles do not now exist. They do, and many of them are very substantial. In early 2018, for instance, Blackstone itself began raising capital for its first permanent-capital infrastructure fund, Blackstone Infrastructure Partners, and by mid 2019 had attracted some $14 billion from around eighty investors. By late 2022, total commitments to the fund had swelled to $31 billion.

Nonetheless, across the wider landscape of infrastructure and housing investment by asset managers, the reality is that fixed-term, closed-end fund structures remain the norm. Of the 1,720 unlisted funds investing exclusively or principally in residential property that were active globally in 2021, for example, a mere 163 (9 per cent of the total) were open-ended vehicles.[55] Meanwhile, using Preqin data, Aleksandar Andonov and colleagues have identified 5,649 institutional-investor commitments to unlisted infrastructure funds between 1990 and 2020, the vast majority of which occurred after 2007. Of these commitments, 92 per cent (5,189) were to closed- rather than open-ended funds, with the number of separate funds to which those commitments were made totalling 538 (closed) and 46 (open). Conscious that the ratio of numbers of commitments might not reflect the ratio of dollar amounts committed, the authors of the study in question attempted to analyse the latter as well. This proved impossible for private institutional investors (for which available data on dollar commitments were 'sparsely populated'), but broadly doable for US and UK public investors, for which the relevant data were 'nearly complete'. For US public investors, the value of total commitments to closed-end infrastructure funds was approximately eight times that committed to open-ended funds ($77 billion versus $10 billion). For UK public investors, the ratio was eighteen times ($18 billion versus $1 billion).[56]

---

55 Gabor and Kohl, 'My Home Is an Asset Class: The Financialization of Housing in Europe', 2021, pre-publication version.

56 A. Andonov, R. Kräussl and J. Rauh, 'Institutional Investors and Infrastructure Investing: Internet Appendix', 20 April 2021, p. 3 – at oup.com.

Identifying why fixed-term, closed-end funds remain dominant in infrastructure and residential real estate is harder than
identifying the fact of such ongoing dominance. One might have
expected open-ended funds to have made greater inroads by now:
as well as better matching asset and liability maturity for investors, they typically charge lower fees than closed-end funds. A
number of factors seem to be in play in sustaining the hegemony
of the closed-end model.[57] Whereas there are well-established
mechanisms for the calculation of performance fees on such
funds (i.e., carried interest based on realised gains), mechanisms
for calculating performance fees on open-ended funds tend to
be more variable (usually based on net-asset value estimations),
and often more opaque. This unsettles some investors, and can
also make it difficult for asset managers to attract and retain
experienced staff.

Furthermore, given that asset managers typically have relatively high staff turnover, investors can sometimes be reluctant to
commit capital for the long term, since the likelihood of the team
originally entrusted with their capital still being in place will progressively decline as the months and years go by. Indeed, this is
one reason why some institutional investors actually prohibit the
allocation of capital to alternative-asset funds without a fixed
duration. Last but not least, even the most long-term-oriented
investors may on occasion need to access their capital, and it is
not always straightforward to exit from open-ended real-estate
or infrastructure funds, even after initial lock-up periods have
expired. Liquidity is usually generated not by selling assets, but
by attracting capital from new investors to replace that of those
who are exiting, and this process (and the price at which such
new capital can be raised) is notoriously sensitive to market
conditions.

But whatever the exact reason may be, the key point is that
real-asset investment by asset managers continues to occur
principally through the closed-end-fund model. As a result,
short-termism is utterly institutionalised: even before buying an
asset, the manager of a closed-end fund knows that the asset will

57 Probitas Partners, 'Infrastructure Investing: The Closed-End Fund
Market', March 2018, p. 15.

have to be sold in a few years' time; and the longer the asset is held, the more the knowledge of the necessity of impending disposal burns into the manager's consciousness, inevitably shaping everything about how that asset is handled – the aggressiveness with which revenues are generated from it, and the care with which monies are invested in its operation, maintenance and renewal. And of course, just because asset managers *can* hold assets for the long term in open-end funds, it does not mean that they always do. It is quite possible for the open-end fund structure to serve as cover, so to speak, for an investment strategy that is just as short-termist as that which is characteristic of closed-end funds. The difference is simply that, while the former fund structure merely permits short-termism (inasmuch as it does not preclude it), the latter fund structure compels short-termism.

This, then, is what is distinctive about the ownership of housing and other crucial infrastructures by asset managers. Unlike most other private-sector owners, the manager of a closed-end real-asset fund is – must be – singularly focused, both strategically and financially, on maximising the value of portfolio assets less to existing shareholders than to prospective buyers of those assets. As soon as an asset is acquired, the overriding concern necessarily becomes: How can the asset best be readied for profitable sale? No sooner is the asset manager 'in' than she is explicitly planning her escape.

A World of Asset Churn

The implications of all this are legion. The real-asset asset-management landscape is characterised by intense churn, as managers buy residential or infrastructural assets of various sorts only to put them in the shop window and sell them on just a handful of years later – often to other asset managers, who then recommence the same cycle.

I touched on a striking example of this ceaseless churn in Chapter 2, specifically in the care-home sector. It concerned the Four Seasons care-home chain in the UK. Founded by the Scottish entrepreneur Robert Kilgour in 1988, Four Seasons remained a relatively small-scale, low-key operation until the late 1990s. But in 1999 this changed irrevocably. In that year, the chain, with thirty-six homes, was bought by the asset manager Alchemy Partners. Five years later, Alchemy sold the chain, by now the UK's largest privately owned operator, with some 300 care homes and approximately 14,600 beds, to another asset manager, Allianz Capital Partners. But Allianz remained invested for even less time than Alchemy: in 2006, after just two years of ownership, it sold Four Seasons (further expanded to 415 care homes and 19,000 beds) to a third asset manager, the Qatar-backed Three Delta.

It was then that serious financial trouble first struck: Three Delta had funded the deal mainly with debt, and mounting difficulties with making interest payments saw the business taken over by its creditors in 2009. But that was by no means the end of the story, least of all in terms of the involvement of asset managers. In 2012, having stabilised the business, Four Seasons' creditors sold it to yet another (fourth) asset manager, Terra Firma, in yet another highly leveraged deal. Once again, however, the deal ended in failure. Increasingly struggling in the mid 2010s with rising costs and cuts to local-authority care fees, Four Seasons began selling off homes – but even this was not enough to prevent another debt default, and in 2017 Terra Firma ceded control to one of the business's main creditors. This creditor was H/2 Capital Partners – a US-based asset manager, and thus the fifth to have controlled the business in less than two decades. In 2019, Four Seasons entered administration. Now holding fewer than 200 care homes, it remains in administration at the time of writing. The story of Four Seasons is a story of the recurrence of short-term asset-manager opportunism.

A different but no less revealing example concerns Copenhagen Airport. In 2005, the Australian asset manager Macquarie bought a controlling interest in the airport through one of its listed funds, Macquarie Airports (MAp). In 2008, approximately half of this equity was transferred into a new, ten-year closed-end Macquarie vehicle, its European Infrastructure Fund III (MEIF3); MAp sold its own remaining stake in 2011. By the beginning of 2017, MEIF3, despite its imminent winding-up, remained invested in the airport. With the clock ticking on the fund, however, Macquarie launched a 'strategic review' of its holding in the airport (widely interpreted as a precursor to sale) in May 2017, prompting the Danish government to say that it would 'consider strengthening the regulatory regime to ensure future owners are focused on the long-term nature of the asset'.[58]

In September 2017, MEIF3 did indeed sell its airport holding. Lawmakers were not happy: Macquarie's perceived short-termism, combined with Goldman Sachs' historical investment in the national energy company Ørsted (representing the first stage in that enterprise's privatisation), led three opposition parties two years later to call for a ban on foreign investors owning Danish 'critical infrastructure'. In fact, no such ban materialised, but in 2021 Denmark did introduce a new regulatory regime whereby all foreign investments in critical infrastructure had to undergo prior screening. The irony, of course, was that, at nine years, by alternative asset managers' standards MEIF3's investment in Copenhagen Airport *was* long-term.

A particularly noteworthy historical–geographical locus of churning in real assets by asset managers – and of the displeasure that such churning commonly occasions among those affected – has been the UK's PPP landscape. As we have seen, contracts awarded under the UK's long-running PPP programme, the PFI, have generally been for twenty-five years or more. But that did not stop equity investors in PFI vehicles, led by asset managers such as Amber Infrastructure, Innisfree, Infrared Capital Partners and Semperian PPP Investment Partners, developing from the early 2000s a lively secondary market in which controlling interests in those vehicles could be actively traded – largely between asset managers. Twenty-five years is, after all, far beyond the standard investment horizon of such firms and their closed-end-fund managers.

One study found that as many as 622 PFI stakes worth a collective £3.88 billion changed hands between 1998 and 2010.[59]

---

58   Z. Bentley, 'MEIF3's Copenhagen Exit Prompts Danish Regulatory Review', 16 June 2017 – at infrastructureinvestor.com.

59   'Secondary Market? It's First for Profit', 7 November 2012 – at infra structureinvestor.com.

In one case, that of the Calderdale Royal Hospital in Halifax, England, equity in the project changed hands no fewer than nine times between 1998 and 2012.[60] As one commentator has recently noted, one of the main reasons that the PPP model has latterly fallen somewhat out of favour in the UK has been precisely the 'frustration among the authorities and the general public with concession owners selling assets midway through their life – and pocketing, according to some perceptions, outsized capital gains in the process'.[61] PFI is much like Copenhagen Airport or Four Seasons, but on a more generalised and institutionalised basis.

What is so instructive about the dynamic of rapid asset churn embedded in the closed-end-fund model is the light it shines on exactly how such funds principally generate investment returns. For all asset managers' and institutional investors' pervasive rhetoric of real assets being an asset class favoured specifically for the stable and predictable income flows they generate, such flows ultimately – and perhaps paradoxically – are not how most housing and infrastructure funds mainly make money. How could they be, if assets are only ever held for a few years (and, in some cases, even just a few months)?

This is not to say that these income flows are unimportant. On the contrary, they are indispensable. But their significance lies less in their substance as actual fund earnings than in the signal that they send to the market. They are, in short, more a means to an end than an end in itself. We will turn to the means in the following section. But the end is clear, and crucial: to maximise the disposal consideration.

The wealth that, say, housing rents or road tolls *directly* create for a closed-end fund manager and its limited partners while the housing or road is under the manager's control is largely incidental. The reality is that the flows of income generated by a portfolio asset create wealth for investors in such a fund primarily *indirectly* – specifically, by persuading third parties that

60   D. Whitfield, 'PPP Wealth Machine: UK and Global Trends in Trading Project Ownership', December 2012, p. 30 – at european-services-strategy. org.uk.

61   Bentley, 'Is It Time to Take a Closer Look?'.

the asset is worth buying, and at a premium price. This reality is structurally rooted in the closed-end model.

The ceaseless churn of assets substantiates this reality. And so also do relevant data. Andonov and his co-authors, for example, expressly asked the question: What principally drives the returns generated by closed-end infrastructure funds – dividend yields or asset sales? The answer was asset sales. Indeed, the utter triviality of yields (i.e., recurring income) qua *yields* was underlined by the authors' analysis of the significance of speed of exit from a fund's investments. They found strong evidence that, the quicker the exit, the more beneficial the impact on fund returns, the positive relation between performance and exit rates being driven mainly by 'relatively quick exits within the first 5 years after the investment date'.[62]

That asset managers often exit investments with what appears to be unseemly haste, long before a fund is due to be wound up, is frequently interpreted as a largely performative phenomenon. As I noted in Chapter 1, funds' internal rates of return (IRRs) are arguably the key metric on which asset managers compete with one another, and earlier asset disposal generates a higher IRR. Thus, by this line of argument, the hegemony of the IRR measure actively shapes investment practices, motivating precisely the kind of rapid asset churn we have been discussing.

Clearly, this performative aspect is significant; it does create a perceived need for speed. But the fascinating and vital element of the study by Andonov and his colleagues is that it found that quicker investment exits were in fact associated with superior fund performance not just on IRR measures, but also according to measures of investment return not influenced by the timing of cash-flows. In other words, for closed-end infrastructure funds, quicker exits *are* return-enhancing.

So much, in short, for the 'long-term stable dividend yields' that real-asset asset managers brazenly invoke. What the evidence both before our eyes and in fund performance data shows is that actually holding the asset – let alone stewarding it – is really not what the business is about. Managers of closed-end

62   A. Andonov, R. Kräussl and J. Rauh, 'Institutional Investors and Infrastructure Investing', *Review of Financial Studies* 34 (2021), pp. 3883, 3902.

funds are essentially glorified traders. Their business is buying (low) and selling (high), and the shorter the gap between the former and latter events, the better. Hence, the guiding strategic maxim for real-asset asset managers can be further clarified thus: get in – and then get out as quickly as possible.

The Golden Rules of Asset-Manager Society

What, then, are the means to the asset manager's end of maximising the disposal consideration when assets – as they typically must be – are sold? What do asset managers do in order to increase prospective sales proceeds in short order? There are three golden rules.

Rules one and two

The first and most obvious rule is simply to maximise revenues. If an asset manager has acquired a piece of farmland or an apartment block or a wind farm, it will always endeavour to capture as much revenue as possible, and as soon as possible: all other things being equal, the more cash an asset generates, the greater its market value will be. Thus, whether it is the municipal waterworks in Bayonne, New Jersey or the Metro Line 9 subway in Seoul, the asset manager's imperative is, where possible, to swiftly increase rates.

Another of the striking lessons of the Chicago parking concessions examined above has been that this compulsion to maximise revenue can often have deleterious effects that spiral beyond the immediate impact on those paying to use an asset. In the city's 2008 parking-meters deal with the MSIP-led investor consortium, the rise in parking rates that followed the deal was bad enough: whereas the city had been taking in around $20 million per annum from the meter system before the deal, steep rate increases saw annual meter revenues jump to more than $80 million by 2011, by which time Chicago had become the country's most expensive city for curb-side parking.[63] But for users,

---

63 Farmer, 'Cities as Risk Managers', p. 2165.

this increased cost was compounded by the contractual conditions the city agreed to in order to ensure that MSIP was able to achieve those rate increases. Specifically, the agreement mandated that the city 'employ vehicle immobilization (the costly "boot" vehicle clamp) and license suspensions for drivers who repeatedly did not pay parking fees, with fines to be set at a level "necessary to deter parking violations"'. Fines and suspensions thus increased dramatically after the deal, with a 'disproportionate impact on low-income and minority drivers, many of whom end up in bankruptcy owing to their inability to pay'.[64]

There are also often significant harmful effects associated with the implementation of the second golden rule of real-asset asset management. To ready an acquired asset for profitable disposal, it is just as important for an asset manager to minimise the costs of operating that asset as it is to maximise the revenues arising from its operation. Assets are valued by the market on the basis of cash-flows, and these represent a net rather than gross measure. Operating expenditures must be cut rapidly, unless doing so jeopardises revenue generation; indeed, revenue maximisation itself is only pursued if it does not incur offsetting cost increases.

The imperative to cut operating costs typically impinges on two main stakeholder constituencies. The first is an asset's users. If the apartment you live in, the land you farm, the water main supplying your home or the hospital you are taken to for surgery is acquired by an asset manager, and if that manager then seeks to cut the cost of maintaining its new asset, you will more likely than not suffer accordingly. The second constituency is the workers employed to carry out this asset maintenance. As we saw in Chapter 1, it is not Blackstone or Brookfield or Macquarie's own investment professionals who clean hospital floors, man toll-road booths and respond to residential-tenant complaints about leaking taps. All those tasks are outsourced under service contracts. Workers' wage-cheques suffer to the degree that the asset manager is successful in squeezing labour costs.

64   P. Ashton, M. Doussard and R. Weber, 'Sale of the Century: Chicago's Infrastructure Deals and the Privatization State', 24 November 2020 – at metropolitics.org.

Blackstone's widely discussed investment in US single-family housing in the wake of the global financial crisis represents something of a case study in the rapid implementation of the alternative asset manager's twofold revenue-maximisation and cost-reduction agenda – and in the implications of such implementation for key stakeholders. The main vehicle that Blackstone used to pursue this investment was Blackstone Real Estate Partners (BREP) VII, a ten-year closed-end fund that it launched in 2011. BREP VII and affiliated funds controlled the company that Blackstone established in 2012 to buy and let housing – Invitation Homes.

During 2012 and 2013, Invitation Homes' focus was primarily on buying: some 40,000 homes had been acquired by the end of the latter year. But the focus then shifted decisively to making Invitation Homes as marketable as possible to third-party investors. On the one hand, rents were ratcheted up. An average monthly Invitation Homes housing rent of $1,424 in 2014 rose to $1,600 for the nine months ending on 30 September 2016. At the same time, Blackstone took a cleaver to company costs. The average annualised amount that Invitation Homes spent on general repairs and maintenance, and on making homes ready to be re-leased after tenants moved out, declined from $1,362 per home in 2014 to $1,146 in the nine months ending on 30 September 2016. In short, the company paid progressively less to what it called its 'market-level personnel': the people on the ground who it used to keep its rental homes in habitable shape.[65]

This had two predictable sets of consequences. First, Invitation Homes did indeed rapidly become highly marketable to prospective investors. With revenues growing and costs declining, its operating profit margin jumped from 51.8 per cent in 2014 to 61.4 per cent for the nine months ending on 30 September 2016.[66] At that point, Blackstone judged that the time was already ripe to begin the process of exiting its investment, only four years after having established Invitation Homes – whose portfolio now contained approximately 48,000 homes – and fully five years before BREP VII would be wound

---

65   Invitation Homes Inc., 'Form S-11', 6 January 2017, p. 17.
66   Ibid.

up. In a January 2017 IPO, 77 million shares were successfully sold to the market, generating proceeds of some $1.5 billion. Moreover, Blackstone's funds continued to control the company, retaining approximately 73 per cent of Invitation Homes shares after the IPO.

Second, tenant dissatisfaction escalated in the face of rising rents and declining investment in repairs and maintenance: the self-same changes that made Invitation Homes more valuable to the market as an investment proposition made it less tolerable to tenants as an accommodation provider. One journalist reported widespread tenant allegations of 'slumlord-like' behaviour on the part of the company.[67] Another, noting that the Better Business Bureau had received more than 600 complaints about Invitation Homes in the course of just three years, quoted tenants who described the company as 'the worst landlord I've ever encountered'.[68]

To be clear, such dissatisfaction was not unique to Invitation Homes among US residential rental operators controlled by asset managers. Tenants of the Pretium Partners–backed Progress Residential have similarly complained of 'unfair rent hikes, shoddy maintenance and excessive fees': one lease seen by the *Washington Post* stipulated fees such as '10 per cent of the rent if the payment is more than five days late; $7.95 a month for a firm picked by Progress to collect utility payments; $9.95 a month for failing to buy renter's insurance; and a $35 "convenience fee" each time rent is paid with a credit card' – not to mention a $200 'administration' fee in the event of Progress filing for eviction.[69] Comparable claims have recently surfaced with regard to Greystar Investment Management's rental operations, too.[70]

---

67   M. Conlin, 'Spiders, Sewage and a Flurry of Fees – The Other Side of Renting a House from Wall Street', 27 July 2018 – at reuters.com.

68   J. Kraus, 'Former Tenants Share Horror Stories of Renting from Real Estate Investment Firm Invitation Homes', 4 February 2019 – at newschannel5. com.

69   P. Whoriskey, S. Woodman and M. Gibbs, 'This Block Used to Be for First-Time Homebuyers. Then Global Investors Bought In', *Washington Post*, 15 December 2021.

70   H. Vogell, 'When Private Equity Becomes Your Landlord', 7 February 2022 – at propublica.org.

Indeed, such concerns reached a new pitch during the coronavirus pandemic. No less than three separate congressional committees undertook investigations of the pandemic-era business practices of US corporate residential landlords, focusing in particular on their eviction practices, and landlords controlled by asset managers such as the Amherst Group, Cerberus Capital Management and the aforementioned Pretium were squarely in the spotlight.[71] Eviction moratoria introduced by federal and local governments during the pandemic evidently did not stop landlords from filing and completing evictions, which were concentrated in communities of colour. 'They're willing to destroy someone's life', remarked the planning scholar Elora Lee Raymond, an expert witness at a hearing held by one of the congressional committees.[72]

In the case of Invitation Homes during its existence as a Blackstone-controlled entity, tensions ran especially high in California, the company's second most important regional market after Florida. There, Invitation Homes tenants stormed Blackstone offices on three separate occasions in protest at rent hikes and alleged property neglect. In October 2017, 'more than three dozen renters of homes across Los Angeles burst through the front door of Blackstone's headquarters in Santa Monica, shaking noisemakers, honking sirens and chanting through megaphones: "Hey, Blackstone, shame on you," "Slumlord," and, "You are being evicted, Blackstone!" Blackstone executives rushed out of the building through the emergency exits and the back door.'[73]

The corporate response to this seeming indignity? When, the following year, Californians voted state-wide on a proposal to enhance the ability of Californian municipalities to control rents (specifically by revoking 1995's Costa–Hawkins Rental Housing Act, which substantially constrains that ability), Blackstone–

---

71 The committees in question were the Senate Committee on Banking, Housing and Urban Affairs, the House Committee on Financial Services and the House Select Subcommittee on the Coronavirus Crisis.

72 Cited in E. Rios, 'Four Corporate US Landlords Deceived and Evicted Thousands during Covid, Report Reveals', *Guardian*, 4 August 2022.

73 Conlin, 'Spiders, Sewage and a Flurry of Fees'.

Invitation Homes donated a reported $6.8 million to the ultimately successful campaign against the proposal.[74] Blackstone's eyes remained firmly set on the prize of further profitable disposals of Invitation Homes stock, an end to which rent maximisation continued to be indispensable. In 2019, with just two years remaining until termination of BREP VII, Blackstone sold its last shares in Invitation Homes. Its funds had made an estimated $3.5 billion in total profit from the seven-year investment.[75]

One could cite any number of other examples of how the real-asset asset manager's imperative to engineer quick, profitable exits from its investments results in similarly deleterious outcomes for users. But perhaps none is as shocking as the impact of growing asset-manager involvement in the US care-home sector in the past two decades.[76] A recent study by Atul Gupta and colleagues sheds a remarkable light on this issue. They studied the acquisition by asset managers of some 1,674 care homes, in 128 separate deals, between 2000 and 2017, comparing the effects of ownership by these asset managers with for-profit ownership more generally. As in the case of Blackstone and single-family housing, we see the familiar combination of immediate upward pressure on revenues and downward pressure on operating costs. Thus, on the one hand, the amount billed by the care home – and paid for primarily by taxpayers, through Medicare – was 11 per cent higher per stay for homes owned by asset managers.[77] At the same time, less was spent on patient care. In particular, the

74 D. Sirota and A. Perez, 'How California Public Employees Fund Anti-Rent Control Fight Unwittingly', *Guardian*, 23 October 2018.

75 R. Dezember, 'Blackstone Moves Out of Rental-Home Wager with a Big Gain', *Wall Street Journal*, 21 November 2019.

76 An especially disquieting example has been related in depth by Y. Rafiei, 'When Private Equity Takes Over a Nursing Home', *New Yorker*, 25 August 2022.

77 A. Gupta, S. Howell, C. Yannelis and A. Gupta, 'Does Private Equity Investment in Healthcare Benefit Patients? Evidence from Nursing Homes', NBER Working Paper 28474, February 2021, p. 3. Notably, Tong Liu has found an identical outcome in the case of asset-manager acquisitions of US hospitals, which for the privately insured have led to an 11 per cent increase in total healthcare spending. See T. Liu, 'Bargaining with Private Equity: Implications for Hospital Prices and Patient Welfare', July 2021 – at ssrn.com.

number of hours per patient-day supplied by frontline nursing assistants was 3 per cent lower.[78]

Given that nurse availability is known to be the most important determinant of quality of nursing-home care – frontline nursing assistants 'provide the vast majority of caregiving hours and perform crucial well-being services such as mobility assistance, personal interaction, and cleaning to minimise infection risk and ensure sanitary conditions' – Gupta and his colleagues suggested that the lower availability of this vital resource in asset-manager-owned homes was probably responsible for the most troubling of their findings: higher mortality. Going to an asset-manager-owned care home increased the probability of death (relative to for-profit homes more generally) by about 10 per cent for short-stay Medicare patients, implying that some 20,150 US lives were lost between 2004 and 2016 specifically due to asset-manager ownership of care homes.[79] In some circumstances, it seems, asset-manager society kills.

Rule three

If asset managers that run closed-end funds are incentivised to squeeze operating expenditures associated with real-asset investments, they have an even greater incentive to avoid capital expenditures – that is, expenditures that are expected to provide utility beyond the very near term. After all, if the overriding objective is to exit within, say, three to five years of investment, there will in general be no reason to spend money whose returns would be realised wholly or primarily beyond that limited time horizon. It would be economically irrational to do so; and the closer to exit the asset manager edges, needless to say, the smaller the incentive becomes to invest for the long term.

And thus we arrive at the real-asset asset manager's third and final golden rule: to avoid, generally speaking, any capital expenditure. Of course, this would be problematic in any context: however 'presentist' in orientation they may in certain cases be, all commercial operations require some degree of investment for

78 Gupta, Howell, Yannelis and Gupta, 'Private Equity Investment in Healthcare', p. 4.

79 Ibid., p. 3.

the long term, whether in employee training, upgrading of IT systems, or any other resource. But it would be difficult to think of a context in which an inherent bias against capital expenditure is more problematic than the ownership and stewardship of real assets such as housing and infrastructure. Such assets are differentiated from other assets in which the private sector invests precisely by their long-term nature: all but the most cosmetic spending on maintaining or upgrading real, physical assets generates benefits extending well into the future. Capital expenditure is their very lifeblood. Insofar as closed-end asset-manager funds are disincentivised to entertain such spending by dint of their intrinsic short-termism, they are arguably the least suitable owners conceivable for housing and infrastructure assets. As proponents of open-ended fund structures are wont to argue, 'having to exit an asset simply because of fund life is counter-productive to growing businesses for the long-term'.[80]

This is not to say that closed-end funds never countenance significant capital expenditure; they sometimes do. But they typically do so only under special circumstances of two main kinds. The first is where capital spending is externally compelled. The most common instance of this is when asset managers acquire regulated real assets and in the process commit to carrying out certain types and levels of capital investment.

Such compulsion, according to Paul Finch, has been a silver lining – perhaps the only one – in the sorry tale of the UK's PFI contracts. Commenting on a 2019 article in the *Sunday Times* detailing a substantial shortfall in repair and maintenance spending on major publicly owned and operated UK hospitals, and suggesting that the same was true of similarly held educational infrastructure, Finch highlighted by way of contrast 'one of [PFI's] most useful attributes: the requirement for consortia to maintain buildings in a proper condition for the period of their ownership (up to 30 years). When the buildings are handed back to the public sector, they have to be in a state comparable to their post-snagging condition in the second year of their operation.' Finch conceded: 'you pay a price for this, and critics say that the price is too high.'[81] One might also add that the liquid secondary market in PFI equity described above will surely have encouraged some owners to skimp on maintenance while in temporary control of PFI assets. Nevertheless, Finch's broader point is well taken: mechanisms exist in some circumstances to require capital spending by asset managers.

The second set of circumstances under which short-termist asset managers undertake substantive capital investment in real assets is where there is a high probability of their being able to monetise future returns on such investment upon exit by effectively incorporating the capital cost (plus a profit) in the disposal price. Typically, this is only possible in situations where capital spending enables the asset owner immediately to lift the rates levied on the users of that asset, by at least an amount corresponding to an acceptable rate of return.

Imagine a hypothetical asset manager that owns a fibre-optic telecoms network. If $1 billion invested in upgrading that network will not enable higher rates to be charged to the companies that use it to deliver data services, such investment will be very hard to rationalise. If it enables annual rates to be lifted by a total of $20 million, the logic will still be weak – payback will take fifty years (an eternity for an asset manager), even before factoring in the time-cost of money. But if annual rates can immediately be lifted by $50 million or even $100 million, the investment potentially makes more sense. Crucially, this is not so much because the asset manager will itself necessarily reap the ongoing rewards five, ten and more years hence; it ordinarily will not. Rather, it is because the market will immediately be able to see that the investment delivers positive returns, thus allowing the asset manager to sell the network profitably and with the requisite haste. Again: the inflated rates are a means to an end, not the end itself.

Blackstone's programme of housing investment in the period since the global financial crisis once more provides a textbook example – only this time not in the United States but in Sweden. In December 2016, two closed-end Blackstone funds combined forces to acquire a 46 per cent ownership share and a

81 P. Finch, 'Dismiss PFI If You Will – At Least the Repairs Get Done', 12 February 2019 – at architectsjournal.co.uk.

65 per cent voting share in D. Carnegie & Co., the owner of over 16,000 Swedish apartments, of which around 10,000 were located mostly in the suburbs of Greater Stockholm. By the end of 2018, by which time Carnegie had been renamed Hembla and owned more than 21,000 apartments, Blackstone had increased its ownership share to 61 per cent.

Much of the Hembla housing stock had not been substantively upgraded since its construction in the 1960s and 1970s. Should Blackstone invest in such upgrading? Sweden's system of 'soft' rent control allows landlords to raise rents if they undertake renovations that improve a unit's physical condition and quality. The question Blackstone faced, therefore, was: if it carried out renovations, could it secure an immediate rent increase of an order that (a) demonstrated to other potential investors that the expenditure generated adequate returns, and would thus encourage them to compensate Blackstone for said expenditure if and when Blackstone decided to sell Hembla, but also (b) did not negatively impact occupancy?

Blackstone wagered that it could – and it was right. In 2018, for example, it spent 903 million Swedish kronor (SEK) renovating 1,626 apartments. It succeeded in immediately increasing the average annualised rent on these apartments by 491 SEK/m^2 (from 1,021 to 1,512).[82] If we assume that the average size of the renovated apartments matched the average size of all Hembla apartments at that time (79m^2), this represented a cumulative annualised rent increase of 63 million kronor. And there was seemingly negligible impact on occupancy: vacancy rates across the whole Hembla portfolio rose only marginally in 2018, from 1.3 to 1.5 per cent.[83]

And the market did indeed valorise Blackstone's investment. In September 2019, less than three years after it had taken control, Blackstone offloaded its majority stake in Hembla to Germany's Vonovia for 12.2 billion SEK (around €1.1 billion), the exit realising a reported profit of approximately 6 billion SEK.[84]

---

82 Hembla, *Annual report 2018*, pp. 59–60.

83 Ibid., p. 83.

84 S. Thór, 'Blackstones Vinst på Hembla-affären Cirka 6 Miljarder', 23 September 2019 – at fastighetsnytt.se.

Meanwhile, large numbers of Hembla tenants were themselves also 'exiting' – although in their case generally not voluntarily. Unable to bear the average rent spikes of some 50 per cent, many tenants of renovated apartments moved out not because they wanted to, but because they had to. Hembla is one of the landlords that has been at the centre of a growing political storm in Sweden around practices of so-called 'renoviction' – that is, eviction of tenants from their homes resulting from renovations, whether the 'eviction' is initiated by the landlord or by the embattled tenant herself.

There *are* circumstances, then, in which closed-end funds undertake significant capital spending on real assets in their portfolios. But this is generally only when they are compelled, or when what might appear to be investment for the long term can be monetised in the short term. Otherwise the incentive for such expenditure is intrinsically absent. The implication of this should be self-evident: housing and infrastructure assets under this type of ownership do not ordinarily receive the capital investment they need, and so they physically deteriorate.

The UK's privatised utility system, in which asset managers have been increasingly active investors since the turn of the millennium (see Chapter 2), represents an important example of this phenomenon, from water to electricity, gas and telecoms. Commentators at the *Financial Times* have consistently highlighted the pertinent issues. In 2018, for example, Jonathan Ford drew attention to exactly the 'time horizon mismatch' discussed above: 'buyout funds have a limited seven- to 10-year life after which they liquidate and distribute any profits, while the capital investments utilities make may only pay off in decades. That means the owner may be tempted to skimp on investment.'[85]

Then there is the fact that most utility businesses are natural monopolies. Why incur the expense of physically upgrading, say, a gas distribution network if dissatisfied customers cannot switch to a different network? Already in 2008, Ford's colleague Martin Wolf had declared Britain's privatised utility model 'broken' precisely because private owners' monopoly power had served

---

85 J. Ford, 'Private Equity and Utilities Don't Mix', *Financial Times*, 18 June 2018.

as 'an obstacle to [capital] investment'; cossetted by monopoly conditions, owners had been sweating their infrastructure assets rather than spending money on improving them.[86] Foremost among such under-investors were asset managers – a fact that led Ford, a decade later, to a robust conclusion. Perhaps, he wrote, managers' closed-end funds 'have a role to play in financing [utility companies] that operate in competitive markets, in short-term concessions, or else in assets they are contractually obliged to keep in good repair. But companies with permanent licences and captive customers are a different matter.'[87]

Exhibit A in Ford's withering critique of asset managers, utility businesses and systematic infrastructure under-investment was Macquarie, most notably in its ownership of Thames Water. As we saw in Chapter 2, Macquarie took control of Thames, the UK's largest water and wastewater company, in 2006. It did so using closed-end funds.

Concerns about underinvestment in Thames Water's infrastructure surfaced relatively early in Macquarie's tenure. In 2013, however, they became headline news, when Ofwat, the industry regulator, challenged Thames's proposal to raise customer rates by 8 per cent, charging that the company had historically 'under-invested on sewer flooding and on sewer treatment, and failed to adequately maintain some of its wastewater network'.[88] Still, the challenge did not appear to elicit any significant behavioural change. Critics continued to point to repeated ongoing water and sewage leaks as evidence of chronic underinvestment. For leaks that resulted in extensive pollution of the Thames and other rivers with untreated sewage between 2012 and 2014, the company was ultimately prosecuted by the Environment Agency, and in March 2017 it was fined £20 million, the judge in the case castigating the company for 'inadequate investment, diabolical maintenance and poor management'.[89]

---

86 M. Wolf, 'Britain's Utility Model Is Broken', *Financial Times*, 12 June 2008.

87 Ford, 'Private Equity and Utilities Don't Mix'.

88 L. Tobin, 'Ofwat Threat to Pull Plug on Thames Water Bills Rise', *Independent*, 13 September 2013.

89 M. Robinson, 'How Macquarie Bank Left Thames Water with Extra £2bn Debt', 5 September 2017 – at bbc.com.

In 2016–17, Thames Water managed to miss the leakage-reduction target set for it by Ofwat by 47 million litres *per day*.[90] As Ford pointed out, this clearly meant that 'customers were not getting the service they were paying for – being, for instance, more exposed to an interruption in supply'.[91] In early 2018, amid a burst of cold weather, ruptured and leaking pipes left 12,000 Thames households without water.[92] Ofwat finally ran out of patience, and in June of that year it fined Thames a record £120 million for its longstanding underperformance with regard to leakage problems. But Macquarie had no need to worry. It had sold its final shares in Thames Water (to a Canadian pension scheme and the Kuwait Investment Authority) the previous year, just in time for the winding-up of the funds through which it had invested. Macquarie, as Ford caustically remarked, 'had gone, leaving others to take its hit'.[93]

If, under Macquarie's decade-long period of control, Thames Water did not spend the money on infrastructure that customers, courts and regulators expected, it certainly did spend extravagantly on something else: dividends paid to shareholders, Macquarie foremost among them. Over the two years (2016 and 2017) when it was failing so colossally to achieve its leakage reduction targets, for instance, Thames paid out dividends of £239 million. In an analysis carried out for the BBC, Martin Blaiklock, a world-renowned expert in infrastructure finance, estimated that the returns made by Macquarie's funds from its investment in Thames Water averaged between 15.5 and 19 per cent per annum. Such returns, Blaiklock commented, were 'twice what one would normally expect'.[94]

In other words, while some suffer the costs of asset-manager society, others appropriate its often-extravagant financial gains. Those gains, and their distribution, are the subject of Chapter 5.

---

90   'Thames Water Fined £8.55m for Failing to Stop Leaks', 14 June 2017 – at bbc.com.

91   Ford, 'Private Equity and Utilities Don't Mix'.

92   G. Plimmer, 'Water Companies Criticised after Thousands of UK Homes Lose Supply', *Financial Times*, 5 March 2018.

93   Ford, 'Private Equity and Utilities Don't Mix'.

94   Robinson, 'How Macquarie Bank Left Thames Water with Extra £2bn Debt'.

The Tragedy of the Horizon

Given the expectation that extreme weather events and associated environmental hazards such as flooding will increase
in frequency and intensity as climate change proceeds in the
decades ahead, it is quite possible that the historical case of
Macquarie and Thames Water – hinging as it did on weather,
water and waste – represents a harbinger of things to come.

Moreover, inasmuch as it seemed to epitomise Ford's 'time
horizon mismatch' – the discrepancy between asset managers'
short-term horizons and the longer timeframe over which capital
expenditures typically repay themselves – the case may also be
propitious in a more fundamental and worrying sense. More
perhaps than any other development in human history, climate
change demands a long-term perspective while at the same time
perversely convincing people that the big changes are not happening yet – and thus that significant remedial action need not
now be taken. Thus are our horizons repeatedly and disastrously
squeezed.

Speaking in 2015 in his capacity as both governor of the Bank
of England and chairman of the Financial Stability Board, Mark
Carney provided an influential reading of climate change and
this particular temporal mismatch. Climate change, he ventured,
represents nothing less than, in his words, the 'tragedy of the
horizon'. Because 'the catastrophic impacts of climate change
will be felt beyond the traditional horizons of most actors', those
actors have little direct incentive to do anything about it. The
main constituency of actors of interest to Carney at that time
was central banks, Carney noting that the horizon for monetary
policy only 'extends out to 2–3 years'.[95] But it could equally
well have been asset managers, whose horizon, as we have seen,
is usually similarly constrained. Why invest for a future you will
not see?

I will have more to say about asset-manager society in the
age of climate crisis in Chapter 6. But it is worth noting here
that asset managers are already widely establishing and raising

95   M. Carney, 'Breaking the Tragedy of the Horizon – Climate Change and
Financial Stability', 29 September 2015 – at bankofengland.co.uk.

capital for explicitly labelled 'climate' or 'transition' investment funds. Among the plethora of these, one fund that was launched in 2021 stood out from the crowd. This was Brookfield Asset Management's Global Transition Fund, which aimed to raise up to $12.5 billion to invest in assets that would 'catalyse the transformation of carbon-intensive businesses' and 'accelerate the global transition to a net-zero carbon economy'.[96] Two things about this fund immediately made it notable.

The first of these was the fund's time horizon. Rather than the type of open-ended 'perpetual' structure of which the industry has recently made so much promotional play, and which one might think would be appropriate for the long-term problem that is climate change, the Brookfield fund was a typical twelve-year closed-end vehicle – a perfect metaphor, if you like, for the structural incongruity of real-asset asset management in the era of climate crisis.

The other notable feature of the new fund was the first-named of the five investment professionals charged with running it. In an irony that was almost terrible in its beauty, this was none other than Mark Carney himself, who the previous year, direct from the Bank of England, had joined Brookfield as vice chair and head of transition investing. Of his tragedy of the horizon, nothing was now to be heard.

---

96 J. Stutts, 'Brookfield's Transition Fund Targets 10% Returns', 18 November 2021 – at newprivatemarkets.com. In the event, Brookfield raised around $15 billion for this fund, from more than 100 different investors.

5

Who Gains?

The Leaders

A native of Pennsylvania born in 1947, Stephen Schwarzman has been a financier his whole professional life. Upon graduating from Yale in 1969, he joined Donaldson, Lufkin & Jenrette, an investment bank. An MBA (Harvard) followed, and he returned to Wall Street and banking. His employer on this occasion was Lehman Brothers. It was there that Schwarzman met Peter Peterson, Lehman's chairman and CEO. In 1985, the two men left Lehman to set up the Blackstone Group. Still just thirty-eight, Schwarzman, already a multi-millionaire, installed himself as Blackstone's CEO. He remains CEO thirty-seven years later. At the time of writing, his net worth is estimated to be in excess of $40 billion.

Bruce Flatt is much younger than Schwarzman. A Canadian born in 1965, Flatt began his career as an accountant at Ernst & Young. In 1990, aged twenty-five, he joined Brascan, a sprawling conglomerate with historic roots in the construction and operation of electricity and transportation infrastructures, only for his new employer to more or less implode during the recession of the early 1990s. Cyclical resource assets were subsequently sold off, and the company re-emerged from the crisis as a leaner entity, more focused on real estate, power systems – and asset management. It was also a company within which Flatt was rapidly ascending the executive ranks. In 2002, he became CEO; in 2005, Brascan was renamed Brookfield Asset Management. Flatt remains CEO seventeen years later. His net worth is estimated at around $3 billion.

Martin Stanley was born in the UK in 1963. He started his career in 1986 at Manweb plc, the operator of the electricity distribution network for Cheshire, Merseyside and North Wales. He later joined TXU Europe Group, an energy services business involved in the generation, supply and trading of electricity and gas. In 2004, aged forty-one, Stanley joined Australia's Macquarie Group and helped to establish Macquarie's first European infrastructure funds, directing a number of early landmark deals, including the 2006 acquisition of Thames Water (see Chapter 4). For over a decade, Stanley has led Macquarie's real-assets investment business, first as global head of Macquarie Infrastructure and Real Assets (2010–18) and then as head (2018–21) and chairman (2021–) of Macquarie Asset Management. There are no publicly available estimates of Stanley's net worth, but he has clearly done well for himself: in the year to 31 March 2021, for instance, he received total remuneration of A$20 million.[1]

'Teachers, Nurses and Firefighters'

Unsurprisingly, these riches are not what one hears about when asset managers in the real-assets space and those supportive of their business model explain what such asset managers do – and, more importantly, why. The preferred narrative certainly highlights wealth gains, only not the gains enjoyed by asset managers themselves. Instead, asset management, it is said, is about delivering financial returns to a constituency that nobody in their right mind could consider unimportant, still less undeserving. The discourse is encapsulated in a line that Blackstone has used when providing an overview of its business in its annual report. 'To the extent our funds perform well', the firm explains, 'we can support a better retirement for tens of millions of pensioners, including teachers, nurses and firefighters.'[2] Insofar as the money that Blackstone invests is the money of teachers, nurses,

---

1 Macquarie Group, *Annual Report for the Year Ended 31 March 2021*, p. 122.

2 The Blackstone Group Inc., *Annual Report for the Fiscal Year Ended December 31*, 2020, p. 7.

and firefighters, they are the ones who benefit when its funds generate significant returns. How can one argue with that?

It would be difficult to overstate the sheer power of this discourse in shaping economic outcomes. If it serves today to legitimise the investment practices of asset managers that buy housing and infrastructure, it has in fact long circulated as a narrative of justification for asset management more generally, and especially for asset-management practices that many observers deem problematic. Private equity – so often associated by critics with job losses and 'asset stripping' at acquired companies, alongside exorbitant fund-manager remuneration – is a case in point. Consider the response of industry advocates, for example, when in 2008 the Service Employees International Union filed a citizens' initiative to the Washington legislature to limit investment in private-equity funds by the State Investment Board (SIB), which managed $62 billion in public pension money. Private equity, protested SIB executive director Joe Dear, was the Board's highest-returning asset class. If he could no longer invest in private equity, the losers, he said, would be ordinary union pensioners who depended on those returns for their retirement income.[3]

In the real-assets context, one of the most forceful proponents of this argument that asset management firms provide a socially beneficial public service by generating income for ordinary pension-savers is the Global Infrastructure Investor Association (GIIA), a leading trade body for asset managers and institutional investors specialising in the infrastructure asset class. Its members, the GIIA emphasises, invest 'on behalf of the citizens they represent' – thus performing a civic service. From 'teachers and council workers to firefighters and factory workers', the GIIA enthuses, 'millions of people' are 'directly benefitting' from the proceeds of its members' investment funds. Indeed, given that much of the capital for infrastructure investment 'comes from the cumulative savings from millions of individual pensions', those same council and factory workers not only benefit from infrastructure investment but enable it – thereby 'improving

---

3 'Pounding Private Equity', *Wall Street Journal*, 23 August 2008.

global infrastructure, and supporting local and national economies'.[4] It is, in every sense of the term, a virtuous circle, centred on a storied (if mythical) figure: the everyday 'investor-citizen'.

It is important to consider what this discourse amounts to at its core. As we saw in the previous chapter, critics of the 'financialisation' of housing, farmland and infrastructure frequently argue that the ownership of such assets by financial institutions like asset managers is categorically more problematic than ownership by 'non-financialised' corporate actors: it is preferable, these critics imply, for housing to be owned by property companies, electricity networks by energy companies, parking systems by parking companies, and so on. Asset managers and their supporters, however, claim the exact opposite. Not only is 'financialised' ownership not worse, they say – it is better.

This, they argue, is because such an ownership model entails a simple, direct and transparent alignment of interests between the asset manager and, behind him or her, all those teachers and factory workers she dutifully represents. In running their businesses, executives of property companies, energy companies and parking companies are required to consider all manner of different sets of stakeholders, from local communities to employees, from customers to shareholders. Even with the privileging of the fourth of these groups in the contemporary era of the elevation of 'shareholder value', corporate executives repeatedly pledge their attentiveness to the interests of the other three groups, making for a messy mix of strategic priorities.

Asset managers are more single-minded. Their job is to make money for those whose capital they manage, period. Indeed, Blackstone's Schwarzman raised hackles when, in 2015, eight years after the company's IPO, he insisted that the firm bore a fiduciary responsibility *only* to its limited partners (that is, investors in its funds) and not *also* to its shareholders (that is, investors in the firm's own equity capital).[5] In the case of

---

4 Global Infrastructure Investor Association, 'Closing the Gap: How Private Capital Can Help Deliver Our Future Infrastructure Needs', March 2019, pp. 4, 14 – at giia.net.

5 S. Willmer, 'Blackstone's Schwarzman Says Duty Isn't to Public Shareholders', 1 February 2015 – at bloomberg.com.

asset management, Schwarzman was saying, there is a pure and unencumbered alignment of interests between manager and 'managee'. And the particular managee on whose behalf asset managers most often claim to be labouring is, of course, the ordinary saver for retirement. If one cares for the prospects of that individual, then, by this logic, one ought to celebrate, not scorn, the asset manager.

An example of this discourse in action – being put to work successfully in the service of a specific political-economic outcome – came in 2019 in the UK. One of the marquee proposals of the opposition Labour Party in the run-up to the general election of that year was to renationalise the country's energy, water and other key utility infrastructures. These infrastructures, as we have seen, have offered a fertile terrain of investment for international asset-management firms in the past two decades. Not only, moreover, did Labour propose to expropriate private infrastructure owners, but to do so at prices set by parliament, which might be below market prices.

While Labour's proposal initially seemed popular with the public, opinion rapidly soured as industry bodies – among them the GIIA – launched a series of attacks. Predictably, these attacks were ostensibly made on behalf of the UK public in general. Compensating at below market value, said Water UK, the sector's trade body, would scare off future investment in infrastructures 'on which ordinary people depend'. No less worryingly, it would hurt people's retirement savings: 'These pension pots, which are sustaining the lives of millions of UK pensioners, are at risk', intoned the head of the Energy Networks Association, a counterpart trade body.[6] Labour, of course, proceeded to lose the election.

On the face of it, there is indeed some merit in the thesis that it is 'ordinary people', in their capacity as current or future pensioners, who benefit from successful practices of real-asset asset management – and that, accordingly, asset managers should be respected, and perhaps even lauded. After all, pension schemes have always been the biggest single category of contributor of

6 Both cited in J. Ford and G. Plimmer, 'Investors Attack Labour's Renationalisation Plans', *Financial Times*, 29 May 2019.

capital to the funds managed by asset managers; and that is no different in respect of 'alternative' funds – hedge funds, private equity, infrastructure and real estate – than of traditional bond and public-equity funds. The Preqin database, for example, identifies a total of 5,189 separate institutional-investor commitments globally to closed-end infrastructure funds between 1990 and 2020, of which some 62 per cent (3,217) were pension-plan commitments.[7] Indisputably, many millions of individuals have indeed received a boost to their retirement savings when the various infrastructure funds to which those 3,217 separate commitments were made have generated strong returns.

Nevertheless, we should not take the altruistic, public-service-like claims of real-asset asset managers and their supporters at face value. For one thing, there are the undoubted costs to be weighed against the putative benefits. A singular strategic focus on the interests of the contributors of investment capital – if such a focus is indeed what asset managers genuinely have – can all too easily mean a downgrading of other interests, not least those of the users of the housing and infrastructure in which asset managers invest. That is to say, any gains that 'the people' (as pension-savers) make from real-asset asset management may not fully compensate them for the costs they incur as a result of it (see Chapter 4).

More pointedly, the fact is that the claims regularly made regarding these gains to ordinary savers simply do not measure up. Scratch beneath the surface, and a very different picture emerges of who exactly gains, and in what relative proportions, when funds are established by the likes of Blackstone, Brookfield and Macquarie, and proceed to invest their clients' capital in housing and infrastructure assets. The more one understands the actual mechanics and structures of the real-asset asset management business, the more misleading seems the GIIA's rose-tinted notion of a virtuous circle with the humble teacher or factory-worker at its centre.

What follows in this chapter is a deep examination of those structures and mechanics. Far from being a kind of beneficent

---

7 A. Andonov, R. Kräussl and J. Rauh, 'Institutional Investors and Infrastructure Investing', *Review of Financial Studies* 34 (2021), p. 3888.

centrifugal force that democratises wealth by liberally spreading it outwards and downwards to the masses, the picture that emerges of the asset management sector is instead one of a distinctly centripetal force that takes the profits of real-asset investments and forcefully concentrates them, distributing them disproportionately inwards and upwards, and thus bolstering the wealth of an existing global elite increasingly represented by the executives of asset-management firms themselves.

Sharing the Spoils?

To enable us to get a handle on who realises any gains generated by asset managers' real-asset funds, let us begin with a hypothetical and highly simplified example of such a fund. It raises $300 million to invest, and it can invest in housing, infrastructure, or both – what it invests in is immaterial for our purposes. Like the majority of unlisted real-estate and infrastructure funds, it is a closed-end vehicle, in this case with a ten-year life. The asset manager itself does not contribute capital to the fund. All the fund's limited partners are assumed at this point to be pension schemes – not a very realistic assumption, clearly, and one we shall relax later in the chapter, but useful for now for illustrative purposes. The fund invests the entirety of its committed capital across a series of assets. No dividends are paid out to the fund and its partners during the fund's life. All acquired assets are successfully disposed of prior to the fund's termination. We shall now examine the quantum and distribution of fund proceeds under two possible scenarios – one where the fund performs well, and one where it does not.

Scenario one

In the 'successful' scenario, we assume that the acquired assets are sold for a total of $690 million, realising a profit of $390 million. Thus, the fund has achieved a total multiple of invested capital (MOIC) – a commonly-used measure of overall return in the asset-management industry – of 2.3, i.e., $690 million divided by $300 million.

But the individual saver whose pension pot has been invested by the fund does not earn a total return multiple of 2.3. Why not? The reason is that these figures represent gross returns – the returns generated by the fund, not those received by its respective institutional partners, still less by those whose money those respective partners have put into it. How, then, can we translate the fund's return into the pension-saver's return?

The first crucial distinction to make is between the gross and net returns delivered by the fund itself. If its gross returns are those identified above (the so-called 'gross MOIC'), its net returns are those accruing after management fees, performance fees and fund expenses have been deducted. As we saw in Chapter 1, typical management fees on real-asset funds are 2 per cent of committed capital per annum, while the typical performance fee is a carry – effectively, a profit share – of 20 per cent. If we use these standard fee percentages and further assume that fund expenses amount to 4 per cent of committed capital in total over the life of the fund, we arrive at figures for our hypothetical fund of $60 million in management fees (2 per cent × 10 years × $300 million), $78 million in carried interest (20 per cent × $390 million profit) and $12 million in expenses (4 per cent × $300 million). This gives total fees and expenses of $150 million. Deducting these from the gross sales proceeds of $690 million, we see that the fund has delivered net proceeds to limited partners (LPs) of $540 million, equating to a net MOIC of 1.8.

Two real-world reference points are useful to consider here. Firstly, research carried out by Ludovic Phalippou has shown that in the private-equity world – whose fee structures are the model on which the fee structures of closed-end infrastructure and real-estate funds have long been based – average gross and net MOICs have historically stood at around 2.3 and 1.7, respectively.[8] In other words, the estimation in our hypothetical example that 0.5 points of gross return are 'absorbed' by fund expenses and manager fees – the difference between 2.3 and 1.8 – is not unreasonable; if anything, it understates the real

---

8   L. Phalippou, 'An Evaluation of the Potential for GPFG to Achieve Above Average Returns from Investments in Private Equity and Recommendations Regarding Benchmarking', January 2011, pp. 25–6 – at ssrn.com.

extent of typical expenses and fees. Secondly, the average net MOIC on closed-end infrastructure and real-estate funds raised in the period 2002–18 was approximately 1.3.[9] Thus, our hypothetical real-asset fund, with a net return to LPs of 1.8 in this first scenario, would indeed in reality represent a highly successful fund of this type – much more successful than average.

This 1.8 return on investment does not represent the individual pension-saver's return, however, as there is a second crucial distinction to make – between the return earned by the pension scheme (in this case, from its commitment of capital to the real-asset fund) and that which is earned by the scheme members. It is not only asset managers that charge fees; pension schemes also do, of course.

Most such schemes levy charges that are calculated as a proportion either of contributions to the scheme or (more commonly) of the market value of a member's assets.[10] In our hypothetical example, we will assume an annual charge on the latter basis of 1 per cent; as a benchmark, the UK average in 2019 was 1.09 per cent.[11] If the market value of the savings capital invested in our real-asset fund remained constant over the life of the fund, total lifetime fees to pension-scheme managers in respect of that capital would be $30 million (1 per cent × 10 years × $300 million). In reality, however, the market value of the capital invested in the fund would be revised each year – in this case, given the fund's success, upwards – thus inflating the annual fee. Let us therefore assume total pension-manager fees of $40 million (implying an average market value of the savings capital over the ten years of $400 million). This would mean that, instead of growing from $300 million (the amount originally invested) to $540 million (the net fund proceeds to LPs after asset-manager fees and expenses), the total retirement-savings capital at the end of the ten years would have increased

---

9 Andonov, Kräussl and Rauh, 'Institutional Investors and Infrastructure Investing', p. 3897.

10 This applies to defined-contribution pension plans, which are the most common variety; fees or charges levied on defined-benefit plans function somewhat differently.

11 J. Gray, 'Large Majority Unaware of Annual Pension Charges', 27 November 2019 – at pensionsage.com.

to $500 million. The pension-saver's return on invested capital would therefore be 1.6 ($500 million ÷ $300 million) – not 1.8, and certainly not 2.3.

But this measure, though revealing, fails to capture the disparities that exist in the distribution of returns on successful funds. Let us now examine things in another way. As we saw, the fund raised and invested $300 million of limited-partner (savers') capital, and made a profit in our first scenario of $390 million – albeit a profit whose value is in practice somewhat eroded by inflation, given the fund's ten-year life. In what proportions are these profits realised?

The individuals whose retirement savings were invested in the fund take $200 million in profit – they put $300 million in, and this grew to $500 million at termination. The pension-scheme manager captures $40 million of the profit: it put no money of its own in, but generates $40 million in fees. The asset manager, meanwhile, earns profits – the fees and expenses it charges, again without a capital contribution – of $150 million.

This, one might think, is a good outcome for the savers: they take the largest profit share of the three. But, in the case of both the asset manager and the pension-scheme administrator, the millions of dollars earned are shared between only a small number – perhaps only a handful – of individuals. This applies in particular to the asset manager's carried interest of $78 million. Usually, only an asset-management firm's most senior executives, together with those investment professionals actively involved in managing a particular fund and its portfolio investments, will share in the carry. To understand this, in other words, is to begin to appreciate how it is that the average Blackstone employee now earns more than $2 million per annum, how Macquarie's Martin Stanley earned $20 million in one recent year, and how in turn Bruce Flatt and Stephen Schwarzman of Brookfield and Blackstone are worth $3 billion and $40 billion, respectively.[12]

In the case of those saving for retirement, by contrast, the millions earned by virtue of investment in our successful

12 On average Blackstone remuneration, see A. Gara, 'Pay at Private Equity Firms "Dwarfs" Sums on Offer to Investment Bankers', *Financial Times*, 15 February 2022.

hypothetical fund would be shared between potentially millions of individuals, and certainly hundreds of thousands. A good way to approach the question of how many savers would typically stand 'behind' pension-scheme commitments of $300 million to a real-asset fund (as per our hypothetical case) is to ask what types of pension scheme are in the habit of making single capital commitments on such a scale to individual funds of this kind. The answer to this question is: large US public-pension schemes such as the Pennsylvania Public School Employees' Retirement System (with around 500,000 members), or the California Public Employees' Retirement System (with more than 2 million). If, for example, the first of these two schemes provided the full $300 million in our case, then the $200 million in savers' profit generated by the fund would represent, on average, an extra $400 in each member's pension pot – or $40 extra per year. This is arguably nothing to be sniffed at; but, needless to say, it is a long way from Schwarzman-scale earnings.

Scenario two

In our second scenario, the investments that the fund makes are not successful. In fact, they are an outright failure, with the assets being sold for a cumulative $210 million, representing a $90 million loss. How are the fund's proceeds distributed in this less rosy scenario?

In terms of fund expenses and manager fees, there is only one difference from the first scenario: no carried interest is earned because there is no profit on investment. Management fees and fund expenses are the same as they were in that first case, however, totalling $72 million. The result is that only $138 million of the $210 million in gross fund proceeds accrues to the LPs, who have therefore 'earned' a net MOIC of less than 0.5 ($138 million ÷ $300 million), and whose face loss – the amount invested in the fund minus the amount realised upon its termination – is $162 million.

The first thing to observe about this second hypothetical scenario is that such disasters do happen. For all the de-risking frequently extended to real-asset asset managers (see Chapter 4), some funds are failures, which has highly damaging consequences – not least for invested pension schemes. Consider the experiences of the aforementioned Pennsylvania Public School Employees' Retirement System (PSERS). In the early to mid 2000s, PSERS began aggressively to increase allocations to alternative asset classes, including real assets. Because the fees charged on real-asset funds are much higher than on traditional bond or public-equity funds, the payments that PSERS made to asset managers ballooned: by 2019, such payments had grown to more than $700 million *each year*. Only two of the approximately seventy-five other US public pension schemes tracked by Pew Charitable Trusts were paying higher fees relative to assets under management.[13]

PSERS ended up losing large amounts of the money it committed to real-asset funds. This was vividly the case for several real-estate funds launched in 2006 and 2007, shortly before the global financial crisis struck and led to a widespread collapse in property values, to which PSERS had committed significant sums. To take four prime examples, it lost $65 million of the $180 million it had invested in the real-estate asset manager Beacon Capital's Strategic Partners V fund (launched in 2007); $223 million of the $291 million it had invested in two real-estate funds launched by Broadway Partners (2006 and 2007); $67 million of the $281 million it had put into Carlyle's Europe Real Estate Partners III fund (2007); and fully $446 million of the $654 million it had sunk into two Morgan Stanley real-estate funds (both 2006).[14] These were nothing less than catastrophic losses.

If all parties gained from the investment activity illustrated in our first hypothetical scenario (albeit to widely varying degrees), how are the fund's losses apportioned in this second hypothetical scenario? We can approach this question, first of all, from the asset manager's perspective. It does not lose anything: it did not put any of its own capital into the fund. It is true that its total fees are much lower in this scenario than in the first, given

13   J. DiStefano, 'Why PSERS Investment Strategy Has Failed to Pay Off for Pa. Taxpayers and School Employees', *Philadelphia Inquirer*, 8 August 2021.

14   'PSERS Real Estate Data as of 9/30/2019', at psers.pa.gov.

that no carry is earned. But it is also true that its guaranteed annual management fees provide a form of insurance against fund failure: they are paid regardless of fund performance.

Of course, as we have seen, alternative asset managers do in fact usually commit some of their own capital to the funds they manage. But the proportion is typically small, averaging perhaps 2 per cent of total capital commitments. In our second hypothetical case, then, 2 per cent would equate to $6 million invested by the asset manager and around half of that being lost. Such a loss would be little more than a trifle, dwarfed by the $72 million received in management fees and fund expenses.

Arguably, the only substantive loss that asset managers potentially face when their funds fail is a loss of future business. If they fail to provide the level of returns expected by their clients, or at least if such failure occurs on a sufficient scale or with sufficient frequency, asset managers can expect to see those clients take their business elsewhere. PSERS's historic actions appear to bear this out. Although, after the debacle of its 2006–07 real-estate fund commitments, PSERS continued to commit capital to various Carlyle real-estate funds over the next decade, its records indicate that it did not invest in any further Beacon Capital, Broadway Partners or Morgan Stanley real-estate funds.

Nonetheless, the pivotal fact remains: the asset manager avoids partaking in any of the monetary losses sustained by our hypothetical fund in this second scenario. The losses must be absorbed elsewhere in the investment chain. To remind ourselves of those losses: after the manager's fees and expenses have been deducted, only $138 million of the $300 million originally invested in the fund is returned to the LPs.

When such failures occur in the real world, institutional investors whose capital has been eroded often make stinging criticisms of the asset manager responsible for the losses. David Carey and John Morris narrated a colourful example in their book about Blackstone. In 1989, the still-youthful firm had made its third ever private-equity investment, paying $330 million for the Pennsylvania-based Edgcomb Metals Company. As was customary, the deal was highly leveraged – but still, some $38.9 million of limited-partner equity capital was invested.

Almost immediately, the acquisition proved a disaster. Just a year later, Edgcomb, nearly bankrupt, was sold at a substantial discount. Blackstone's LPs lost $32.5 million (84 per cent) of their capital, even before accounting for fund-management fees. In a telephone conversation, the chief investment officer of Presidential Life Insurance, one of the LPs to have lost money, held nothing back, reportedly calling Stephen Schwarzman 'a complete idiot', before adding: 'I never should have given you a dime!'[15]

Criticisms of this type give the impression that among those who substantively absorb losses when asset managers' funds fail are institutional investors – the funds' LPs – themselves. In the specific case of Presidential, a life insurance company, that impression would indeed be fair. When such companies invest capital, whether directly or via asset managers, it is generally their own capital. It is true that the capital derives from customer premiums, but only in some cases is the insurance company investing directly on behalf of policyholders, in the sense that the latter's projected death benefits are explicitly linked to investment performance. More often, the insurance company is investing on its own behalf: taking policyholder premiums and investing them in the hope of boosting the profits generated by its core underwriting business. It is possible, of course, that Presidential's 'complete idiot' comment was made partly out of concern for customers with performance-linked policies. The likelier scenario, though, is that the individual who lambasted Schwarzman was preoccupied with the impact of the Edgcomb losses on Presidential's own balance sheet and corporate profitability.

In the case of our hypothetical fund, however, the LPs are not insurance companies, but pension schemes – the self-same LPs, more importantly, that Blackstone invokes when it explains that its activities support teachers, nurses and firefighters. And when it comes to the question of where and by whom in the investment chain losses on failed investment funds are absorbed, pension

---

15   D. Carey and J. E. Morris, *King of Capital: The Remarkable Rise, Fall, and Rise Again of Steve Schwarzman and Blackstone* (New York: Crown Business, 2010), p. 75.

schemes and their managers are different to life insurance companies like Presidential. The money they invest *is* their members' money. Thus, even if a pension-scheme manager receives significantly less back in proceeds from a real-asset fund than it originally invested in that fund, it does not directly incur losses itself. The invested capital is wholly retirement-savers' capital. The scheme manager, like the asset manager itself (at least in our hypothetical case), has no 'skin in the game', being a pure intermediary. Furthermore, and again like the asset manager, the pension-scheme manager reliably earns management fees each year irrespective of investment performance.

This does not mean that pension-scheme managers simply do not care about investment performance: they do, not least because, if their fees are based on the market value of members' invested assets, poor performance translates into lower annual management fees. But because they have no skin in the game, and because they rarely charge performance fees themselves, pension-plan managers are likely to care much less about investment performance, or to care about it in a much less visceral way, than life-insurance LPs (or indeed than asset managers, not to mention those whose retirement savings are being invested). Less is directly at stake in a commercial sense. This is especially the case for scheme managers such as PSERS, which face essentially zero risk of loss of customers, inasmuch as members cannot simply switch to alternative scheme providers if they are dissatisfied: if you work for a public school in Pennsylvania, PSERS manages your pension, whether you like it or not.

Therefore, all of the losses resulting from investment in our hypothetical real-asset fund in the second, disastrous scenario ultimately fall on the shoulders of individual retirement savers. Not only that, but the loss that those savers collectively sustain is of course greater than the figure of $162 million given above. The $138 million that is returned to LPs upon fund termination is net of the fund manager's expenses and fees – but the amount returned to savers is lower still, by an amount equivalent to the pension-scheme manager's own cumulative fees charged over the course of the fund's ten-year life. Let us assume that, in this second scenario, where the market value of the fund's assets falls, these fees only amount to $20 million in total, compared to $40 million in the first scenario. This reduces the net proceeds returned to scheme members to just $118 million, representing an overall loss of $182 million, and a dismal net MOIC of 0.4.

It is no wonder, therefore, that the greatest ire in cases of substantial underperformance by real-asset funds is expressed not by LPs such as Presidential or PSERS, but by those who are the real losers – the individuals saving, unsuccessfully, for retirement. After years of seeing their pension scheme consistently generate below-benchmark returns in the light of its ill-fated allocations to alternative asset classes, for example, Pennsylvania's public-school teachers finally lost patience when, in mid 2021, PSERS announced that large numbers of scheme members would henceforth be charged an average of $240 in additional annual pension contributions, precisely to offset the impact of the scheme's investment failures. In June of that year, in the Philadelphia Common Pleas Court, lawyers filed a suit in relation to PSERS's failures, initially on behalf of Kevin Steinke, a middle-school teacher in Delaware County, but proposing it as a class-action suit representing the approximately 100,000 other school employees hired since 2011.[16]

Given what we now know about the position of structural privilege enjoyed by asset managers and pension-scheme managers in being able to avoid any losses sustained by investment funds, it is interesting to note who exactly was being sued in the PSERS case. It was not the actual asset managers that PSERS had used. It was not even PSERS itself: as an arm of state government, it is generally protected from liability under the state's Sovereign Immunity Act. Instead, lawyers had to satisfy themselves with suing two consultants to PSERS, alleging that they had been 'grossly negligent' in their dealings with the scheme and that their advice had led to 'significant and traceable losses' from the alternative investment vehicles to which PSERS had committed so much capital.

What, then, do our two scenarios tell us about who gains within asset-manager society? They tell us that, when investments

16 J. DiStefano, 'Delco Teacher Sues Over PSERS Moves', *Philadelphia Inquirer*, 24 June 2021.

perform well, everyone in the investment chain wins, including those whose retirement savings are increasingly invested in real-asset funds; but, proportionately speaking, the asset manager is comfortably the biggest winner of all. Our scenarios also tell us, however, that when investments perform badly, there is only one loser, and this is not the pension-scheme manager, still less the asset manager. Asset managers' fund prospectuses really should be clearly adorned with the motto: 'Heads I win, tails you lose'.

Whose Capital?

Whose retirement savings?

In October 2009, the Brazil-based asset manager Vision Brazil Investments closed to new investors its debut property vehicle, the Brazil Real Estate Opportunities Fund I. In total, it had raised $210 million, all of which was to be invested domestically – some in commercial property, and some in residential property, including seven affordable housing projects in Rio de Janeiro and São Paulo. Geographically, the capital raised by the fund had a very different complexion from the assets that the fund would acquire. Fifteen institutional investors had committed to it, and all were from Europe and North America. These fifteen included both public and private pension schemes.[17] One, for example, was the local government pension scheme of the UK city of Wolverhampton.[18]

The reason for highlighting this particular fund is as follows. When organisations such as the GIIA laud asset managers for the fact that they invest on behalf of 'citizens' and their retirement savings, exactly who those 'citizens' are is rarely, if ever, specified. The 'citizen' is, rather, a free-floating signifier, unmoored from geographical location and typically also from social structure. Ostensibly, this citizen is, so to speak, all of us. But, of course, the reality is that the citizen in question is *not* all of us.

17 Z. Hughes, 'Vision Closes Debut Real Estate Fund on $210m', *Private Equity Real Estate News*, 21 October 2009.

18 City of Wolverhampton Council, 'Response to Request for Information: Reference FOI 001870', 15 January 2018 – at wolverhampton.gov.uk.

To the extent that asset managers invest on behalf of those with pension pots, generating capital gains for them, they do so for some people much more than for others. The gains enjoyed by 'citizens' by virtue of asset managers' investment of pension-scheme capital are in fact highly unequally distributed. Such inequality is social: within any given country, pension wealth is relatively concentrated among particular groups. The inequality is also geographic: some countries and national citizens enjoy substantial retirement savings; some have almost none. And, as the Vision Brazil example sharply illustrates, there is often a clear-cut spatial disjuncture between where capital gains are captured by asset managers and where in the world they are allocated to savings beneficiaries.

We can start with the geographical aspect of this issue. As we saw in Chapter 3, the vast majority of the capital committed to real-estate and infrastructure funds comes from institutional investors based in North America, Europe and to a lesser extent the Asia-Pacific region. As far as pension schemes, in particular, are concerned, the geographical centre of gravity is even more firmly fixed in Europe and North America: with the exception of Australia, whose superannuation schemes are major contributors to asset managers' funds, the bulk of the Asia-Pacific institutional capital that is invested via asset managers is the capital not of pension schemes, but of sovereign-wealth funds, banks and insurance companies (on which more below). Insofar as all the retirement-savings capital invested in the Brazil Real Estate Opportunities Fund I, mentioned above, derived from Europe and North America, that fund was representative of the broader industry pattern.

Figures for pension assets by country bear this out. The OECD has estimated that, of $56 trillion of global retirement savings in 2020, some $54 trillion was held in OECD countries, and that North America and the UK alone accounted for nearly 80 per cent of the OECD total. As a percentage of annual economic output, total assets in retirement savings plans comfortably exceeded 100 per cent in countries such as Australia, Canada, Denmark, the Netherlands, the UK and the United States; at the other end of the spectrum, such assets represented less than 1 per cent of economic output in countries including Albania, Greece and Serbia.[19] In short, when asset managers invest retirement savings, by definition they are overwhelmingly investing the savings of citizens of the Global North. It is thus overwhelmingly to citizens of the Global North that any gains remaining after the deduction of asset-manager and pension-scheme fees accrue, whether those gains ultimately emanate from dwellings and tenants in Brazil or from toll roads and car drivers in Boston.

Then there is the social dimension. By claiming that its funds help grow the retirement savings of 'teachers, nurses and fire-fighters', Blackstone implies that those savers who profit from the success of its funds are ordinary savers. But this is simply not the case – or, at least, the main beneficiaries among retirement savers are assuredly not such individuals. In every country in which there exist retirement savings that pension-scheme administrators invest partly via real-asset funds, such savings are unequally distributed across the population. Any gains delivered by asset managers' real-asset funds to retirement savers cannot help but benefit those with greater savings more than those with limited savings.

Take the United States – easily the most important territory in this regard, given that more than half of all global retirement savings are US-based savings, accounting for $36 trillion of the $56 trillion total in 2020. A study by Teresa Ghilarducci and colleagues has shown just how unequally such US savings are held.[20] In 2010, median retirement-plan wealth among US workers aged from fifty-one to fifty-six was $67,000; but this average figure masked enormous differences between those in different socio-economic classes. Median wealth of this kind for those in the top lifetime-earnings quintile was $294,700 (the figure for the ninetieth percentile of the wealth distribution within the same earnings quintile was $837,800). Meanwhile, median retirement

19   OECD, 'Pension Markets in Focus 2021', 2021, pp. 8–11 – at oecd. org.

20   T. Ghilarducci, S. Radpour and A. Webb, 'Retirement Plan Wealth Inequality: Measurement and Trends', *Journal of Pension Economics and Finance* 21: 1 (2022), pp. 119–39.

wealth for those in the lowest earnings quintile was zero: 51 per cent of those in that quintile had no retirement savings at all – most often, the authors found, because their employer did not sponsor a retirement plan, and less often because workers opted not to participate in such a plan. The upshot was that, in the same year (2010), the top lifetime-earnings quintile held half of all US retirement savings, while the bottom earnings quintile held only 1 per cent. And things had become progressively more unequal: in terms of share of total retirement savings, the top quintile fared better in 2010 than it had in 1992, whereas the bottom quintile fared worse.

All of which is to say that the generic 'citizen' that the GIIA and other champions of Western asset management identify as being the pre-eminent beneficiary of the sector's operations in fact has a predominant social location as well as a predominant geographical one. Saving for retirement, he or she is almost always based in North America or Europe, and is generally a high earner. Certainly, the likes of Blackstone do invest the retirement savings of some teachers, nurses and firefighters – the outsized allocations to real-asset funds by the Pennsylvania Public School Employees' Retirement System, for example, have shown us as much. But, compared to the universe of workers more widely, such workers do not have significant retirement savings. As and where asset managers generate capital gains for pension-scheme members, those gains are in reality captured disproportionately not by teachers, nurses and firefighters, but by bankers, lawyers and consultants.

Beyond pensions

As we saw in Chapter 4, Blackstone's infrastructure team spent much of 2018 and 2019 raising capital for a new open-ended fund, Blackstone Infrastructure Partners, to which, by the middle of the latter year, around eighty investors had committed a total of approximately $14 billion. Among this large cast of clients, one name stood out: the Public Investment Fund (PIF) of Saudi Arabia, that country's sovereign-wealth fund. It stood out primarily in view of the scale of its commitment: PIF had invested no less than $7 billion in Blackstone's new vehicle. This, it transpired, was in accordance with a deal that PIF had struck with the US-based asset manager in May 2017 – it would match all other investors' cumulative commitments to the fund, up to a maximum of $20 billion.

In the illustrative scenarios explored in the previous section of this chapter, we assumed that all external investors in our hypothetical real-asset fund were pension schemes. Clearly, however, that was not a realistic assumption. If 62 per cent of the approximately 5,000 separate institutional-investor commitments globally to closed-end infrastructure funds between 1990 and 2020 were pension-fund commitments, then it follows that nearly 40 per cent of investments were not made by pension schemes.

The key narrative ordinarily enrolled in support of what asset managers do is, as we have seen, that those whom such firms are ultimately making money for are ordinary citizens saving for retirement – the 'teachers, nurses and firefighters' invoked by Blackstone. We have already established that, in fact, alternative asset managers' own executives benefit from such firms' investments by orders of magnitude more than retirement savers ever do, all while the latter (alongside other providers of the capital that asset managers invest) bear essentially all the risk of investment underperformance. To this critique, we must now add another. To wit: Blackstone and other asset managers that invest in housing and infrastructure often raise capital from – and hence aim to generate investment returns for – economic actors around which it would be considerably harder to spin a positive public-relations story.

Who or what are these other actors? Peter Whoriskey and his colleagues at the *Washington Post* highlighted one important such constituency in a recent report about housing investment by the New York–based asset manager Pretium Partners. To raise funds for Progress Residential, its housing investment vehicle, Pretium had approached, among others, high-net-worth individuals – 'people wealthy enough to put up at least $2 million'. The reporters found that two particular individuals who committed funds for this venture, for example, were Vikrant Bhargava, who made his fortune in online gambling, and, via a Cayman Islands trust, Stephen Bronfman, the Canadian heir to the Seagram spirits dynasty.[21]

Meanwhile, alongside high-net-worth individuals, the three other most important categories of investor in real-asset funds (aside from pension schemes) are all institutional actors. Insurance companies are one; banks are another – and indeed, these two types of investor, both of which invest via asset managers principally to boost profits and shareholder returns, accounted between them for nearly 20 per cent of the roughly 5,000 historic commitments to closed-end infrastructure funds mentioned above.[22] The third category – returning us to the example of Blackstone Infrastructure Partners – is sovereign-wealth funds (SWFs).

Consider Saudi Arabia's PIF itself. Does Blackstone perform a socially beneficial role by investing on behalf of this entity? Hardly. It would be spurious to suggest that PIF, one of the world's largest SWFs, exists to benefit ordinary Saudi citizens. As the country was enduring one of its worst economic crises in decades in early 2020, for instance, and the government was trebling value-added tax while slashing domestic spending, PIF was busy buying stakes in international companies ranging from Boeing to Facebook. Its overseas spending spree, observed Anuj Chopra, belied 'deep and unpopular austerity measures' at home. One observer wondered aloud 'how Saudi citizens view their savings and collective national nest egg being spent on international equity markets at a time of a national economic crisis'. Why indeed, asked Chopra, were PIF's vast resources – its assets were valued at around $500 billion in 2021 – 'not instead used to prop up struggling small and medium enterprises choked by the pandemic?'[23]

Given the persistence of significant domestic socioeconomic problems such as high youth unemployment, the consensus

21   P. Whoriskey, S. Woodman and M. Gibbs, 'This Block Used to Be for First-Time Homebuyers. Then Global Investors Bought In.', *Washington Post*, 15 December 2021.

22   Andonov, Kräussl and Rauh, 'Institutional Investors and Infrastructure Investing', p. 3888.

23   A. Chopra, 'Saudi Wealth Fund "Shopping Spree" Belies Economic Pain', *Agence France-Presse*, 12 June 2020.

has instead gained ground that Saudi Arabia's PIF is in fact best viewed as a political instrument – a vehicle used by the government to project influence and control globally. Such an impression was certainly given sustenance by PIF's acquisition in 2021 of Newcastle United football club in the UK, a takeover described by Amnesty International as 'a blatant example of Saudi sportswashing'.[24]

The example of PIF and Newcastle United is perhaps extreme. Nevertheless, the scholarly literature on SWFs more generally, which is to say beyond the borders of Saudi Arabia and the Middle East – which is host to two additional major SWFs in the shape of the Abu Dhabi and Kuwait investment authorities – increasingly takes the same line: namely, that, in Manda Shemirani's words, 'investor states use their SWFs in order to exert political power and influence', including, but not only, 'over the recipient state'.[25]

The importance of investors other than pension schemes to asset managers' fundraising, and hence to their overall business model, is frequently underappreciated. A key reason for this is that commentators tend to focus, as indeed I have thus far, on the number of investments that different types of investor make in asset managers' funds. This metric can be highly misleading, for the simple reason that not all such investments are of an equal monetary value – as the above example of PIF and Blackstone's open-ended infrastructure fund makes abundantly clear. To assess their relative significance in monetary terms (which, to the asset manager, are the only terms that matter), it is important to consider, as far as one is able, different types of investors' respective shares of committed capital. Only then can one determine who asset managers are really making money for when they are not simply making it for themselves.

In this regard, Aleksandar Andonov and his colleagues have helpfully provided descriptive statistics for the varying size of the different types of institutional investor in infrastructure funds

24   P. Wintour, 'Saudi Crown Prince Asked Boris Johnson to Intervene in Newcastle United Bid', *Guardian*, 15 April 2021.

25   M. Shemirani, *Sovereign Wealth Funds and International Political Economy* (New York: Routledge, 2016), p. 7.

globally in the 1990–2020 period. Quantified in terms of average assets under management, this metric ranged from $163 billion at one extreme (SWFs) to $3 billion (endowments and foundations) at the other. Notably, banks and insurance companies were much closer to the former end of the size spectrum, with average assets under management of $158 billion, while pension schemes were much closer to the latter, weighing in at $25 billion in the case of public schemes and $11 billion for private schemes.[26]

Of course, the fact that a particular investor is large does not necessarily mean that each of its investments in an asset manager's funds will be correspondingly large. Large SWFs can sometimes make smallish individual commitments; small endowments can sometimes make relatively large commitments. In general, however, larger investors make larger average fund commitments. This stands to reason. It is inefficient for large investors to make large numbers of small commitments, each of which needs to be independently researched, negotiated and monitored. Equally, small investors, like all investors, aim to spread investment risk, which militates against putting all of one's capital eggs in one or a small number of fund baskets.

Because the average size of commitment to asset managers' real-asset funds varies between different categories of investor, the shares of overall fund capital contributed by those different types of investor can depart substantially from their respective shares of the number of investment commitments. Unfortunately, data showing shares of contributed capital for each main investor type are not publicly available for either infrastructure or real-estate funds. But certain data reported by Preqin for private-equity funds – a reasonable proxy for real-asset funds, for reasons we have already established – can help to substantiate the key point, which is that neither the number of commitments by investors in different categories, nor indeed the number of investors within each such category, necessarily tells us very much about how much capital different types of investor invest.

In particular, consider again the example of SWFs. In 2018, private-equity funds globally managed $2.97 trillion of investor

---

26 Andonov, Kräussl and Rauh, 'Institutional Investors and Infrastructure Investing', p. 3890.

capital. More than half of this – some $1.54 trillion – was from just 359 investors, referred to by Preqin as the 'Billion Dollar Club' – meaning that each such investor had at least $1 billion invested in private equity. Of the total population of institutional investors of all sizes globally with investments in private equity, only 1 per cent happened to be SWFs. But when it focused on its more exclusive subset of larger 'Billion Dollar' private-equity investor, Preqin found the SWF share to be higher: 4 per cent of Club members were SWFs. And the SWF share of invested capital – the measure that really matters – was much higher still. No less than 14 per cent – $215 billion – of the $1.5 trillion collectively held in private equity by the Club was capital from just fourteen SWFs.[27]

In other words, one really should not read too much into alternative asset managers' pronouncements that pension schemes – and, in particular, teachers, nurses and firefighters saving for retirement – are the third-party constituency they represent. It is certainly true that pension schemes are important real-asset (and private-equity) clients. But so, too, are banks, insurance companies and SWFs – much more important than either asset managers' own proclamations, or indeed much of the existing independent analysis of the alternative asset-management sector, would lead one to believe. Only about one in fifty of historic commitments to closed-end infrastructure funds globally have been made by SWFs like Saudi Arabia's PIF.[28] But we can be sure that the SWF share of the capital committed to and invested by those infrastructure funds, and thus of the returns that such funds have generated, has been far higher than that.

Asset-manager society is nothing if not a creature of the modern world – a world riven by inequalities of wealth and power. Asset managers take those inequalities as they are – inequalities embodied in the very capital committed to their investment funds – and actively reproduce them. The very last thing they do is challenge or alleviate such inequalities. Indeed,

---

27 Preqin, 'The $1bn Club: Largest Investors in Private Equity', June 2018 – at preqin.com.

28 Andonov, Kräussl and Rauh, 'Institutional Investors and Infrastructure Investing', p. 3888.

arguably the signal lesson of Blackstone's 2017 deal with PIF is that, if asset managers like Blackstone really do have a proto-typical investor whose interests they faithfully serve, it is not a humble Pennsylvanian schoolteacher or Californian firefighter, but rather the likes of Yasir Al-Rumayyan, the chairman at one of the world's most profitable companies, the oil giant Saudi Aramco; of north-east England's most popular football club, Newcastle United; and of the world's most notorious sovereign wealth fund – which is, of course, the Public Investment Fund of Saudi Arabia.

Unequal Returns

In strictly financial terms, the commitment to Blackstone's new infrastructure fund that Saudi Arabia's PIF made in 2017 was notable not only for its size but also for the preferential terms that PIF secured. Throughout this book, including in my examination of a hypothetical fund earlier in this chapter, I have assumed both relatively standard fee terms – the 'two and twenty' model, at least for closed-end funds – and that all investors in the same fund pay the same fees. In reality, however, investors do not always pay the same fees. Terms vary both between and within funds: they are negotiable.

Perhaps unsurprisingly, the greatest source of leverage in fee negotiations with asset managers such as Blackstone is scale: how much capital does an investor potentially bring to the table? 'Fee reductions are customary across the industry for investors of scale', Blackstone has acknowledged. As we have just seen, the investors with the greatest scale are sovereign wealth funds such as PIF. Hence, in an unambiguous demonstration of their power, they typically secure the best terms. And if any capital commitment justified preferential treatment, then PIF's invest-ment in Blackstone Infrastructure Partners, the asset manager argued, was surely it. It was, after all, 'a decade-plus investment that is more than 10 times larger than any fund commitment we've received in firm history'.[29]

29   Cited in G. Tan, 'How Blackstone Landed $20 Billion from Saudis for New Fund', *Bloomberg*, 21 October 2018.

In the event, there were two dimensions to PIF's preferential terms. First, its basic fees were lower than those of other investors. Second, each year from the third year of the fund's life, PIF's costs would be lowered by an amount equal to 15 per cent of the total annual fee revenue that Blackstone generated from other investors in the fund – this was, in essence, a revenue-sharing agreement. Interestingly, in reporting on the agreement between Blackstone and PIF, the institutional investor whose fee terms *Bloomberg* compared with PIF's fee terms was none other than the Pennsylvania Public School Employees' Retirement System (PSERS), whose historic investments in real-estate funds I discussed earlier.[30] PSERS had itself committed $500 million to Blackstone Infrastructure Partners. It would pay a 0.75 per cent management fee for the first two years and a 0.9 per cent fee thereafter; its performance fee was a carry of 12.5 per cent; as we have seen, the fees charged by open-ended funds, such as this one, are lower than those charged by closed-end funds. PIF's management fee was 0.75 per cent on its first $10 billion commitment, and 0.65 per cent on any additional investment. Carried interest would be charged at 10 per cent. And then, of course, there was its revenue share.

As we have seen, different constituencies occupying different positions in the asset-management investment chain bear different risks and enjoy markedly different levels of financial reward. In the case explored in our two hypothetical scenarios, there were three such constituencies – the asset manager itself, the pension schemes that committed capital to the asset manager's fund (that is, the fund's limited partners) and the individual members of those pension schemes. The fact that there are varying fee terms for different limited partners points to another key issue. Even if they were to invest in and exit from a fund at the same points in time, it is unlikely that all investors in a particular fund would earn the same return on investment after fees had been paid. PIF's net multiple of invested capital (MOIC) from its commitment to Blackstone Infrastructure Partners will inevitably be different to, and higher than, PSERS's net MOIC from its commitment to the same fund. This leads one to

30 Ibid.

ask: Which LPs, in general, do best? Which do worst? And what are the implications for the wider question about asset-manager society with which this chapter is concerned: Who gains?

That *Bloomberg*'s report happened to compare PIF's fee terms with Blackstone Infrastructure Partners to the terms negotiated by PSERS was fortuitous; but it was also highly apposite. Research has repeatedly shown that public institutional investors such as PSERS consistently earn lower returns from their investments with alternative asset managers, such as private-equity firms, than institutional investors do in general. This is partly due to systematically unfavourable fee arrangements, such as those that PSERS was able to negotiate with Blackstone (at least compared to PIF's terms).[31] But higher fees, it seems, are not the only explanation for inferior returns. Other explanations put forward include public investors' 'politicized governance structures', their 'inability to compensate and attract talented staff members', and their 'inability to select or access better-performing asset managers'.[32]

The aforementioned research that has exposed public investors' lower returns generally does not focus specifically on investment in real-asset funds. But a recent study has demonstrated that the underperformance of investors such as public pension schemes (representing public-sector workers) indeed also applies in that specific context. In its analysis of net returns from closed-end infrastructure funds to which institutional investors committed capital between 1990 and 2020, the study found that public investors received an IRR that was 1.81 percentage points lower than that received by private investors, and a multiple of invested capital that was 0.038 lower.[33] On the face of it, these look like small numbers. But, as the authors of the study pointed out, the gap is in fact substantial when considered not in isolation, but rather with reference to absolute expected returns. The 1.8 percentage point lower IRR of public investors represents

---

31   J. Begenau and E. Siriwardane, 'How Do Private Equity Fees Vary Across Public Pensions?', February 2020 – at ssrn.com.

32   Andonov, Kräussl and Rauh, 'Institutional Investors and Infrastructure Investing', pp. 3884–5.

33   Ibid., p. 3884.

an underperformance of fully 30 per cent of the expected real annual return on infrastructure if the latter is assumed (in line with recent historic industry norms) to be around 5 per cent. Needless to say, this is not a small number.

In the boosterist discourse surrounding and buttressing asset-manager society, public-sector employees, as we have seen, invariably enjoy pride of place. It is for them, it is said, that asset managers make money. But, in reality, such employees – the firefighter, the nurse, the teacher – are utterly peripheral to the rewards ledger. Not only do they hold only a very limited proportion of the vast retirement-savings capital that asset managers invest – and, of course, an even smaller share of total invested capital from all institutional sources. They also suffer the indignity of realising subpar rates of return from the managed investment of those meagre resources.

Asset Management and Fiscal Extractivism

Extractivism versus mutualism

The recent history of the investment strategy of AP3 – the third of Sweden's five main public pension funds – looks much like that of leading public pension schemes in other territories of the Global North, and with comparable consequences for the evolution of its investment portfolio. Until as recently as 2005, less than 5 per cent of AP3's capital was allocated to alternative asset classes such as private equity, real estate and infrastructure: the vast bulk was invested in publicly listed shares. By 2020, however, the proportion allocated to alternatives had grown to 25 per cent, with real estate leading the way.[34]

It is a revealing exercise to examine what some of those newly favoured alternatives consisted of. One of the unlisted real-asset funds in which AP3 was significantly invested (it owned nearly 20 per cent of fund units) in 2020, for instance, was the UK asset manager Innisfree's PFI Secondary Fund II.[35] Digging into the investments made by that closed-end fund, one finds, in turn,

---

34 AP3, *Annual Report 2020*, p. 26.

35 Ibid., p. 74.

near the top of the list, a thirty-year concession contract with North Lanarkshire Council in Scotland to build (at a capital cost of £158 million), finance and operate twenty-four primary and secondary schools. Thus, the retirement savings of, among others, Swedish schoolteachers have more or less directly funded the construction and maintenance of a portfolio of Scottish schools.

It would be easy to see this – the public's savings capital explicitly funding public-use infrastructure, including across national borders – as a relatively novel phenomenon. Indeed, such was essentially the thrust of the narrative I related in Chapter 2. As they increasingly arrogated substantial pools of capital to themselves from the 1960s through to the 1980s, pension schemes and other major institutional investors, as we saw, invested – as Sweden's AP3 also did until recently – almost exclusively in 'traditional' asset classes, and especially publicly listed company shares, only beginning to turn to alternatives in general, and to real assets in particular, towards the end of the twentieth century.

This narrative holds. But if one now winds the clock back to *before* the 1960s, one finds that the phenomenon of the public's savings capital explicitly funding public-use infrastructure is not in fact novel. This was very much a common way of things, for example, in the United States in the first half of the twentieth century. Local governments raised money for building infrastructure such as roads, sewers and schools principally by issuing bonds, and among the main buyers of those bonds were public pension schemes, which in that era were restricted in most states to investing in debt raised by public bodies. As late as 1942, municipal bonds accounted for approximately 70 per cent of all US public-pension investment holdings.[36] Insofar as the yields on such bonds were lower than yields on financial assets with equivalent risk profiles, public retirement savings indirectly subsidised the construction of public-use infrastructure. Only after World War II, when rules on investment by public-pension schemes were progressively relaxed and scheme administrators

36   M. R. Glass and S. H. Vanatta, 'The Frail Bonds of Liberalism: Pensions, Schools, and the Unraveling of Fiscal Mutualism in Postwar New York', *Capitalism: A Journal of History and Economics* 2 (2021), pp. 427–72.

went in search of higher returns in corporate bonds and stocks, did the share of municipal bonds in US public-pension investment portfolios start to fall, dropping to below 20 per cent by 1957, and to below 1 per cent by 1972 – which was effectively the point at which we picked up the story in Chapter 2.

The point of rehearsing this history here is that it accentuates by way of contrast a key, historically specific characteristic of the contemporary scheme of things. Today, in buying into infrastructure funds, public pension schemes, among others, once again often find themselves in the position of explicitly supporting the construction of public-use infrastructures: witness AP3 and the North Lanarkshire school system. But the intermediary who controls, channels and profits from such support is now of a radically different nature.

In the pre-war US context, the owner of the physical infrastructure and the issuer of the financial assets enabling the circulation of capital into and through the built environment was the local state. Michael Glass and Sean Vanatta have helpfully conceptualised this particular pre-war political-economic constellation in terms of 'fiscal mutualism' – a kind of virtuous circle redounding to the benefit of the state (the linchpin of the circle) and of taxpayers.[37]

Today, by contrast, the owner of the infrastructure and the issuer of the relevant financial assets is not the local state, but increasingly an extra-local private-sector asset manager. Thus, if the arrangement described by Glass and Vanatta represented fiscal mutualism, what we see around us now can perhaps best be thought of instead as a form of fiscal *extractivism*. The public's capital is once again being mobilised to fund public-use infrastructures. Yet the linchpin of this investment cycle is today a private-sector actor actively extracting tribute from the fiscal domain.

Fiscal extractivism and shareholder loans

That fiscal extractivism is an appropriate conceptualisation for asset-manager society is underscored by a series of important further fiscal considerations. Coincidentally, we can approach

---

37 Ibid.

these by way of another example of pertinent connections between the UK asset manager Innisfree and the country of Sweden. In this case, however, the example involves Innisfree investing *in* Sweden as opposed to attracting limited-partner capital *from* Sweden.

In 2010, in Sweden's first public–private partnership (PPP) in the healthcare sector, Innisfree led a consortium, named Swedish Hospital Partners (SHP), to secure a contract to build and operate (until 2040) the New Karolinska Solna hospital in Stockholm. Its partner in the consortium was the Swedish construction company Skanska. As is typically the case with such PPPs (indeed, with asset-manager-led investments in general), much of the funding for the consortium vehicle, and thus for the project, was raised with debt – initially reported to be around 5 billion Swedish kronor (SEK) in this instance.[38]

So far, so unremarkable. In 2014, however, certain matters with acute fiscal significance came to light when the International Consortium of Investigative Journalists revealed hitherto undisclosed information about tax arrangements in Luxembourg set up by PricewaterhouseCoopers for several of its clients – including Innisfree. It turned out that among the lenders to SHP were two Luxembourg-based Innisfree funds themselves, which had lent the consortium over 500 million SEK at the notably steep interest rate of 9 per cent. Reporters who investigated this arrangement for Sveriges Television (SVT) calculated that, over the course of the PPP contract, SHP would pay around 1.3 billion SEK in interest to Innisfree – its part-owner.[39]

There are a number of layered issues in play here. One is the tax implications of leverage per se. Taxable commercial entities pay tax on profits earned after, not before, debt-financing expenses. This has significant consequences in asset-manager society, inasmuch as the modus operandi of alternative asset management is, as we have seen, precisely to leverage portfolio investment (see Chapter 1). The result of asset managers loading

---

38 'Karolinska Hospital PPP Financial Close', *Project Finance*, 21 June 2010.

39 S. Bergman and J. Dyfvermark, 'New Karolinska – Advanced Tax Scheme in Luxembourg', 26 November 2014 – at svt.se.

debt onto portfolio companies used to hold acquired infrastructure or housing is to saddle those companies with ongoing interest payments that suppress the same companies' taxable profits. Frequently, the debt is of such a magnitude that little or no tax is paid, even where underlying operating profitability is strong. Under its much-criticised tenure, for example, Martin Stanley's Macquarie added in the region of £2 billion in debt to Thames Water's balance sheet, so that the latter ended up paying almost no UK corporation tax for a decade. Thus, returning to Stockholm, part of the concern in Sweden with the volume of debt shouldered by the Innisfree-controlled SHP has been related to exactly the same dynamic: such leverage, SVT's report noted, would 'reduce [SHP's] taxable profits in Sweden'.

The second key feature of the case of SHP and the Solna hospital was, of course, the specific identity of the recipient of these tax-suppressing interest payments – namely, Innisfree itself. Essentially, the reason that the state would not make gains (in the form of tax receipts) in this case was that the asset manager would do so: such is the crux of fiscal extractivism. During the course of the relatively brief history of asset-manager society, the particular type of loan advanced by Innisfree to SHP has indeed represented a common vehicle of said extractivism. A so-called shareholder loan, it involves one or more shareholders lending money to the company in which equity is held (see Chapter 1). The higher the interest rate, the higher the interest payment to the shareholder, and hence the lower the tax payment to the government.

Examples involving real-asset investments by asset managers abound. In 2017, Jonathan Ford reported on two cases in the UK, both involving Macquarie. One related to the company Arqiva, which controls vital elements of the UK's telecommunications infrastructure, and in which Macquarie and IFM Investors (another asset manager) are the second- and third-largest members of the controlling investor consortium. In the three years to mid 2016, Arqiva earned £822 million of cumulative operating profit – but this was more than negated by interest charges of approximately £1.5 billion, of which roughly half went on servicing shareholder loans bearing interest at an attractive 13–14 per cent. Interest rates were even higher in Ford's second example, the Wales and West gas distribution network, which a Macquarie-led consortium owned between 2005 and 2012, and financed with shareholder loans bearing interest rates of 15–21 per cent.[40]

Meanwhile, Jason Ward has recounted an instructive Australian example. Upon buying the care-home chain Allity from Lend Lease Group in 2013, using its fifth buyout fund, the asset manager Archer Capital provided Allity with a loan paying it (Archer) interest of 15 per cent. Despite subsequently recording profits before interest of around A$300 million in both 2014–15 and 2015–16, Allity reported zero taxable income in either year. Ward concluded that there was 'little doubt that the sole purpose of this shareholder loan at a 15% interest was to reduce taxable income on profits'.[41]

Alternative mechanisms of fiscal extractivism

Before returning one last time to Solna and SHP–Innisfree, it is important to note that shareholder loans are not the only mechanism that asset-management firms active in the real-assets space use to extract at source income that one ordinarily would have expected to flow to the state as tax revenues.

Perversely, some alternative such mechanisms include ones designed and proffered by the state itself. Many Western governments, for example, allow companies that generate the bulk of their revenue from the letting of real estate to incorporate themselves as real-estate investment trusts (REITs). In doing so, such companies are able to shield most of their profits from income taxes, and to distribute such profits in the form of shareholder dividends. It is no accident that, where national provisions allow, asset managers almost always use REIT structures to hold their real-estate portfolios, including their housing portfolios. In Blackstone's case, for instance, Invitation Homes – its original

---

40 J. Ford, 'Lax Regulation Has Turned Britain into a Rentier's Paradise', *Financial Times*, 1 October 2017.

41 J. Ward, 'Tax Avoidance by For-Profit Aged Care Companies: Profit Shifting on Public Funds', May 2018, p. 26 – at cictar.org.

US single-family housing rental operation – was, as it remains, a REIT; so too are the various companies through which Blackstone holds most of its Spanish residential-property assets – one of the largest of these being Fidere Patrimonio, which owns thousands of rental units located principally in Madrid, and in which Blackstone funds own around 99 per cent of the shares.

Other available extractivist mechanisms tend to be asset managers' own creations, however. Consider, for example, that, in 2021, Macquarie invested €43 million in a 50 MW solar power plant in Spain, but that Macquarie owned no equity in the plant either before or after this investment. How can we account for this? The explanation is that this was a debt investment, made not by one of Macquarie's numerous equity funds but by one of its growing number of private debt funds, in this case its Green Energy Debt Fund. Upon announcing the investment, Macquarie disclosed that, over the previous decade, its private debt funds had invested a total of approximately €2.7 billion worldwide in around forty renewable-energy projects.[42]

Asset managers' private debt funds, sometimes also referred to as private credit funds, operate in much the same way as the equity funds with which we are more familiar. They pool money from external investors (their limited partners), and their general partners earn fees by managing and investing that client capital. But instead of using the committed capital to buy shares and take asset ownership and control (the staple operation of asset-manager society), private debt funds invest by making long-term loans, which constitute 'private' debt inasmuch as it is not issued or traded in an open market; and such funds generate income in the form of interest payments, as opposed to dividends and capital gains. Although such funds have existed for decades, they have risen to prominence only since the global financial crisis. As banks increasingly withdrew from what they considered to be 'risky' lending, asset managers stepped into the breach. The

---

42 'Macquarie Closes €43 Million Debt Investment in Spanish Concentrated Solar Power Plant Sponsored by Q-Energy', 23 September 2021 – at macquarie.com.

total client capital managed by private debt funds increased from less than $200 billion in 2007 to over $800 billion by 2019.[43] A year later, that figure had reached $1 trillion.[44]

Although it remains relatively marginal within the broader firmament of the asset-management business, certain aspects of the private-debt-fund phenomenon are particularly significant for our purposes. For one thing, much of the debt that such funds provide serves precisely to help finance real-asset acquisitions made by other asset managers' equity funds. In other words, when one asset manager buys an infrastructure or real-estate asset on a leveraged basis, it increasingly frequently does so with the use of debt supplied not by a bank, but by another asset manager.

While some asset managers, such as Oaktree Capital Management, are credit-fund specialists, most of the firms with a significant presence in private-debt asset management are the same firms that dominate equity-based alternative asset management. Thus, debt funds run by one such firm often make loans to companies acquired or owned by the equity funds of a direct competitor. 'Marquee names such as Ares, Apollo and Blackstone might compete for an acquisition', noted a report in the *Financial Times*, 'and then end up as partners in the debt financing.'[45] The Spanish solar plant in which Macquarie made its 2021 debt investment, for example, was owned by a rival asset manager, the Madrid-based Q-Energy.

More pointedly still, private debt funds serve as quintessential instruments of asset-manager society's signature fiscal extractivism. Like shareholder loans, debt financing of real assets that is organised through private investment funds has the effect of suppressing *de jure* government taxes on operating profits by imposing a de facto asset-manager debt-servicing 'tax'. In short, one way or another, fiscal duty is essentially privatised and siphoned off.

43   'Private Debt', at preqin.com.

44   BCG, 'The $100 Trillion Machine', July 2021, p. 2 – at bcg.com.

45   J. Rennison, E. Platt and S. Indap, 'Private Credit Joins Private Equity to Freeze Out Banks', *Financial Times*, 13 July 2021.

Extractivism at large

Of course, if the taxes not paid by, say, SHP, Allity or Fidere Patrimonio on operating profits effectively were paid in equivalent measure by asset managers (and their limited partners) on the interest payments and dividends that such managers extract, then there would be no net gain to the asset manager or loss to the state – and no fiscal extractivism. But there is, for one thing, a crucial geographical issue at stake here: Where are any such taxes paid? For example, do Blackstone and the limited partners in its relevant real-estate funds pay tax on dividends received from Fidere Patrimonio in Spain – which is where all Fidere Patrimonio's housing tenants pay their rent – or elsewhere in the world?

Coming back to our example of SHP, Innisfree and Solna helps to sharpen the issue. Insofar as SHP operates in Stockholm, commentators in Sweden were surely entitled to think – as many expressly said they did upon SVT's disclosure of details of Innisfree's shareholder loans – that it was in Sweden that any taxes arising from SHP's activities should be paid. But the effect of the shareholder loans was to transfer part of the tax liability, in the first place, to the location of domicile of the relevant Innisfree funds, which was Luxembourg. It was highly significant, then, that SVT's report, mentioned above, worried specifically that the high-yielding Innisfree loans would reduce taxable profits 'in Sweden'. Fiscal extractivism is territorial as much as it is political and economic.

Interestingly, uncovering the territoriality of the fiscal extractivism effected by real-asset asset managers has seemingly become something of a speciality of Scandinavian investigative journalists. Five years after Sweden's SVT revealed the machinations centred on SHP and Stockholm, the Norwegian broadcaster TV 2 revealed an uncannily similar case in Norway involving an investment I discussed in Chapter 1: BlackRock's ownership of the Tellenes wind farm. The key similarity was that local taxable profits were being suppressed by interest payments on high-yielding loans advanced specifically by the controlling investment fund, in this case Global Renewable Power II, which, like the relevant Innisfree funds in the case of SHP, was based in a tax haven. 'This is how what is actually a profit from Tellenes wind farm', the tax lawyer Gregar Berg-Rolness told TV 2, 'ends up as interest income for a company in the Cayman Islands.' Berg-Rolness went on: '[T]his is a scandal. International capitalists are told, "just come and help yourself".'[46] So striking are the similarities that a cynic might suspect a pattern.

Moreover, it is well known that methods of tax minimisation are systematically embedded in such geographical transfers. The SVT report on SHP–Solna, for example, observed that the Luxembourg tax rate that Innisfree's funds would pay on their interest income would be 'near zero'. Likewise, research published by Corporate Watch in 2013 showed that offshore-based shareholders in various UK water companies had historically issued some £3.4 billion of quoted Eurobond loans to those companies, generating interest payments that suppressed tax liabilities in the UK – and on which those shareholders themselves paid no tax. Among the relevant water companies were three that were owned either by individual asset managers (South Staffordshire Water – owned by Alinda Capital Partners) or by investment consortia led by asset managers (Thames Water – owned by a Macquarie-led consortium; and Yorkshire Water – owned by a consortium led by Citi Infrastructure Investors).[47]

Indeed, everything that we now know about the secretive circuits of capital making up asset-manager society suggests that the ultimate winner from the state's losses is the asset manager itself; it is both principal architect and prime beneficiary of fiscal extractivism. Nowhere, perhaps, is this dynamic – namely that of the asset manager capturing gains that one might have expected to flow to the state – clearer than in relation to the taxation of carried interest, which is therefore the final issue we will consider.

Carried interest, as we have seen, is the real-asset asset manager's main performance fee, calculated as a percentage of the profits that a fund generates. In the United States (the domicile

46   S. Figved, I. Fredriksen and K. A. Kleppe, 'TV 2 avslører: Inntekter fra norsk vind sendes til en skattefri øy i Karibien', 24 November 2019 – at tv2.no (my translation).

47   R. Clancy, 'UK Water Companies Avoid Paying Tax', *Telegraph*, 15 February 2013.

of most major asset managers), as in many other countries, asset-management firms that are incorporated as partnerships, as most such firms conventionally have been, pay tax on carried interest at the capital gains rate. The logic of this tax treatment, such as it is, turns on the notion of risk: the asset manager, it is said, has put capital at risk, and thus carry represents a return on invested capital, and should be taxed as a capital gain. But critics insist that carried interest should be treated as a payment for services rendered (the management of clients' assets), and hence taxed like regular income.

To some ears, this may sound like a fiscal triviality – but it absolutely is not. Generally speaking, in most countries, the rate of capital gains tax – and thus the rate that asset managers have paid as tax on carry – has historically been much lower than the rate of income tax – the rate that critics believe asset managers *should* pay on carry, and which the companies owned by asset managers *would* pay on profits were they not shielded from the tax authorities by the mechanisms of tax suppression mentioned above.

If anybody had been in any doubt about how much this tax treatment mattered to asset managers' financial bottom line, such doubt was summarily dispelled when, in 2010, President Obama moved to close the carry tax-loophole in the United States. The industry united in indignation. The response specifically of Blackstone's chief executive, Stephen Schwarzman – himself worth $40 billion – was nothing short of jaw-dropping: he compared the threat from Obama to Hitler's invasion of Poland.[48]

Obama's gambit failed, and, both in the United States and farther afield, the carried-interest tax provision survives. Writing in the *New York Times* in 2017, James Stewart called the US provision 'a tax loophole for the rich that just won't die'.[49] Like the proverbial cockroach that not even a nuclear explosion can kill off, the most recent demonstration of the loophole's remarkable obduracy came in 2022. Critics were jubilant when

48   J. Alter, 'Schwarzman: "It's a War" Between Obama, Wall St', *Newsweek*, 15 August 2010.

49   J. Stewart, 'A Tax Loophole for the Rich that Just Won't Die', *New York Times*, 9 November 2017.

it was reported that 'closure' of the loophole would be one of the means of funding the US Inflation Reduction Act (on which, see Chapter 6). But the fine print revealed that the proposal was not in fact to close the loophole, only to modestly circumscribe asset managers' ability to exploit it. And, in the event, even that weak proposed inhibition proved too much for the country's political economy to accommodate. Only once the carried-interest proposal was scrapped did the legislation pass.[50]

It would, perhaps, be difficult to think of a better illustration in microcosm of the main themes explored in this chapter. Notwithstanding all manner of (ultimately self-serving) claims to the contrary, asset-manager society, as we have seen, primarily benefits and strengthens a wealthy global elite. Once one strips away the foliage, it becomes clear that, in terms of its root-and-branch structures and mechanics, this is in fact precisely what asset-manager society is designed to do. The disproportionate capture of the financial gains accruing from asset-manager society by a small elite is just as integral a feature – a necessary rather than contingent outcome – as the widely socialised social and economic costs we examined in Chapter 4. Both the tax treatment of carried interest and the inability or unwillingness of policymakers to modify it stand as testament to this fact.

All that remains for us to examine is where things might now be headed, as the global financial crisis – so fundamental to the consolidation and expansion of asset-manager society over the past decade – increasingly recedes in history's rear-view mirror, as the recent ravages of Covid-19 subside, war rumbles on in eastern Europe, a period of relative macroeconomic stability is shattered by the abrupt return of inflation concentrated in food and energy markets, and intersecting global crises of housing and climate escalate daily. What, in short, is the future of asset-manager society?

---

50   J. Politi, 'Kyrsten Sinema Backs Joe Biden's Flagship Climate, Health and Tax Bill', *Financial Times*, 5 August 2022.

6

The Future

Problems, Problems ...

The identification of 'problems' always depends on perspective: what looks like a significant concern to some will seem a minor irritant to others, and perhaps an opportunity to others still. So it was that, in 2021, as peoples and institutions the world over struggled to come to terms with the continuation of the coronavirus pandemic and to adapt their lives and activities to the new realities it had created, those people and institutions identified problems of widely varying kinds.

Many saw the pre-eminent problem as a lack of investment, and in particular a lack of investment in precisely the kinds of assets we have been examining in this book: housing and other critical infrastructures of socioeconomic production and reproduction. This camp included the consultancy McKinsey. 'We all need places to live', three of its consultants wrote,

> but housing stock hasn't kept pace with demand ... While real-estate prices rise, affordable housing remains in very short supply: Some 165 million people in 22 advanced economies are overburdened by housing costs ... We need to generate economic growth investing in assets like infrastructure to broaden and sustain our prosperity, yet infrastructure investment gaps have proved persistent ... In all, we have estimated that the world needs to spend about $3.7 trillion annually on infrastructure for the next 15 years.[1]

---

1 J. Woetzel, A. Madgavkar and J. Mischke, 'Global Wealth Has Exploded. Are We Using It Wisely?', 26 November 2021 – at barrons.com.

Meanwhile, others highlighted entirely different types of 'problem'. Not least among those were alternative asset managers. In mid 2020, a report by the *Financial Times* had observed that these firms were struggling to find opportunities to invest all the money that institutional investors had committed to their funds: the industry as a whole had '$1.5tn in so-called "dry powder" burning a hole in its pocket'.[2] A year later, the problem had seemingly worsened, with the amount of industry dry powder having grown to $2.3 trillion. In short, alternative asset managers, as Steve Gelsi wrote, continued in 2021 to face 'a problem most people wish they had – they have more money than they know what to do with'.[3]

Given this particular juxtaposition of problems, it is probably unsurprising that we have latterly seen a hardening among elites of a consensus that has been growing and crystallising now for several decades – namely, that each such problem is in fact the solution to the other. Asset managers can solve the trillion-plus-dollar housing-and-infrastructure investment problem; housing and infrastructure can solve asset managers' trillion-plus-dollar dry-powder problem. As the McKinsey consultants concluded, with what seemed like impeccable logic: 'There is no shortage of money and no shortage of opportunities to spend it more productively.' All that was required was to facilitate the reconciliation of surplus capital on the one hand with investment opportunity on the other.

In this final chapter, I explore the nature of this consensus and its likely implications for the future of asset-manager society – and thus of society itself.

---

2 J. Ford, 'Private Equity Fees Have Become a Rentier's Bonanza', *Financial Times*, 30 August 2020.

3 S. Gelsi, 'Private-Equity Powerhouses Are Sitting on Piles of Uninvested Cash', MarketWatch, 25 August 2021 – at marketwatch.com.

Asset-Manager Society After the Pandemic

Rich countries

One of the many things for which the peak pandemic years of 2020 and 2021 were notable was the massive intervention and spending conducted by governments in the Global North. As they put economies and societies into lockdown, governments from Canada to Singapore and from Spain to the United States borrowed heavily in order to give direct support to strained households, businesses and health services. 'As the private sector shut down', wrote Adam Tooze, 'the public sector expanded ... Government spending made up for the loss of private incomes and spending.'[4] The United States alone saw government debt rise by nearly \$3 trillion in 2020. Relative to national economic output, the biggest incremental public debtor was the UK, whose government, in the twelve months from April 2020 to April 2021, borrowed £299 billion – 'the highest figure since records began in 1946'.[5] The state, remarked the *Financial Times*'s Martin Sandbu in December 2020, was 'back in a big way'.[6]

Also notable was the response of the financial markets. For several decades, the orthodoxy among mainstream economists and politicians of the Global North had been that the bond markets effectively disciplined debt-fuelled government 'excess'. If governments funded public expenditures through substantial increases in borrowing, the market would lift interest rates on government debt in order to instil greater fiscal prudence. The US president Bill Clinton famously acknowledged this orthodoxy in the mid 1990s when, upon being advised to rein in his own spending plans, he lamented being hamstrung by 'a bunch of fucking bond traders'. And this was plainly the orthodoxy behind the austerity measures widely introduced after the 2007–09 financial crisis: governments had borrowed to excess

---

4 A. Tooze, 'What If the Coronavirus Crisis Is Just a Trial Run?', *New York Times*, 1 September 2021.

5 B. King, 'How Much is Covid Costing the UK and How Will We Pay?', 22 June 2021 – at bbc.com.

6 M. Sandbu, 'The Post-Pandemic Brave New World', IMF, December 2020 – at imf.org.

to bail out the banks, the argument went, thus requiring a period of judicious (if painful) fiscal belt-tightening.

But 2020 seemingly shattered this orthodoxy; the markets did not react as the experts expected. As Tooze observed, 'Governments around the world issued debt as not seen since World War II, and yet interest rates plunged. As the private sector shut down, the public sector expanded. As government deficits grew, the monetary system responded elastically.' The lesson appeared to be clear: the markets were simply not worried by the huge volumes of extra debt taken on by the governments of the world's richer countries. 'Budget constraints don't seem to exist', reflected Tooze; 'money is a mere technicality.' In short, the pandemic had 'erased' the supposed 'hard limits of financial sustainability'.[7] The economic thinking underlying the political economy of austerity had been decisively repudiated – or so it seemed.

For those of a Keynesian persuasion (Tooze included), this was nothing less than revelatory. 'The world discovered', Tooze went on to say, 'that John Maynard Keynes was right when he declared during World War II that "anything we can actually do, we can afford".'[8] Tooze was quick to note that this declaration must be geographically circumscribed – if it is true, it is, as we shall see, true only for rich countries. Nevertheless, the implication was profound: the limits to government ambition are political, not financial; if rich-country governments choose not to spend, it is not because the expenditure is unaffordable. Unsurprisingly, all of this gave a considerable fillip to those who for years had been agitating in vain for governments to put public money to work in addressing society's key challenges – not the least of which were the need for infrastructure and housing investment highlighted in the McKinsey report mentioned above.

Confidence that the considerable long-term silver lining to Covid-19 might be a new era of big government, spending generously on investments with significant public benefit, was especially high in the United States. On the one hand, it was already widely appreciated that the need for such investment was

---

7   Tooze, 'What if the Coronavirus Crisis Is Just a Trial Run?'
8   Ibid.

disproportionately urgent in that country. In the 2021 iteration
of its influential 'report card' on the state of US infrastructure,
for example, the American Society of Civil Engineers (ASCE)
rated eleven of seventeen categories of national infrastructure
in the D-range – indicating 'mostly below standard', exhibit-
ing 'significant deterioration' and 'strong risk of failure' – and
estimated the funding gap over the following decade at $2.6
trillion.[9] Meanwhile, January 2021 saw a new, Democratic president come to power. Whereas Donald Trump had frequently
talked about stepping-up infrastructure investment during his
presidency without taking meaningful action, Joe Biden's team
quickly set about drafting legislation to that end, the new president's initial proposals calling for $2 trillion in government
infrastructure spending over four years. Thus, as Tooze noted,
there was great 'excitement' on the US left; the atmosphere was
'intoxicating'. 'If money *was* a mere technicality', advocates
enthused, 'what else could be done? Action on social justice,
climate change, the Green New Deal, all seemed within reach.'[10]

Few of those heralding the 'return of the state' registered the
pinched nature of that return, however. For all that governments
in the Global North borrowed and spent on a grand scale in
2020–21, the ownership and control of what they were spending money on did not change. The rescue packages provided
zero challenge to the default existing distribution of economic
resources and assets as between the public and private sectors.
Indeed, in many countries, the emergency funding called forth
by the pandemic merely hastened and amplified the longstanding
pattern of such resources and assets increasingly flowing towards
the private sector. The UK was arguably the emblematic case. By
late 2021, the total value of contracts awarded to private firms
by the UK government in response to Covid-19 had reached
nearly £50 billion. Serious concerns were widely expressed
about the processes that had governed the awarding of these

---

9 American Society of Civil Engineers, 'A Comprehensive Assessment of
America's Infrastructure: 2021 Report Card', March 2021 – at infrastructure
reportcard.org.

10 Tooze, 'What If the Coronavirus Crisis Is Just a Trial Run?' (emphasis
in original).

contracts – covering everything from personal protective equipment to the provision of test-and-trace services. That the assets those contracts represented would be acquired specifically by the private sector was, however, more or less taken for granted.

President Biden's initial proposals for infrastructure investment likewise spoke volumes about his country's underlying political-economic realities. Promises were made of modest amounts of government spending on public housing and certain other long-neglected publicly owned infrastructures (schools and transit). But more space in the proposal text was given over to encouraging private-sector financing – most notably, of electricity-generating facilities and transmission networks, as well as vehicle-charging networks.[11] In this, Bidenism in fact represented a continuation of, rather than a break from, Trumpism; Trump's stillborn infrastructure plans had themselves been based on 'using federal dollars as up-front investment to entice private enterprises to provide most of the financing'.[12] It scarcely required spelling out that the economic returns ultimately generated by assets funded largely or wholly by the private sector would likewise be largely or wholly privatised. What this certainly was not was a Rooseveltian vision for a new era of large-scale, publicly financed, publicly owned infrastructure, despite much of the rhetoric surrounding the proposals in early 2021.

Crucially, alternative-asset-management firms sensed this fact, even if Biden's supporters on the left did not. It is enormously telling that, from the outset, asset managers appear to have seen Biden's infrastructure plans as an opportunity, not as a threat. Having digested the proposals and taken the pulse of lawmakers in Washington, by mid 2021 such firms were confidently eyeing, in Lee Harris's words, a 'federal infrastructure windfall … a public asset bonanza'. They were particularly encouraged by the fact that talks around the funding of what traditionally had mainly been municipally owned assets such as roads, bridges and water-supply networks explicitly included allowances for public–private partnerships (PPPs). 'If federal dollars are

11 'The American Jobs Plan', 31 March 2021 – at whitehouse.gov.

12 B. Alexander, 'Privatization Is Changing America's Relationship with Its Physical Stuff', *Atlantic*, 12 July 2017.

shaved down enough, if the final [PPP] language is sufficiently business-friendly, or both', Harris observed, 'the forthcoming infrastructure package could mean open season for private-sector entrance into municipal utilities.'[13]

There was nothing in the eventual legislation for infrastructure investment to suggest that the asset managers' faith had been misplaced. Passed in November 2021 after a tortuous passage through the House of Representatives, the Infrastructure Investment and Jobs Act (IIJA), for one thing, offered a relatively derisory amount of public capital – just $550 billion in new federal funding, which was far less than groups such as the ASCE had urged. Federal dollars had indeed been, in Harris's words, 'shaved down', including for public transit, which was allocated only $39 billion of new money, while funding for public schools and housing was to be provided for – if at all – in later legislation.

Moreover, 'buried deep in the 1,039-page law', there were, confirmed Allan Marks, various statutory changes that 'could radically reshape how we [in the US] approach infrastructure investments'.[14] Foremost among these were changes pertaining to private investment in and control of assets – especially, though not exclusively, in the transportation sector. The IIJA both expanded several existing programmes that leveraged additional private-sector investment in infrastructure, and introduced new opportunities for private investment via asset concessions and PPPs.

If Covid-19 heralded the 'return of the state' in rich countries, then, it is essential to be clear that this was the return of a particular *kind* of state. It was not a state newly persuaded of the merits of public ownership of critical infrastructures of socioeconomic reproduction. The state was not 'stepping up' as asset owner, or indeed as service provider, at least beyond the extent to which the latter was absolutely necessary. The state that has 'returned' remains first and foremost a handmaiden of

13   L. Harris, 'Eyeing Federal Infrastructure Windfall, Private Equity Courts Public Utilities', *American Prospect*, 22 July 2021 – at prospect.org.

14   A. Marks, 'Biden Signs Infrastructure Law', *Forbes*, 16 November 2021 – at forbes.com.

private property and private-property rights – in other words, a quintessentially neoliberal state.

By late 2021, furthermore, the seemingly radical notion that 'anything we can actually do, we can afford', had receded almost as quickly as it had materialised the year before. 'That idea disappeared very quickly as soon as the market conditions changed, and once you saw a little bit of inflation coming up', Daniela Gabor told the *New Republic*'s Kate Aronoff. 'Now', said Aronoff, 'grandstanding about fiscal prudence is back.'[15] Such grandstanding reached a new pitch the following autumn: plans announced by the short-lived UK government of Liz Truss to introduce substantial, unfunded tax cuts and energy-consumption subsidies saw gilt investors throw a fit of pique, which commentators widely interpreted as evidence that the bond markets had resumed their disciplinary stance and needed to be obeyed.

The reality is that, across the Global North, governments have for several decades been widely, if unevenly, withdrawing from the ownership and funding of housing and other essential infrastructures, and for all the hoopla about the state suddenly being 'back', Covid-19 changed that trajectory not one jot: not in Australia, not in Europe, and certainly not in the United States. US municipalities – the principal owners of US public infra-structure – have increasingly been considering public–private partnerships not necessarily because they want to, but because federal funding has dried up – declining by around 75 per cent in real terms since the late 1970s in the case of water infrastructure, for example.[16] In the midst of the pandemic, faced with a 'dire' need for capital, municipalities were widely welcoming asset managers' PPP proposals.[17] Biden's legislation barely scratched the surface of that need for capital (least of all in relation to water supply), which will instead increasingly be met by other capital providers.

---

15 K. Aronoff, 'The White House's New Climate Strategy: Let Businesses Solve It', *New Republic*, 4 November 2021 – at newrepublic.com.

16 E. Douglass, 'Towns Sell Their Public Water Systems – and Often Regret It', McGraw Center, 8 July 2017 – at mcgrawcenter.org.

17 Harris, 'Eyeing Federal Infrastructure Windfall'.

Poorer countries

The coronavirus pandemic was experienced very differently in different parts of the world, with significant variance between richer and poorer countries. The level and nature of government intervention and spending designed to support domestic companies and households was one important axis of such variance. While many poorer countries also locked down to varying degrees at various points, few provided cushioning payments to those most impacted on anything like the scale seen in much of the Global North. The International Monetary Fund (IMF) reported in October 2021 that almost 90 per cent of the active fiscal support deployed during the Covid crisis up to that point had been concentrated in 'advanced' economies and China.[18]

Needless to say, this dearth of support was not due to any lack of will. Rather, it resulted from the markedly different structural circumstances under which the governments of poorer countries are compelled to operate. Like the governments of countries in Western Europe and North America, most governments in the Global South would have needed to borrow on a massive scale to fund substantive social and economic Covid-support mechanisms; but unlike the former, the latter governments were not able to do so – or, more importantly, not at non-punitive interest rates. As the IMF's head of fiscal policy Vitor Gaspar remarked, the varying state responses to the pandemic highlighted a 'great finance divide' – between countries with ready access to cheap finance, and those without.[19]

In the process, of course, the pandemic demonstrated that Keynes's forthright declaration, cited above – that anything we can actually do, we can afford – is something of a rich-country conceit. Who belongs to the 'we' to whom Keynes referred? In reality, poor countries did not belong even when Keynes wrote those words, and they assuredly do not belong today. As Tooze observed in the early part of the pandemic, 'conservative scaremongering' about the volume of sovereign debt has traditionally analogised national to household finances, representing such

---

18 C. Giles, 'Covid-19 Demonstrated "Power" of Government Spending, Says IMF', *Financial Times*, 13 October 2021.

19 Cited in ibid.

debt as 'a burden on the profligate; a moral obligation that must be honoured on pain of national bankruptcy and ruin'. But, as Tooze went on to say, while this analogy is 'profoundly misleading' for rich countries (whose governments typically borrow in their own currency, and primarily from their own citizens), there are certainly national circumstances in which it is apt: specifically, 'when you are an impoverished and desperate country dependent on foreign creditors who will lend to you only in the currency of another country, most commonly that of the US'.[20] Many poorer countries, Tooze reminded readers, were in precisely this position when Covid-19 struck. The idea that such countries could afford 'anything they could actually do' would have struck them as, at best, fanciful.

Hence, if the state that 'returned' to the Global North during the pandemic was the big-borrowing, big-spending state, such a state made barely an appearance in the world's poor countries. There, Covid instantiated not even a whiff of change to the fiscal status quo: business-as-usual persisted. And this continues to mean a massive need for investment in infrastructure production and renewal. Estimates as to the quantum of investment that is required vary significantly. But the specific numbers – $40 trillion was one recently floated estimate for low- and middle-income countries – are less important than the sheer scale of investment need that they denote.[21] Just as the world's poorer countries were largely unable to marshal significant fiscal resources during 2020–21 to support domestic economies and societies ravaged by the pandemic, so they have widely struggled to marshal such resources in the service of infrastructure investment over a much longer period of time – and so they continue to struggle today.

Into that distinctive opportunity space – namely, countries with a greater need for infrastructure investment than in the Global North, but run by governments with inferior fiscal capacity to meet that need – a range of actors have eagerly entered in recent times. China is one such, as is well known. The Belt

---

20   A. Tooze, 'Should We Be Scared of the Coronavirus Debt Mountain?', *Guardian*, 27 April 2020.

21   'G7 Backs Global Infrastructure Plan to rival China's Belt and Road, US Says', Reuters, 12 June 2021 – at reuters.com.

and Road Initiative (BRI), launched in 2013, is a global-scale Chinese strategy for regional integration held together by selective infrastructure investment in dozens of countries located predominantly in Africa and Central and South Asia. Projected ultimately to encompass investments worth more than $1 trillion, most BRI projects involve transportation or power assets, both fossil-fuel-based and renewable. It is very much a state initiative, directed from the commanding heights of the Chinese government and carried out by an array of state-owned enterprises financed by state-owned banks.

As we saw in Chapter 2, however, China's state–industry–finance complex has been joined in the business of infrastructure investment in low- and middle-income countries, and over broadly the same time-span, by private-sector asset managers from the Global North, among others. In the period since the global financial crisis, but especially during the past decade, leading industry names from North America and Europe have allocated growing sums of fund capital to investment in non-Western real assets such as renewable-energy power plants, road concessions and farmland. Covid-19 may have temporarily slowed the flow of private money from institutional-investor capital pools in the Global North to infrastructure and land projects in the Global South, but it did no more than that.

Indeed, in mid 2021, steps were taken that will likely see this flow accelerate sharply. As Daniela Gabor, among others, has noted, such investments, while made by the private sector, nonetheless commonly entail some degree of state involvement – though state and finance come together here in very different ways than in the case of the Belt and Road Initiative. In particular, to encourage private-sector asset managers to make infrastructure investments they might ordinarily consider excessively risky, Western (and sometimes host-country) governments use state or quasi-state vehicles – notably national and multilateral development banks – to de-risk the projects in question (see Chapter 2).

Gabor has described this phenomenon of Western governments 'escorting' Global North asset managers into de-risked infrastructure assets in the Global South as nothing less than a new development paradigm, dubbed 'the Wall Street Consensus'. In fact, she suggests that it represents a 'strategic Western response' precisely to the BRI.[22] The 'strategic' part appeared debatable when her article was published in early 2021, inasmuch as, up until then, de-risking had been largely ad hoc rather than coordinated. That June, however, the leaders of the Group of Seven (G7) economies announced plans for a new partnership, called Build Back Better World. It appeared to be everything Gabor had alluded to: a strategic, coordinated mechanism; oriented to infrastructure investment in poorer countries; professedly an axis of competition with China; and, most crucially of all, to be effectuated by de-risking – specifically using 'catalytic investments from our respective development finance institutions' to 'mobiliz[e] private-sector capital'.[23] A year later, in mid 2022, the partnership was formally launched, albeit repackaged and rebranded as the Partnership for Global Infrastructure and Investment (PGII). It aimed to 'mobilize' some $600 billion in global infrastructure investment by 2027.[24]

A century earlier, Rudolf Hilferding and Vladimir Lenin famously proposed that the state in the West had become an agent of private finance capital, and that the latter effectively operated on the global stage as a form of national capital. 'Thus finance capital, literally, one might say, spreads its net over all countries of the world', Lenin wrote. 'The capital-exporting countries have divided the world among themselves in the figurative sense of the term.'[25] It is impossible to say how efficacious the G7's PGII initiative will be, but in the explicit offering of succour to the ongoing export of asset-manager society to the Global South, the shades of Lenin and Hilferding are unmistakable.

---

22 D. Gabor, 'The Wall Street Consensus', *Development and Change* 52: 3 (2021), p. 454.

23 'President Biden and G7 Leaders Launch Build Back Better World (B3W) Partnership', 12 June 2021 – at whitehouse.gov.

24 'President Biden and G7 Leaders Formally Launch the Partnership for Global Infrastructure and Investment', 26 June 2022 – at whitehouse.gov.

25 V. I. Lenin, *Imperialism: The Highest Stage of Capitalism* (New York: Dover, 1987 [1917]), pp. 66–7.

Crisis After Crisis

When societies emerge from periods that are widely recognised to have been periods of crisis, there is typically an equally wide-spread recognition that the societies in question are returning to some kind of normality, that the winds of crisis have ebbed. With Covid-19, however, such a recognition has been notably absent. This is not just a reflection of the fact that it is more or less universally accepted that this particular coronavirus will always be with us. Nor, indeed, has it to do principally with the war in Ukraine, or (in large parts of the world) the sharp rise in inflation for which that war and its geopolitical fallout are partly responsible – an economic shift I will consider directly later in the chapter.

More fundamentally, the absence of a sense of abatement of crisis reflects a recognition that, even if societies are increasingly able to live with Covid-19 without treating its circulation *as* a crisis, and even if we can survive the latest outbreak of the 'virus' that is inflation, our emergent post-Covid reality nonetheless can scarcely be considered calm or stable, never mind 'normal'. In fact, there is a growing recognition that societies were already widely in crisis even before Covid-19 struck. If Covid-19 now is (or will soon be) endemic, then so also now, it appears, is crisis itself.

There are several components to this growing sense of endemic, even permanent crisis, but two arguably stand out. The first is housing. As we saw in Chapter 2, the idea of a systemic 'infra-structure gap' is largely a phenomenon of the new millennium: prior to the year 2000, the phrase 'infrastructure gap' appeared only very sporadically in public discourse. This is worth recalling here because the exact same ideational–discursive pattern is true of 'housing crisis'. The number of articles indexed by Factiva that include this phrase in English has grown exponentially since the turn of the millennium, such that there were nearly twenty times as many such articles in 2021 (around 18,700) as in 2000 (970). On top of this, there are all those articles, including the one by McKinsey consultants with which I began this chapter, which discuss housing crises without labelling them explicitly as such.

In any event, English-language articles today routinely discuss housing crises – crises principally of availability and afford-ability – not only in all English-speaking countries, but also in countries ranging from Denmark to India, Germany, Israel, France, Sweden, Spain and Russia. Furthermore, the notion spe-cifically of a *global housing crisis* is now very much abroad: the subject of numerous scholarly papers over the past decade, the purported global housing crisis has also recently been addressed in articles in popular media such as *Bloomberg* and *Forbes*, and in investigations by multilateral organisations such as the United Nations and World Bank.

The second stand-out component of the perception of endemic contemporary crisis is of course the climate crisis. Again, this is a relatively new phenomenon, dating at most only to the past decade or so. Needless to say, this is not to suggest that it is only in the past decade that the science has demonstrated that climate change is a phenomenon of gargantuan – and perhaps even existential – significance. Rather, it is to suggest that only in the relatively recent past have elites in many countries come to recognise climate change *as a crisis phenomenon*. Until just a few years ago, governments, businesses and the mainstream media tended to view climate change as something that would occur strictly in the future, and could be dealt with in the future. Both such cognitive deferrals have now been widely (though not universally) abandoned. Climate change, it is increasingly accepted, is a crisis in the here-and-now: consider that broad-sheet newspapers such as the *Guardian* now include 'Climate crisis' as a permanent news category alongside 'Politics', 'Society' and 'Sport'. And the Factiva article-count data are even more striking here than in the case of housing: a paltry thirty-eight articles naming the 'climate crisis' were published in 2000; in 2021, that number had risen to nearly 84,000.

Around the world, therefore, we live in what is widely understood today to be an age of deep-seated crisis both in the provision of shelter and in the maintenance of a habitable geo-physical environment. And, while the housing and climate crises are, of course, very different from one another, what is crucial to recognise for our purposes is that they share a key attribute: they are both, in considerable measure, real-asset crises, and hence crises of acute relevance to asset managers.

This particular crisis characteristic is especially obvious in respect of the housing crisis – precisely a crisis in the ability of individuals and households to secure affordable access, whether through renting or ownership, to the real asset that is residential property. But it is also true of the climate crisis. Whether focused on mitigation of climate change or adaptation to it, the locus of efforts by governments, businesses and households to address the climate crisis is very often also real assets – as defined in this book. Pertinent such assets include energy infrastructures, where the greatest urgency is to replace fossil-fuel-based systems with zero-carbon alternatives; transportation infrastructures, which likewise need to be weaned off fossil fuels; farmland, which needs to become a net sink rather than source of greenhouse-gas emissions; and infrastructures of water supply, which require massive expansion and upgrading to cater for shifting irrigation requirements and withstand shifting and intensifying patterns of drought. Last but not least, real assets necessarily implicated in efforts to address the climate crisis also, of course, include housing itself, the 'greening' of which – for example, through the replacement of gas-fired central-heating systems – has barely begun.

The central point is that, given that they turn fundamentally on society's most important real assets, the ways in which the twin housing and climate crises are approached in the coming years and decades will inevitably play a disproportionately significant role in shaping the future of asset-manager society around the world. Will evolving climate policies facilitate, and potentially even encourage, the widespread ownership and operation of energy and transportation infrastructures by private-sector asset managers? What – to the extent it exists – of housing policy? Over the next few pages, I attempt to read the runes by taking stock of significant recent and ongoing developments in each sphere.

Housing crisis

As we saw in Chapter 2, the financial crisis of 2007–09 fostered highly opportune investment conditions for asset managers in several housing markets, not least the United States. On the one hand, the crisis saw widespread and significant falls in prices, making housing cheaper to acquire. At the same time, the crisis increased the supply of housing for sale – many households were forced sellers – while decreasing the capacity of ordinary home-buyers to purchase such housing. With the shift in monetary policy after the crisis leading to a substantial fall in interest rates, and thus in the cost of any debt that asset managers raised to finance acquisitions, material conditions for major programmes of institutional housing investment were as close to perfect as can be imagined.

But perhaps even more important in the long term would be a parallel shift in ideational conditions. Historically, there was a certain reticence among many asset managers regarding investment in housing. Homeownership is widely idealised by consumers and politicians – and a dwelling owned by an asset manager is a dwelling that by definition is not owner-occupied. Circumspect asset managers did not want to be seen to be tram-pling on the homeownership 'dream', and hence typically trod warily around this asset class.

Something very significant happened as a result of the finan-cial crisis, however. After the crisis, people certainly still widely dreamed of homeownership – and yet a new, sobering cognitive reality set in. Across the geographical breadth of asset-manager society, in countries ranging from Australia to the United States, Sweden and the UK, homeownership rates, after decades of growth, had peaked in the early to mid 2000s before beginning to fall back. Commentators now widely mused that perhaps there was a 'natural' limit to levels of homeownership in a liberal-capitalist society. The *Economist*'s claim that, in reaching nearly 70 per cent, the US homeownership rate had been 'artificially' swelled, suggested that there was indeed a natural ceiling, and that it was lower than that figure.[26]

Whatever the exact 'natural' limit was, the crucial implication was that there would *always* be renters – at least three in ten households in the US case – and hence that buying housing as an investor, explicitly to let it, would not necessarily be perceived

---

26 'Help for Housing Markets?', *Economist*, 25 June 2008.

as an impediment to someone's aspiration to homeownership. Instead, it could be credibly positioned as an effort to provide an essential service for which there was, and would always be, a healthy and natural demand. One did not need to subscribe to the view – one increasingly widely disseminated in the wake of the financial crisis – that what was emerging were 'rentership' or 'post-homeownership' societies, in order to believe that the private-rental sector had a legitimate role to play within a necessarily variegated housing system.

Indeed, the shift in ideational conditions went further than that. Not only was there a growing acceptance of renting, and thus of landlordism. The argument increasingly circulated that the dream of homeownership for all was positively damaging, as well as being unattainable. In fact, the argument went, it was precisely the blinkered pursuit of that goal that had got countries such as the United States into the mess that was the financial crisis in the first place: if governments had not allowed lenders to give mortgages to people who could not afford them, the collapse would not have happened. Some people, it was implied, needed to be excluded from homeownership for the good of both themselves and the financial system.

Given that this thesis was highly beneficial to asset managers that stepped up investment in residential property after the crisis, it is unsurprising that they were among its most enthusiastic proponents. The Blackstone partner Byron Wien, for instance, writing in 2012, traced the financial crisis to irresponsible lending underwritten by the 'government-encouraged goal of creating an "Ownership Society" where most families could realise the American dream'.[27] The firm's chief executive, Stephen Schwarzman, similarly excoriated the US government for 'politically encouraging home ownership before the crisis, even by people who couldn't afford it. Lending standards fell, mortgages were pushed on uninformed and unsophisticated borrowers who could never realistically hope to pay them back.'[28]

27 B. Wien, 'Can Washington Rouse a Good Morning for America?', *Eureka Report*, 16 March 2012 – at eurekareport.com.au.

28 S. Schwarzman, *What It Takes: Lessons in the Pursuit of Excellence* (New York: Simon & Schuster, 2019), p. 274.

In short, the narrative around housing ownership was transformed, and this transformation served to one extent or another to naturalise institutional investment – that is, to make housing appear a natural asset class for the likes of Blackstone to own. Now notably subdued on the benefits of owner-occupation, governments and government agencies increasingly accepted, or even actively championed, the acquisition of distressed housing assets by asset managers. In the United States, the Federal Reserve was in the vanguard of this discourse. In 2011, Elizabeth Duke, a Fed governor, first publicly made the case for converting foreclosed single-family homes held by state-owned institutions such as the government-sponsored enterprises (GSEs) Fannie Mae and Freddie Mac into rental properties to be owned by private financial institutions.[29] Sales of pools of GSE-owned homes to large investors soon followed. Meanwhile, in Spain between 2013 and 2015, SAREB, the state-controlled 'bad bank' established in 2012 to take toxic real-estate assets off the balance sheets of the country's ailing banks, similarly favoured the bulk-sale of wholesale portfolios to institutional investors. Blackstone happened to be among them. In 2014 it bought at least three separate property portfolios from SAREB.

If policymakers' growing acceptance, and even promotion, of 'rentership' served to lubricate asset-manager investment in housing in the distressed market conditions of the immediate post–financial crisis years, it further helped sustain such investment when distress eventually lifted – which, of course, it did at varying rates in different countries (lasting considerably longer in Spain than the United States, for instance), and to varying degrees for different population cohorts. Some observers had thought that asset managers' interest in residential property would wane once rock-bottom prices – and hence the opportunity to reap significant capital gains simply by holding assets and awaiting market recovery – were no longer available. But such observers were wrong.

Investors like Blackstone learned two very important things while buying into housing-market distress in the first half of the

---

29 E. A. Duke, 'Rebalancing the Housing Market', Federal Reserve, 1 September 2011 – at federalreserve.gov.

2010s. One was that rental homes, much more than the companies purchased by such investors' private-equity buyout arms, provided a predictable and reliable source of recurring income, not to mention one that could be very cheaply financed – which was a valuable combination of qualities in the otherwise volatile world of alternative asset management.

The second, equally important, concerned the available mechanisms for generating capital gains on housing investments. Here, Blackstone's own experience with Invitation Homes, the single-family-housing investment vehicle it launched in 2012, proved highly instructive. Buyers of Invitation Homes' shares at and after the company's 2017 IPO placed a much higher average value on each of its 50,000-plus rental units than Blackstone had originally paid for those units, both because the housing market had recovered *and* because each such unit was on average producing increased rental yields (see Chapter 4). The lesson was that, when buying residential property, one did not necessarily need conditions of market distress – and hence the prospect of generalised price inflation – in order to profit when later selling that property. If there was potential to lift rents, one could make capital gains by buying, letting and then selling housing even if the wider market stood still.

Moreover, across large parts of the world, there was one factor more than any other that boosted residential rent inflation in this period – supply shortages. Rates of new housing construction collapsed in many countries when the financial crisis struck, and subsequent growing shortages of inventory translated into consistent upward pressure on rents: a boon to investor-landlords. Analysis by the *Economist* has shown that the number of homes built per capita across eleven advanced economies more than halved in the five years from 2006.[30] Even as late as 2021, global housing starts per person remained 'considerably below the levels of the early 2000s'.[31]

Far from retreating from housing investment in the mid to late

---

30 'How Long Can the Global Housing Boom Last?', *Economist*, 8 January 2022.

31 International Monetary Fund, *Global Financial Stability Report, October 2021*, p. 21 – at imf.org.

2010s, then, asset managers doubled down, increasing the pace of investment. Preqin data bear this out. Totalling around 750, the number of launches globally of unlisted real-estate funds focused exclusively or primarily on residential assets was more than 30 per cent higher between 2016 and 2020 (inclusive) than between 2011 and 2015.[32]

When Covid-19 appeared on the scene at the beginning of 2020, there was a widespread expectation that the world would see a repeat of the cycle of a decade earlier: defaults on house-hold mortgages would spike as the economy was shut down; foreclosures and falling house prices would swiftly follow; and asset managers and other institutional specialists in distressed real-estate investing would once again swoop in, vulture-like, and make a proverbial killing.

This cycle, we now know, in fact did not repeat: in the heart-lands of asset-manager society in the Global North, at least, emergency government measures provided support for at-risk mortgaged homeowners; perversely, house prices in fact rose rather than sinking. And yet the appetite for residential-property investment among asset managers further increased. The absence of distressed assets clearly did not matter. Having declined by a fifth year-on-year in 2020 to approximately 130, as asset managers paused to take stock of the pandemic, launches of residential-focused funds surged anew in 2021, taking the number of such launches to above 200 in a single year for the very first time; two decades earlier, typically only around ten new residential-focused funds were being established each year.[33] In Europe, one of the centres of feverish housing investment activ-ity during the pandemic, the amount of capital that investors poured into residential property in 2021 – some €105 billion – was more than 50 per cent higher than the annual total just two years earlier (€67 billion).[34]

That asset managers' commitment to housing investment should grow so strongly while the pandemic was still raging – as

---

32   D. Gabor and S. Kohl, 'My Home Is an Asset Class: The Financialization of Housing in Europe', 2021 (pre-publication version).

33   Ibid.

34   G. Hammond, 'Greystar Raises Fresh Funds as Residential Rental Investment Surges past €30bn', *Financial Times*, 7 July 2022.

it obviously was in 2021 – is not hard to explain. As we saw at the beginning of this chapter, the alternative asset-management industry was sitting on some $2 trillion of dry powder at the outset of 2021. Managers needed to find a profitable 'home' for this capital somewhere, and one of the main historic alternatives to housing investment had been dealt a particularly heavy blow by the coronavirus. This, of course, was commercial property: offices, hotels and shopping centres, three of the main pillars of commercial real-estate investment, lost much of their sheen when societies locked down and doubts were widely raised about whether working, travelling and shopping habits would ever return to 'normal'. In 2022, the market for office investment remained 'shaken', and retail was still 'buckling'.[35]

Not only, during Covid, did people suddenly spend much less time in offices, hotels and shopping centres, but the quid pro quo was that they spent much more time within a certain other real-estate space: their homes. As commercial property's star fell among investors, therefore, residential property's ascended: investors' real-estate allocations were 'turned on their head', a 'thriving' residential investment sector still also being supported by what one economist described as 'supranormal rates of rent growth due to [the continuing] shortage of housing'.[36] It turned out that people can work without offices and shop without shops (the other property-investment sector to boom during the pandemic was warehouses, driven by the surge in online retail). But few are willing (or compelled) to live without homes.

Certainly, in countries suffering chronic housing crises, there have recently been sparks of protest, and even occasionally instances of successful political pushback, against asset managers' seemingly unstoppable rush into the residential property sphere. One of the most notable of these has been in Denmark, where the later part of the 2010s saw significant institutional investment in older rental stock, particularly in the capital city of Copenhagen. Financial investors soon came to be linked to sharply rising rents, and the country's new left-wing government

35   A. Carroll, 'A New Balance for Real Estate', PERE, 14 April 2022 – at perenews.com.

36   Ibid.

cried foul. In pledging stricter legislation to control housing costs in the capital, the government in 2019 singled out none other than Blackstone – one of the most active investors in the city – for what it described as 'unsustainable' practices. 'An American private-equity fund is purchasing our houses', exclaimed Prime Minister Mette Frederiksen. 'Does greed know no boundaries? Apparently not.'[37]

The following year, Frederiksen's government acted – albeit not by proscribing the acquisition of housing by investment funds, as some voices had proposed, but by targeting the mechanism that allowed for rents on acquired dwellings to be substantially increased. As in neighbouring Sweden (see Chapter 4), this mechanism had turned on physical property upgrades: Denmark's Housing Regulations Act (1996) enabled landlords to increase rents significantly on units in buildings containing more than six homes when previous tenants vacated them, if they spent a minimum of approximately 250,000 kronor per unit on renovations – which is what Blackstone and others had therefore been doing. New legislation passed in 2020 – dubbed, tellingly, the 'Blackstone-*indgreb*', or 'Blackstone intervention' – stipulated that investors would have to wait five years to raise rents after buying and renovating properties. A blow, of a kind, was struck.

In other countries afflicted by the housing crisis, however, either barely a whimper has been heard from those in power about growing asset-manager investment in housing – Sweden, the UK and the United States would be prime examples of this establishment docility – or else moves to arrest the trend have ultimately come to little.[38] Germany and Ireland are both

---

37 Cited in B. Christophers, 'Mind the Rent Gap: Blackstone, Housing Investment and the Reordering of Urban Rent Surfaces', *Urban Studies* 59 (2022), p. 709.

38 The US case is interesting. It is true, as we saw in Chapter 4, that various congressional committees have recently investigated, and been critical of, the operations of large US residential landlords including those controlled by asset managers – focusing in particular on eviction practices during the coronavirus pandemic. Moreover, high-profile politicians such as Senator Elizabeth Warren have repeatedly highlighted the perceived problems associated with the practices of such landlords. As yet, however, none of this has translated into policy; the critique has failed to gain traction.

instructive examples of the latter outcome. In Germany, attention has been focused on Berlin, where, in the past decade, both
equity-fund investments in housing and rapid rental-price inflation have been concentrated – not, critics say, unrelatedly. In
early 2020, the city's legislature introduced regulation to cap
rents and limit rent increases. Had this regulation held, it would
have had major implications for the ability of investors to earn
profits on housing investment – but just a year later Germany's
highest court ruled that it was unconstitutional, and hence null-
and-void. Later in 2021, Berlin's residents voted in a high-profile
referendum to expropriate private landlords with more than
3,000 apartments in the city (Blackstone was one such); but the
result is non-binding, and nothing may ever come of it.

Meanwhile, in Ireland, asset-manager investment in housing
has been growing rapidly – investment funds reportedly bought
95 per cent of all new apartments completed in 2019, for instance
– and became headline news in 2021 when it was reported that
the UK-headquartered firm Round Hill Capital had 'pushed
out first-time buyers' by purchasing most of the houses in a
new development in the city of Maynooth.[39] Concerned about
public opinion against the backdrop of a housing crisis years
in the making, the government vowed to take swift action to
stop investment funds from bulk-buying dwellings. Its deputy
head, Leo Varadkar, said such investments were 'undesirable'
and militated 'against the principle of home ownership'.[40]

These were strong words, but the government's actual policy
response, when it arrived, was a damp squib: an increase in the
stamp duty to be paid by investment institutions when buying
ten or more homes – notably, exempting apartments from the
higher levy. Opposition politicians were scathing: one described
the higher stamp-duty rate as 'puny, not punitive'; another said
that, in exempting apartments, which in value terms represent a

---

39 B. O'Halloran, 'Just 8,000 Houses Built Last Year Offered For Sale on
Open Market, Says CIF', *Irish Times*, 19 February 2020; M. Brennan, 'Global
Property Investment Firm Buys Most of 170-Home Estate in Kildare', *Business
Post*, 2 May 2021.

40 D. McConnell, 'Government Vows to Act as Investment Funds Buy Up
Whole Estates', *Irish Examiner*, 5 May 2021.

much more important investment class for asset managers than single-family housing, the government had effectively 'hoisted the white flag over [Dublin and said] it's a free for all for vulture funds'.[41] Dermot Desmond, the well-known Irish business-man, was pithier still, observing that international investment funds were 'having a laugh' at the government over its housing strategy.[42]

Given the Irish government's ultimately weak response to demands to take a more vigorous stance towards asset-manager investment in the nation's housing stock, it was perhaps not surprising to hear the prime minister, Micheál Martin, strike a conciliatory tone in comments made towards the end of 2021. The Irish housing market, he said, *needed* institutional investors. The notion that firms like Round Hill have a detrimental impact was, he said, part of an 'overly simplistic narrative around the housing story'.[43]

Across the Irish Sea, the UK government, for its part, has recently been even more accommodating to this aspect of asset-manager society. In mid 2021, Peter Freeman, the chair of Homes England (the government's 'housing accelerator'), announced that he was 'keen to hear' from institutional investors considering investment in the country's affordable-housing sector.[44] A few months later, Homes England launched a co-sponsored report designed indeed precisely to accelerate institutional investment in that sector – its chief investment officer, Harry Swales, insist-ing that such investment had 'a critical role to play in addressing the undersupply of housing in the UK'.[45]

---

41 P. Hosford, 'Government Bid to Curtail Vulture Funds "Designed to Fail"', *Irish Examiner*, 19 May 2021.

42 S. Carswell, 'Investment Funds Are "Having a Laugh" at Ireland's Housing Policy – Desmond', *Irish Times*, 10 October 2021.

43 P. Hosford, 'Housing Market Needs Institutional Investors, Says Taoi-seach', *Irish Examiner*, 28 December 2021.

44 J. Wilmore, 'Homes England "Keen to Hear" from Institutional Inves-tors on Affordable Housing Opportunity', *Social Housing*, 29 June 2021 – at socialhousing.co.uk.

45 Impact Investing Institute, 'Impact Investing Institute, Property Funds Research, Homes England and the Investment Property Forum Launch Ground-Breaking Report on Social Housing Investment', Press Release, 7 October 2021 – at impactinvest.org.uk.

Two years earlier, Bloomberg TV had invited Kathleen McCarthy, Blackstone's then co-head of real estate, to tell viewers about the group's real-estate business and its own relationship to the housing crisis.[46] The host, Erik Schatzker, was particularly keen to discuss housing affordability, which, he said to McCarthy, was 'an enormous problem in some of the cities where you're making a good number of your investments'. 'How does Blackstone think about the affordable housing problem?', he wanted to know. McCarthy meandered somewhat in her reply, but her core message was consistent: 'We think', she maintained, 'we are part of the solution.'

That global asset managers such as Blackstone should claim they were part of the solution to the housing crisis, rather than part of the cause of it, was scarcely noteworthy. What *is* highly significant, however, is that they appear to have persuaded governments in countries like Ireland and the UK that the claim actually rings true.

At the time of writing, in autumn 2022, every passing week brings news of asset managers launching new residential or residential-focused investment funds, and of such funds completing substantial new acquisitions. In the wake of Covid-19, even as the housing crisis becomes increasingly deep and pervasive, politics and policy around the world remain largely obliging to the continuation of this investment trend.

Climate crisis

It is probably an accident of history that broad consciousness of the climate crisis and of the associated need to overhaul vast swathes of the world's built infrastructure of social and economic life has materialised coincidentally with the hegemony of neoliberalism. After all, scientific claims that society's emission of greenhouse gases could influence the climate were already circulating as early as the late nineteenth century; the term 'greenhouse effect' is itself more than a century old. The fossil-fuel industry certainly knew about anthropogenic climate change in the 1960s and 1970s.

---

46 'Blackstone Says Any Real Estate Deal Is Possible', video, 8 November 2019 – at bloomberg.com.

But if it is an historical accident that meaningful awareness of the climate crisis emerged during the neoliberal age, it has been an enormously consequential one. This is for two related reasons. Firstly, becoming 'known' within the context of neoliberal dominion, the climate crisis has predominantly been understood and approached from a neoliberal angle. The significance of this cannot be overstated. For more than a decade now, climate change has been framed by global elites as a quintessential case of 'market failure'. In this way of thinking, we – society – continue to emit greenhouse gases specifically because the market has failed to recognise the full costs of those emissions. And just as important as the diagnosis is the recommended cure. As thinkers such as Philip Mirowski have repeatedly noted, the neoliberal answer to purported market failures is never to replace markets with other mechanisms of allocation, governance or regulation, but rather always to try to make markets work *better*. So it has been, and continues to be, with climate. We can 'solve' the crisis, elites insist, by getting the price – not least the price of carbon – 'right'. This means that governments' role should be limited to, at most, modulating markets and price signals. It definitely should not be one of *substituting* for market (private-sector) actors, including in the financing, provision and operation of climate-related infrastructure.

This brings us to the second and more self-evident reason why it matters that the climate crisis is a crisis specifically of the neoliberal age. Awareness that action needs to be taken on a vast scale, and that this action must hinge to a significant extent on infrastructure transformation, has crystallised at the precise moment in history when – again, very much in line with neoliberal orthodoxy – infrastructures at large have been passing from public into private hands. In such a historic context, it would have been very much against the grain of history for either the renewal of existing infrastructures or the building of new ones to occur as anything other than a process in which the private sector is at the very centre of things.

Hence, from the very start, 'climate infrastructure', broadly conceived, has been understood and effectuated predominantly as a private-sector affair. The data attesting to this fact really are quite striking, but are seldom acknowledged for what they are. Let us focus for the sake of illustration on the specific infrastructure sector in which decarbonisation is widely seen as both most urgent and, fortuitously, most achievable: power generation. To begin with, it is important to note that, as one would expect, the proportion of overall generating capacity of all types owned privately has generally been increasing: the average privately owned share in OECD and G20 countries increased from 48 to 55 per cent between 2000 and 2014.[47] It is also important to note that this average, of course, masks huge variance: in Argentina, Spain and the United States, for instance, the share is now above 90 per cent, while in Croatia and South Africa it is below 10 per cent.

But it is the difference between clean and dirty generating infrastructures that stands out. Approximately three-quarters of new solar and wind capacity installed in recent years represents private-sector investment.[48] And not only is the private sector responsible for, and in control of, the lion's share of new green power infrastructure – it is much less invested in legacy fossil-fuel-based generating infrastructure: over half of total operating global coal-power capacity, for example, is held by governments or state-owned enterprises.[49] Furthermore, the private sector appears to be exiting legacy dirty-power assets with greater haste: 'privately-owned firms are moving out of the coal sector faster than state-owned enterprises, by investing in fewer new plants'.[50] If the future is indeed predominantly green, then the private sector, on this evidence, appears likely to have the leading share in its ownership.

In liberalised power markets where the private sector dominates new (and increasingly green) capacity investment, the role of the state has been mainly what we have discussed several times already: namely, to de-risk said private-sector investment. Wholesale electricity markets are notoriously volatile – never more so, in fact, than during the period of writing of this book

---

47 A. Prag, D. Röttgers and I. Scherrer, 'State-Owned Enterprises and the Low-Carbon Transition', OECD Working Paper No. 129 (April 2018), p. 29.

48 Ibid., p. 16.

49 Ibid., p. 17.

50 Ibid., p. 18.

in 2021 and 2022 – and thus even though the costs of wind tur-
bines and photovoltaic solar panels have declined dramatically
in the past decade, banks are reluctant to lend capital for the
construction of new wind or solar plants unless mechanisms for
mitigating revenue risk are in place. To date, governments have
been the main providers and funders of such mechanisms, which
can mitigate revenue risk either directly (for example, through
feed-in tariffs and procurement auctions) or indirectly (such as
through investment tax credits). To some extent, as we have
seen, similar mechanisms of de-risking have been employed by
governments to incentivise private-sector investment in other
'climate-friendly' infrastructures, from public transit systems
(such as in Seoul) to water desalination plants (such as in
Carlsbad, California).

And of course, asset managers in particular are increasingly prominent in the private-sector ownership of pertinent
infrastructures. Macquarie, for example, is notably active in
mass-transit investment. Needless to say, it is also a longstanding
investor in the water sector, recently consolidating its presence
through investments directed explicitly towards 'climate resil-
ience' projects – one such being its 2021 co-investment with
another asset manager, AVAIO Capital, in a new desalination
facility in Belgium's port of Antwerp. More than any of the
other major alternative asset managers, however, it is Canada's
Brookfield Asset Management that has thus far moved most
decisively into the 'climate infrastructure' space. Water-supply
infrastructure seemingly is not yet an area of active interest for
the firm, but Brookfield is a major investor in transportation
infrastructures, a huge owner of farmland, and, as we saw in
Chapter 3, one of the world's largest owners of any kind of
renewable-power assets.

Can we expect all this to continue? Is the ownership of climate
infrastructures destined to be dominated by private-sector interests in general and asset managers in particular? There are
certainly many on the left who have strenuously resisted, and
continue to resist, the idea that such private-sector dominance
is somehow inevitable. Increasingly, they have found inspiration
and even policy guidance in a previous significant chapter of

infrastructure investment history – the US New Deal. Under President Franklin D. Roosevelt, the mid 1930s saw a vast programme of national infrastructure renewal designed to drag the United States out of the depths of the Great Depression. The Public Works Administration oversaw more than 30,000 individual infrastructure projects involving the construction of roads, bridges, dams, sewerage systems, hospitals, schools and airports. Private construction firms carried out the projects, but otherwise this was overwhelmingly a public-sector enterprise. Almost all the new infrastructure was funded and owned publicly. What is needed today to confront the climate crisis, progressives argue, is a Green New Deal (GND), centred on a large-scale state-funded programme of investment in state-owned, low-carbon infrastructure assets. Books such as Ann Pettifor's *The Case for the Green New Deal* (2019) and *A Planet to Win: Why We Need a Green New Deal* (2019), by four US-based authors, have forcefully made the case.[51]

To date, however, the idea of the GND has circulated meaningfully only on a relatively restricted geographical basis. By and large, it is an idea developed and taken seriously, at least by some, solely within rich countries – principally the UK, the United States and the European Union. This is not surprising. The ability of governments in poorer countries even to consider, let alone implement, transformative programmes of state-financed infrastructure investment is fundamentally constrained, as we have seen. Global North–based GND advocates are generally not unaware of these geo-economic constraints, and the proposals they have elaborated have often made attendant provisions, for instance for equitable cross-border transfers of key technologies. Nevertheless, the constraints remain real and daunting.

Furthermore, even in those Global North countries where the idea has gained most traction, the window of opportunity for the GND as a programme of investment in publicly funded and controlled infrastructure, after having briefly opened, seems already to have been slammed shut. The UK and US cases are

---

51 A. Pettifor, *The Case for the Green New Deal* (London: Verso, 2019); K. Aronoff, A. Battistoni, D. A. Cohen and T. Riofrancos, *A Planet to Win: Why We Need a Green New Deal* (London: Verso, 2019).

exemplary. In the former, the GND sketched by Labour Party policy architects in 2019, on which the Jeremy Corbyn–led party campaigned in the general election of December that year, was explicitly based on decommodification and public ownership of all relevant infrastructures, ranging from energy to water and rail. But Corbyn lost, and, while his successor as leader of the opposition, Keir Starmer, remains committed in principle to the GND, he has publicly distanced himself from the pivotal, broad-ranging public-ownership elements embedded in the original Labour vision, meaning that what is left of the latter is but a shrivelled husk. The furthest that Starmer's Labour has been willing to go is to promise a single publicly owned renewable-energy start-up, the comically named Great British Energy, which, if it ever came to fruition, would struggle to be more than a gnat on the hide of the huge beast that is the UK's wholly private energy sector. Labour's, then, is now more or less the same, pale imitation of a GND to which the governing Conservative Party has itself occasionally given lip service.[52]

Similarly, in the United States, Bernie Sanders's 2020 campaign for the Democrats' presidential nomination incorporated GND proposals containing explicit public-ownership commitments, albeit in his case only of renewable-energy infrastructure and not also of transportation and water assets. Yet the man who beat him to the nomination, and in early 2021 became president, has performed a Starmer-like reformulation. Biden's proposals – and eventually, legislation – for climate infrastructure investment took Sanders's GND and stripped it of its most radical element. 'Public ownership', wrote Ed McNally of Biden's GND in May 2021, 'is nowhere to be seen.'[53]

Instead, the GND, as it is articulated by the liberal establishment today, resounds to the familiar refrain of de-risking. Consider in particular Biden's landmark climate law, eventually sealed in August 2022 after dying a dozen deaths along the way. The incongruously named Inflation Reduction Act does not

52   K. Adam, 'Boris Johnson says Britain Needs Its Own Green New Deal', *Washington Post*, 18 November 2020.

53   E. McNally, 'Whose Green New Deal?' *New Left Review – Sidecar*, 4 May 2021 – at newleftreview.org.

tackle the climate crisis by pledging the US government to build, own and operate wind and solar farms. Rather, its centrepiece is a modification and extension of the country's existing battery of renewable-energy investment and production tax credits, designed principally to incentivise the private sector to continue to build wind and solar facilities.[54]

The de-risking refrain likewise dominated the discourse of 2021's United Nations Climate Change Conference (COP26), which in some respects it was possible to construe as a coordinated attempt to internationalise the GND – or at least what remained of it by that stage. 'The argument the US and other wealthy countries have been making this week', Kate Aronoff reported from the conference, 'is that the primary goal of public climate investments should be to transform desperately needed climate projects into profitable investments, shouldering the risk corporations are unwilling to take to save the world.'[55] Indeed, Aronoff had heard this from the proverbial horse's mouth. 'Blend the finance, de-risk the investment, and ... create the capacity to have bankable deals', the US international climate envoy, John Kerry, had told reporters at the conference. Kerry went on: 'That's doable for energy. It's doable for water. That's doable for transportation.' After COP26, Kerry explained, 'we'll be transitioning my team directly into a hand-holding aid agency that's going to be out there working with' developing nations.[56]

Naturally, leading asset managers have been enthused by this propitious re-versioning of the GND. Moonlighting as both the UN special envoy for climate action and finance and the UK prime minister's finance adviser for COP26, Mark Carney, the

---

54 Although the inclusion in the legislation of so-called direct-pay provisions may create some space for the public sector to assume a more involved role. See R. Cooper, 'The Inflation Reduction Act's Quiet Revolution on Public Power', 18 August 2022 – at prospect.org.

55 Aronoff, 'White House's New Climate Strategy'.

56 The International Monetary Fund, too, is evidently now also on board with the prevailing orthodoxy, having effectively recognised the mobilisation of private finance through state-led de-risking as best practice for the development of climate infrastructure in the Global South. See A. Prasad, E. Loukoianova, A. Xiaochen Feng and W. Oman, 'Mobilizing Private Climate Financing in Emerging Market and Developing Economies', IMF Staff Climate Note No 2022/007, July 2022 – at imf.org.

vice chair of Brookfield Asset Management, wrote in the green-financing report that he published in preparation for COP26 – a report that made no mention of his employment by Brookfield – that the transition to 'net zero' afforded 'enormous commercial opportunities' for private finance.[57] Similarly, in his annual letter to shareholders, penned in August 2021, BlackRock chief executive Larry Fink opined: 'the climate transition presents a historic investment opportunity.'[58]

Fink's comments are especially noteworthy. More than any other representative of the asset-management industry, Fink in recent years has been relentlessly banging the drum of accelerating the climate transition by de-risking private finance. To the degree, therefore, that we are entering an epochal period of investment not just in climate infrastructure, but more particularly in privately held climate infrastructure, what Fink and BlackRock emphatically should not be seen as is merely passive and fortuitously positioned beneficiaries of that development. Rather, if the climate transition does indeed prove to be an 'historic investment opportunity' for real-asset asset managers, it is an opportunity that the likes of Fink and Carney will have actively and assiduously helped to create.

Pettifor, the author of *The Case for the Green New Deal*, explicitly warned about the influence of industry figures on policymakers in a March 2021 interview with CNBC. Pressing the case specifically for a European GND led and controlled by the state, Pettifor insisted that the finance sector was ill-equipped to address the climate crisis in a timely, environmentally beneficial and socially just fashion. Governments themselves should be both coordinating and financing the necessary transition, she said. 'I want to see public authority over the system of transformation and not private authority. I want to see the EU leading this', Pettifor added, 'not BlackRock.'[59]

---

57 M. Carney, 'Building a Private Finance System for Net Zero: Priorities for Private Finance for COP26', November 2020, p. 22 – at ukcop26.org.

58 BlackRock, 'Larry Fink's 2021 Letter to CEOs', August 2021 – at blackrock.com.

59 E. Smith, 'Governments – "Not BlackRock" – Should Lead the Economy Away from Fossil Fuels, Economist Says', CNBC, 29 March 2021 – at cnbc.com.

By then, however, it was arguably too late. With respect to climate issues, BlackRock already had its tentacles firmly wrapped around the EU polity. In April 2020, for example, the European Commission had hired the firm to advise on how best to integrate sustainability considerations into the region's banking regulation – and this in the face of campaigners' protests that the firm's investment holdings in both fossil-fuel companies and European banks raised all manner of conflict-of-interest concerns. BlackRock worked on the study for the next year, delivering its report in May 2021. The Commission meanwhile received a rap on the knuckles from the EU's independent ombudsman for its decision to use the firm.

In the United States, the influence of BlackRock on government policy in general, and its climate policy in particular, runs deeper still, being channelled, among other routes, through the ever-present 'revolving door' between the finance sector and the commanding heights of the state. As Adrienne Buller has noted, both Vice President Kamala Harris's chief economic adviser and the deputy secretary of the Treasury were hires from Black-Rock.[60] Most notably of all, there is Brian Deese, who was global head of sustainable investing at BlackRock from 2017 to 2020, before being recruited by Biden to direct the National Economic Council – becoming, in Adam Tooze's words, 'the anchor of climate policy on the Biden economics team'. Is it really any wonder that the climate infrastructure programme that Biden ended up pursuing in 2021–22 was what Tooze felicitously described as 'the Green New Deal recast in the image of BlackRock' – namely a meek, conservative framework designed principally to de-risk private-sector investment, and as such a 'far cry from the bold vision of the original'?[61]

Given that the other domain we are principally concerned with in relation to the future of asset-manager society is housing, it is important to note that, in the 'BlackRock-ification' of contemporary US climate policy, there are uncanny echoes of developments

60 A. Buller, 'The Limits of Privatized Climate Policy', *Dissent*, Winter 2022 – at dissentmagazine.org.

61 A. Tooze, 'America's Race to Net Zero: Does Joe Biden's Climate Plan Go Far Enough?', *New Statesman*, 21 April 2021.

in US housing policy a decade earlier. Then, too, there was an acknowledged crisis to deal with: the flood of post-crash housing foreclosures. Then, too, a liberal new president in whom great hopes were invested had just taken the reins. And then, too, bold and progressive plans were widely mooted: where climate activists would air Green New Deal proposals in 2019–20, in 2009–10 the talk among housing activists was of a modern version of the Home Owners' Loan Corporation, a key plank of Roosevelt's New Deal which, established in 1933, enjoyed significant success in limiting Depression-era foreclosures.

But after 2009, too, such bold aspirations were unceremoniously snuffed out by the president's team. In the event, pallid Obama-era housing policy substantially failed distressed homeowners, resulting in the availability of a glut of foreclosed homes to be acquired cheaply by asset managers. The most visible difference from the later case of Biden, BlackRock and climate was simply that a different 'Black' was implicated. Whereas Biden would hire from BlackRock, Obama's housing-finance policy team within the Treasury hired extensively from Blackstone; and Blackstone, as we know, went on to become the biggest institutional buyer of foreclosed single-family homes. If, under Biden, what we are seeing is the Green New Deal recast in the image of BlackRock, then equally, Obama presided over the housing New Deal recast in the image of Blackstone – the 'Blackstone-ification' of US housing policy, if you like.

Not content with the opportunities for climate-infrastructure investment occasioned by Global North policymakers' watering-down of the GND, and their associated re-commitment to de-risking private-sector investment, BlackRock's Fink has for several years been making the case that de-risking is required with even greater urgency to propel investment in such infrastructure in the Global South, which has historically received only a small share of the investment made by asset managers' infrastructure funds. In this regard, his most audacious suggestion has been that, to meet the demands of the climate crisis, the entire legacy model of multilateral finance centred on the International Monetary Fund and World Bank should be overhauled. Such institutions, Fink says, should no longer be *financiers*, themselves lending money to promote development; they should instead be *insurers*, reducing risk for private investors (like Black-Rock) via mechanisms such as first-loss guarantees.[62] To meet the climate challenge, as Fink later put it, 'we're going to have to change finance'.[63] This was the case Fink would make while glad-handing John Kerry and other policymakers at COP26, in particular on the third full day of the conference, 3 November: so-called 'Finance Day'.

Of course, Fink has also had another important constituency to try to persuade: his limited partners. Whereas the message to policymakers has been that private-sector investment in the infrastructure of the climate transition is too risky in the Global South without public-sector support, the message to limited partners has been that there is, in fact, money to be made. Needless to say, satisfying both audiences has required a nimble rhetorical balancing act. While Pettifor, for instance, worries that Larry Fink will exploit the climate 'opportunity' to make 'huge profits for his business', Fink's clients have worried conversely that he, and they, will not make any profit at all.[64] Blackstone, as it happens, has long negotiated a comparable balancing act in relation to housing: that is, telling its investors that housing is a dependable source of robust profits – while insisting to campaigners and public officials that it is not profiteering from the asset class. At any rate, it is in this light that we must understand Fink's widely reported insistence in his 2022 letter to shareholders that, in targeting 'sustainable' investment opportunities, BlackRock is not pursuing a 'woke', ideological agenda. 'We focus on sustainability not because we're environmentalists', he wrote, 'but because we are capitalists and fiduciaries to our clients.'[65]

The early signs are that Fink's persuasion has worked on both fronts: he has convinced governments to de-risk private investment in Global South climate infrastructure; and he has

62 See, for example, E. Schatzker, 'BlackRock's Fink Urges World Bank, IMF Overhaul for Green Era', Bloomberg, 11 July 2021 – at bloomberg.com.

63 S. Jessop and R. Kerber, 'BlackRock raises $673 mln for Climate-Focused Infrastructure Fund', Reuters, 2 November 2021 – at reuters.com.

64 Smith, 'Governments – "not BlackRock" – Should Lead the Economy'.

65 BlackRock, 'Larry Fink's 2022 Letter to CEOs', January 2022, at blackrock.com.

convinced his limited partners to front-up capital for such invest-ment. The most striking and instructive specific outcome to date is the Climate Finance Partnership – a new unlisted fund that BlackRock closed to investors in late 2021, having raised $673 million. It will invest in climate infrastructure, including renew-able power–generating capacity, in the Global South, initially targeting Kenya, Morocco, Egypt, Peru and Vietnam. It is a classic ten-year closed-end vehicle. (No 'tragedy of the horizon' for investors to worry themselves about here.) Most significantly of all, the private investment is explicitly de-risked. Philanthropic institutions, together with state-owned development banks from France, Germany and Japan, provided $130 million in 'cata-lytic' capital to the fund, and agreed to take any losses before BlackRock itself (which made a typically small commitment, representing just 3 per cent of fund capital at $20 million) and its private limited partners (who invested $523 million).[66]

It is of course always a hazardous business to try to predict the future. But if readers are wondering whether there exists today a prototypical model for the likely future of climate infrastructure investment around the world as the climate crisis intensifies, then BlackRock's Climate Finance Partnership may just be it.

The Return of Inflation

An important component of the story told in this book has been the significant expansion of asset-manager society in the period since the global financial crisis. As we saw in Chapter 2, strong growth in housing and infrastructure assets under management in the 2000s turned into very strong growth in the 2010s.

A large part of the explanation for this expanded rate of growth, I argued, lay in macroeconomics. In the context of long-term low inflation and new, post-crisis demands on monetary policy, the decade or so following the crisis was characterised by rock-bottom interest rates, which boosted institutional invest-ment in housing and infrastructure via asset managers for two principal reasons. First, the decline in yields on fixed-income

---

66   Jessop and Kerber, 'BlackRock Raises $673 mln'.

financial securities motivated investors to look elsewhere for income-generating assets, and real estate (including housing) and infrastructure fitted the bill. Second, real-estate and infrastructure investments, alongside private-equity investments, can generally be readily geared – and plentiful cheap debt was now available to asset managers to help amplify returns from infrastructure and real-estate funds.

Since the beginning of 2021, however, we appear to have entered new macroeconomic territory. Inflation has spiked, more than doubling globally between early 2021 and early 2022, nearing (or even exceeding) 10 per cent in many countries in which rates of above 5 per cent had not been seen since the 1980s. With notable exceptions such as China and Japan, all the world's major economies have been affected. Despite initial confidence in many quarters that the spike would be temporary – a one-off adjustment to the positive shock of economies re-emerging from Covid-19 shutdowns – the signs are increasingly that such confidence was misplaced. Russia's invasion of Ukraine in February 2022 redoubled inflationary pressures. A year-and-a-half into this new inflationary age (if that is what it is), the rate of inflation, far from falling, continues to rise.

To begin with, monetary authorities did not react. Convinced (or simply hopeful) that the uptick in inflation would soon wash through, leading central banks remained in expansionary mode. But in 2022, in the face of accelerating price rises, they were jolted into action and began to tighten policy, first and foremost in the United States, where, in March of that year, the Federal Reserve approved a first increase in rates since 2018. All market expectations are for interest rates to continue to climb, not just in the United States but throughout the world's advanced economies.

What effect would a period of sustained and substantive inflation accompanied by significant increases in interest rates have on asset-manager society? There have been suggestions – at least implicitly – that residential real estate and infrastructure would take a big hit, just like any other asset class. The argument here is that owners' returns would suffer, not least as a result of the increased cost of levering deals as debt finance becomes more expensive, and institutional investors would reduce allocations to real assets accordingly. This view was captured in one asset manager's comment to the *Financial Times* amid the market turbulence of April 2022 – when global stock and bond indices fell sharply – that there was 'nowhere to hide'.[67] There is, the comment intimated, no safe haven for investors as inflation and interest rates climb: not gold, not government debt, and not real assets such as infrastructure and housing.

But sober reflection suggests that the opposite is more likely to be the case: investors will in fact maintain or even increase allocations to housing and infrastructure in an environment characterised by persistently high inflation and increasing capital costs, thus leading to further intensification and extensification of asset-manager society. There are at least four significant grounds for making this judgement.

First, and most obviously, we need to consider where in the economy – sectorally, not geographically – prices are rising. Inflation is not a free-floating phenomenon, somehow applying to all commodities equally. It is always a phenomenon of variegated price rises, driven by increases in the prices of some commodities more than others. Today, the bulk of generalised inflation – the headline rates we read about – is in fact inflation in the prices specifically of energy and food. What do these two have in common? They are both commodities increasingly generated within asset-manager society – that is to say, *by* asset managers with significant holdings of, respectively, energy generation and farmland assets. To the extent that rises in the prices of food and energy offset any rises in the costs incurred in producing those commodities (notably fertiliser costs in the case of farmland and fuel costs in the case of energy), contemporary inflation is positive, not negative, for asset managers holding the relevant assets, and continuation of such inflation would more likely precipitate capital inflows than outflows for investment funds with the appropriate specialisation.

Second, and more importantly, investors have long seen real assets as a better hedge against inflation than almost any other

67   H. Agnew and C. Flood, '"Nowhere to Hide" for Investors in Market Turbulence', *Financial Times*, 11 April 2022.

significant asset class. As we saw in Chapter 2, one of the main explanations that asset managers and their clients have consistently given for their increasing appetite for infrastructure investment since the mid 1990s has been inflation risk; fees that can be charged to users of regulated infrastructure assets, for example, are often explicitly index-linked. The link is less explicit in the case of housing, but research has widely shown that both house prices and rents typically keep pace with or outstrip the rate of inflation over the medium and long term.

Indeed, housing rents are notably better able to follow inflation than rents on commercial property are. One reason for this is that commercial real estate, such as offices or retail premises, tends to be tenanted on multi-year leases, thus limiting the opportunities for landlords to revise rents upwards. Residential leases, by contrast, are typically reviewed annually, reducing the risk to landlords of being encumbered with tenants paying rents set at a time of much lower general price levels. As Mark Allnutt, head of Greystar's European operations, has explained, 'because of the duration of the lease', residential 'has historically been the best inflation hedge of all ... real estate'.[68]

Thus, it is entirely as one would expect that, in our new era of resurgent inflation, investors are turning *towards*, not away from, housing and infrastructure. In early 2022, in the United States, 'with inflation at a nearly 40-year high and at least three priced-in rate hikes', and in the context of a corresponding 'hunt for investing safe havens', *Bloomberg* reported that investor interest in housing was 'soaring'.[69] Meanwhile, unlisted infrastructure funds launched by asset managers were raising capital faster than ever, and were more oversubscribed than ever: in the twelve months to April 2022, the fifteen most oversubscribed infrastructure funds – led by offerings from KKR, Stonepeak and EQT – raised $33 billion more than the cumulative $77 billion they had set out to raise.[70]

---

68 Cited in Hammond, 'Greystar Raises Fresh Funds'.

69 C. Ballentine and A. Kantor, 'Real Estate Is Emerging as a Hedge Against Roaring Inflation', Bloomberg, 24 January 2022 – at bloomberg.com.

70 B. Alves, 'The Top 15 Oversubscribed Funds of the Past Year Raised $33bn Above Target', *Infrastructure Investor*, 7 April 2022.

Asset managers will continue to buy infrastructure and housing for as long as institutional investors continue to give them capital to do so, and as at mid 2022, money was continuing to pour into the relevant funds, with institutional investors widely raising their proportional allocations of investment capital to infrastructure and real estate. This was true both of investors with relatively low existing allocations and those already deeply invested in real assets. An example of the former was the Connecticut Retirement public pension plan, which, in June 2022, proposed to increase its allocation to infrastructure from 4 to 7 per cent, and to real estate from 10 to 12 per cent.[71] An example of the latter was Canada's Ontario Municipal Employees Retirement System, which, the following month, announced its aim to lift its infrastructure allocation from 20 to 25 per cent.[72]

Third, there is an important additional reason that we should expect asset-manager investment specifically in housing to remain buoyant if interest rates do indeed rise markedly. It is true, of course, that buyers of housing – whether owner-occupiers or investors, including asset managers – often use borrowed money; and, in relation to rising interest rates, I will consider the implications of this shortly. But buyers are far from being the only key actors in the housing market that borrow heavily. So also do developers.

As we have seen, rates of new construction of housing have been significantly depressed for the past decade around much of the world. A whole range of factors have militated against meaningful recovery of housing construction in the wake of the financial crisis – in the US context, the economist Mark Obrinsky has highlighted three key ones, namely 'the increasing cost of materials, a lack of labour, [and] continued obstructionism from NIMBYs'. And, as Obrinsky noted, a fourth can now be added to the list: the increasing cost of capital for developers

---

71   J. Peterson, 'Connecticut Retirement Proposes Real Estate, Infrastructure Allocation Increase', IPE Real Assets, 16 June 2022 – at realassets.ipe.com.

72   Z. Bentley, 'How the World's Largest Infra Allocator Is Supersizing Its Portfolio', 1 July 2022 – at infrastructureinvestor.com.

due to rising interest rates.[73] None other than Paul Krugman has highlighted the likely ramifications of this, again with a focus on the United States. Higher interest rates, he recently noted, 'will work largely by depressing housing construction, which was already too low'.[74]

Bad news for renters, certainly – but, by the same token, clearly good news for investor-landlords: enduring and intensifying supply shortages have been the key driver of rising housing rents in the past decade; and asset managers, by their own admission, have invested precisely in those urban housing markets where such shortages of supply – and thus upward pressure on rents – are most pronounced. The negative impact on construction rates from future rises in capital costs will only augment the attractiveness of housing as a relatively scarce asset class.

If we return to the question of how rising interest rates might affect housing and infrastructure asset managers in their capacity as borrowers, it is possible that they would reduce levels of leverage – which could have a negative impact on fund returns and, in turn, the ability to attract investor capital – were interest rates to rise far enough. Arguably more likely, though, is that, if the debt financing available to asset managers from banks became too expensive, managers would simply supply the debt themselves, thus hastening an important trend that I touched upon briefly in Chapter 5: rapid growth in asset managers' private debt funds.

This, then, is the fourth and final reason we should not anticipate a slowdown in the growth of asset-manager society in the event of sustained interest rate rises. What we might expect, instead, is that more purchases of housing and infrastructure by asset managers would be financed by debt also provided by asset managers. Indeed, the early signs are that just as institutional-investor capital is pouring into unlisted housing and infrastructure equity funds at unprecedented rates as inflation spreads in 2022, so also is it pouring into managers' unlisted debt funds. A key part of the reason appears to be that the money

---

73   P. Bergeron, 'Apartment Investors "Very Concerned" about Rising Rates, Inflation Combination', Globe St, 2 May 2022, at globest.com.

74   P. Krugman, 'Inflation, Interest and the Housing Paradox', *New York Times*, 24 April 2022.

loaned by such funds typically pays floating interest rates – and hence, as an investment option, the funds are not threatened by inflation and rising interest rates in the way that traditional fixed-income credit instruments are. Hannah Zhang reported in May 2022 that, while the reality and expectation of rising rates were 'killing traditional bond portfolios', almost all institutional investors were planning to maintain or increase their allocations to private debt, since few other investments 'naturally benefit from rising rates'.[75]

In short, the smart money would be on continuation of business as usual in asset-manager society – even as inflation and higher interest rates take hold. Asset managers will continue to invest in housing and infrastructure. No less inevitably, they will continue to push through price rises for those who rely upon access to and use of the housing and infrastructure assets they own. Asset managers, as we have seen, hardly need an excuse to increase charges – increasing charges is what they do. But if a useful excuse happens to arise – and inflation is assuredly one candidate – one can be certain that it will be put to effective use.

Follow the Money

That essential infrastructures will increasingly be held in private hands, and in particular the hands of asset managers, is certainly the way asset managers themselves see the future unfolding. For historical support for this prognosis, they frequently point to the example of real estate, including residential real estate. Real estate that used to be controlled by owner-occupiers or by the state, they say, has increasingly been transferred into private investor portfolios. In moving in this same direction, they argue, energy, transportation and other such infrastructures are simply following a rational, well-trodden path: from the UK to central and eastern Europe, Southeast Asia and the United States, infrastructure privatisation has tended to follow where housing and commercial-real-estate privatisation led the way.

---

75 H. Zhang, 'Private Credit Boomed Amid Low Yields – and Now It's Set to Flourish', *Institutional Investor*, 11 May 2022 – at institutionalinvestor.com.

Cesar Estrada, of the US asset manager State Street, has offered a particularly vivid rendition of this sequential, teleological thesis:

> The rise of infrastructure in some ways mirrors the growth of the real estate asset class some two decades earlier. Whereas most buildings in metropolitan areas around the world were once owned by corporations, governments or universities, many are now in the hands of pension funds, insurance companies, foundations and other institutions. It's likely that in just a few years, much of the world's infrastructure – now mainly owned by municipalities, state and federal governments, and corporations – will also find new homes in the portfolios of institutional investors and infrastructure funds.[76]

Bruce Flatt, chief executive of Brookfield Asset Management, is more succinct. 'We're in a 50-year transformation of the infrastructure world', Flatt confidently told the *Financial Times* in 2018. 'We're 10 years in; we have 40 left to go. By the end of that 50 years most infrastructure in the world will be transferred to private hands.'[77] In terms of numbers, Flatt reckoned that, of a total $100 trillion-worth of infrastructure that would go private, 'maybe 10 per cent' had done so thus far.

It goes without saying that this development has never been about logic. That it is inherently better for infrastructure – or for that matter, housing – to be funded and owned by private-sector investors than by the state is a nonsense economically. This is not just a matter of the Keynesian nostrum, quoted above, that anything that (rich-country) governments can actually do, they can afford. It is also to do with the fact that one reason such governments can afford that which they choose to do is that they can almost always borrow more cheaply than the private sector can.

Writing about the US infrastructure investment space in 2017, for instance, Brian Alexander observed that 'the current average

---

76 C. Estrada, 'Young, Illiquid, and … Irresistible? The Infrastructure Asset Class, Explained', State St, 2018 – at statestreet.com

77 J. Evans and P. Smith, 'Bruce Flatt of Brookfield on Owning the Backbone of the Global Economy', *Financial Times*, 22 September 2018.

yield on municipal bonds, which is what cities use to build and maintain things like schools, roads, and fire stations, is about 3 per cent'. Meanwhile, private owners backed by asset managers (with their high-leverage model) typically paid 'much higher interest rates', which meant that 'a private owner is more likely down the line to have to, for example, keep the rates high on a toll road'.[78]

Writing two years later, the *Financial Times*'s Jonathan Ford observed that the UK's own long post-1980s history of 'bail[ing] in costly private cash' to finance infrastructure projects had been an expensive disaster. In particular, the private finance mobilised by the Private Finance Initiative was on average vastly more expensive than the public debt that the government could itself have raised to fund the relevant investments had it chosen to do so. Partly to pay off this costly private debt and partly to pad their own profits, asset managers and other private investors active in the UK have for decades been charging inflated infrastructure fees, 'often for very limited or non-existent risks', and with zero evidence of improved operating efficiencies (see Chapter 4). UK households have effectively been paying a premium for 'the privilege of keeping assets off the government's balance sheet'.[79] 'With the country facing fresh [infrastructure investment] demands from the need to decarbonise rapidly', Ford warned somewhat ominously – perhaps with Larry Fink's words ringing in his ears – 'it cannot afford more of the same'.

Ford made another important point. Think, he implored readers, about what it is that a government is in fact spending money on, on the increasingly rare occasions that it borrows to build publicly owned infrastructure (or indeed publicly owned rental housing). What is the payback? Too often, Ford argued, critics of public investment muddy matters by equating infrastructure spending with final consumption expenditure, or even transfer payments. As Ford said, 'there's surely a distinction between [the government] selling bonds to fund current

---

78 Alexander, 'Privatization Is Changing America's Relationship with Its Physical Stuff'.

79 J. Ford, 'Britain Needs Cheaper Infrastructure, Not Accounting Tricks', *Financial Times*, 23 June 2019.

spending, and doing so to create real assets with attached revenues. If you think about it logically', he went on, 'it's hard to see why a properly constituted national infrastructure fund with its own balance sheet – backed by highly rated assets – couldn't finance itself at fine rates.'

Indeed, having long cautioned against 'excessive' state borrowing, even the International Monetary Fund has latterly come to accept that deficits are the very last thing rich-economy governments should worry about in relation to long-term, remunerative investments such as infrastructure. Covid-19, it said, had proved as much, demonstrating that state borrowing 'for "well spent" capital spending would have a positive return, boosting economic performance and not adding to debt burdens in the long term'.[80]

But, of course, Ford's explicit injunction to 'think about it logically', and the IMF's implicit injunction to do the same, ultimately miss the point. The growing historic – and, if we have read the runes correctly, likely future – ascendancy of asset managers over society's vast stock of housing and infrastructure assets has nothing to do with 'logic', economic or otherwise. It is, rather, about power.

Let us return to Bruce Flatt's comment regarding the current trajectory of infrastructure ownership. Note that he talked about infrastructure increasingly moving into 'private hands'. Now, more private ownership of infrastructure does not necessarily mean more *asset-manager* ownership of infrastructure. But Flatt was nonetheless immensely confident that this would indeed continue to be the case. It more or less went without saying. Why so?

The simple answer is that asset managers control the bulk of society's financial wealth. They, in short, have the money – and, as theorists of money from all manner of conceptual traditions have long maintained, money is nothing if not social power objectified. Without money, you do not get the Blackstone-ification of housing policy and the BlackRock-ification of climate policy.

In the final reckoning, in other words, this book has told a remarkably straightforward story. Housing and infrastructure

---

80 Giles, 'Covid-19 Demonstrated "Power" of Government Spending'.

are widely ending up in asset managers' hands not because the latter are the most 'appropriate' or 'suitable' or 'efficient' owners of such assets, as if in some gigantic drama of perfectly righteous market clearance. Rather, this is increasingly such assets' default destination simply because asset managers are cash- and power-rich – arguably more so, in fact, than any other category of economic actor at any time in history.

In 2020, the amount of money managed by the global asset-management sector passed $100 trillion for the first time.[81] At an estimated $103 trillion, the sector's assets under management represented more than 40 per cent of total global financial wealth of all kinds, which stood at $250 trillion.[82] That is to say, four in every ten of the world's equivalent dollars are now controlled by and invested through asset managers. Moreover, the proportion of global financial wealth controlled by asset managers is growing with every passing year. It stands to reason, therefore, that more and more of everything with a positive market value – not just housing and infrastructure – is owned by these firms.

Ultimately, asset-manager society is merely a reflection of the wider society of which it is a part. Consistently proffering evidence of a short-term, speculative profit calculus riding roughshod over concerns around affordable access to a wide range of socially indispensable physical assets, it is perhaps the purest manifestation we have of a world in which money talks.

---

81   Boston Consulting Group, 'The $100 Trillion Machine', July 2021 – at bcg.com.

82   Boston Consulting Group, 'Despite COVID-19, Global Financial Wealth Soared to Record High of $250 Trillion in 2020', June 2021 – at bcg.com.

Acknowledgements

Our Lives in Their Portfolios is my third book with Verso, who have been as fantastic to work with on this one as the previous two. I remain very, very grateful for the support that I continue to receive from all parts of the organisation, not least Sebastian Budgen. As previously, considerable thanks are due to Mark Martin, managing editor, and Charles Peyton, copy editor.

What is true of Verso is also true of Uppsala University, my place of employment now for fourteen years, and where everyone in both the Institute for Housing and Urban Research and the Department of Social and Economic Geography continues to make for a supportive, stimulating and enjoyable working environment.

Five people kindly read the manuscript in draft, and while I can't blame them for any remaining errors of fact or interpretation (those are on me!), they certainly had a big part to play in shaping whatever is good about the book. So I want to thank them wholeheartedly: Nicole Aschoff (at Verso), Benjamin Braun, Julian Dickens, Daniela Gabor and Hettie O'Brien. Nicole, in particular, helped me to better identify those key places in the text where wider implications required explicit drawing-out rather than being taken for granted.

As ever, it's my family – Emilia, Oliver, Elliot and Agneta – that I have to thank most of all.

September 2022

Index